THE EUROPEAN UNION IN THE G8

Global Finance Series

Edited by
John Kirton, University of Toronto, Canada,
Michele Fratianni, Indiana University, USA and
Paolo Savona, University of Rome Guglielmo Marconi, Italy

The intensifying globalization of the twenty-first century has brought a myriad of new managerial and political challenges for governing international finance. The return of synchronous global slowdown, mounting developed country debt, and new economy volatility have overturned established economic certainties. Proliferating financial crises, transnational terrorism, currency consolidation, and increasing demands that international finance should better serve public goods such as social and environmental security, have all arisen to compound the problem.

The new public and private international institutions that are emerging to govern global finance have only just begun to comprehend and respond to this new world. Embracing international financial flows and foreign direct investment, in both the private and public sector dimensions, this series focuses on the challenges and opportunities faced by firms, national governments, and international institutions, and their roles in creating a new system of global finance.

Also in the series

European Union Economic Diplomacy
The Role of the EU in External Economic Relations
Stephen Woolcock
ISBN: 978-0-7546-7930-1

The New Economic Diplomacy
Decision-Making and Negotiation in International Economic Relations
Edited by Nicholas Bayne and Stephen Woolcock
ISBN: 978-1-4094-2541-0

Financial Crisis Management and the Pursuit of Power
American Pre-eminence and the Credit Crunch
Mine Aysen Doyran
ISBN: 978-1-4094-0095-0

Full series listing at the back of the book

The European Union in the G8
Promoting Consensus and Concerted Actions for Global Public Goods

Edited by

MARINA LARIONOVA
*National Research University – Higher School of Economics,
Moscow, Russia*

Routledge
Taylor & Francis Group

LONDON AND NEW YORK

First published 2012 by Ashgate Publishing

Published 2016 by Routledge
2 Park Square, Milton Park, Abingdon, Oxfordshire OX14 4RN
711 Third Avenue, New York, NY 10017, USA

First issued in paperback 2016

Routledge is an imprint of the Taylor & Francis Group, an informa business

British Library Cataloguing in Publication Data
The European Union in the G8 : promoting consensus and
  concerted actions for global public goods. -- (Global finance series)
  1. European Union countries--Foreign relations--21st century. 2. Group of Eight
(Organization) 3. Public goods-- International cooperation. 4. Economic policy--
International cooperation. 5. Economic development--Finance.
  I. Series II. Larionova, Marina.
  337.1-dc23

Library of Congress Cataloging-in-Publication Data
The European Union in the G8 : promoting consensus and concerted actions for global
public goods / [edited] by Marina Larionova.
    p. cm. -- (Global finance)
  Includes bibliographical references and index.
  ISBN 978-1-4094-3323-1 (hardback)
1. European Union. 2. European Union countries--Foreign relations. 3. Group of Eight
(Organization) 4. International cooperation. 5. International economic relations. 6.
International agencies. I. Larionova, Marina.
  JZ1570.E94 2012
  337.1'42--dc23

                                                                          2012012818

ISBN 13: 978-1-138-27918-6 (pbk)
ISBN 13: 978-1-4094-3323-1 (hbk)

Contents

PART I: INTRODUCTION

PART II: THE ANALYTICAL PARADIGM

PART III: THE KEY PLAYERS

List of Figures

List of Tables

Notes on Contributors

Mark Entin is director of the European Studies Institute at the Moscow State Institute of International Relations (MGIMO University) of the Ministry of Foreign Affairs of the Russian Federation.

Peter I. Hajnal is a research fellow at the Munk School of Global Affairs at the University of Toronto and a member of the G8 Research Group and G20 Research Group.

Judith Huigens is a junior lecturer at the Department of Political Science of the University of Amsterdam.

Vitaliy Kartamyshev is a former governance policy officer for Oxfam International's Moscow office.

John J. Kirton is director of the G8 Research Group and co-director of the G20 Research Group and a professor of political science at the Munk School of Global Affairs at the University of Toronto.

Marina Larionova is head of the International Organisations Research Institute at the National Research University Higher School of Economics and the head of international programmes at the National Training Foundation in Moscow.

Sergey Medvedev is the deputy dean of the Faculty of Applied Political Sciences of the National Research University Higher School of Economics in Moscow.

Arne Niemann is a professor of international politics at the University of Mainz.

Victoria Panova is associate professor at the Moscow State Institute of International Relations (MGIMO University) of the Ministry of Foreign Affairs of the Russian Federation and the regional director for Russia of the G8 Research Group.

Mark Rakhmangulov is deputy director of the Global Governance Research Centre of the International Organisations Research Institute of the National Research University Higher School of Economics in Moscow.

Thomas Renard is a research fellow at Egmont, the Royal Institute for International Relations in Brussels.

Igor Tomashov is a PhD student at the Faculty of Applied Political Sciences of the National Research University Higher School of Economics in Moscow.

Vladimir Zuev is head of the International Economic Organisations and European Integration Department at the Faculty of World Economy and World Politics at the National Research University Higher School of Economics in Moscow.

Preface and Acknowledgements

This monograph presents the results of research on the evolution of the European Union as a collective member of both the G8 and the G20, the external and internal factors that have influenced that evolution, models of collaboration, and the future role of the EU in this system of global governance.

The findings are outcomes of the project titled 'The EU as a Global Actor: A European Way to Creating Global Public Goods through Partnerships and Rule-Based Multilateral Institutions'. This project enjoyed the support of the Jean Monnet Programme of the European Commission. It relied on the dedication, talent, and academic rigour of scholars from the International Organisations Research Institute of the National Research University Higher School of Economics (IORI HSE), the Moscow State Institute of International Relations (MGIMO) of the Ministry of Foreign Affairs of the Russian Federation, the Munk School of Global Affairs of the University of Toronto, and Royal Institute for International Relations of Belgium.

The authors appreciate the help of the students and staff at HSE and MGIMO in Moscow and the G8 Research Group at Trinity College in the University of Toronto. We express gratitude for the help of Yuriy Zaitsev, researcher of the Center for International Projects at the HSE Institute for Statistical Studies and Economics of Knowledge, and Ekaterina Prokhorova and Daria Frolova, graduates of the HSE Faculty of World Economy and World Politics, and their contributions to the research through the formation of a structured analytical database of the EU and G8 documents. We owe a special word of thanks to programmer Alexander Grechkin, who translated into reality the idea of creating such a database and software for the functional analysis employed in this research.

We are also grateful to Olga Perfilieva, head of the IORI HSE Centre for International Comparative Studies, and Anna Zaichenko, editor and head of the Operational Release division of the HSE Publishing House, whose editorial skills were essential in ensuring the magic of transforming the drafts into an integrated manuscript.

We owe much to the comments of our colleagues Jacqueline Gower of the King's College London and Sven Biscop of the Royal Institute for International Relations of Belgium. Special thanks are due to several key figures at the Université Catholique de Louvain, namely Tanguy de Wilde d'Estmael, the director of the Inbev-Baillet Latour Chair and chair of the Department of Political Science, Vincent Dujardin, director of the Institute of European Studies, and Laetitia Spetschinsky, research assistant at the Institute of European Studies, for organizational and research support for the intenrship at the Inbev-Baillet Latour and the Institute of European Studies of Arina Shadrikova, IORI HSE researcher.

I must express my deepest appreciation for the inspiration provided by the contributors and continuing support of my colleagues at IORI.

We are indebted to Madeline Koch for her profound professionalism and deft editorial touch.

I would like to reiterate special words of thanks to the European Commission Jean Monnet Programme, the support of which was critical for the project and thus, also, this book.

Marina Larionova
December 2011

List of Abbreviations

3R	reduce, reuse, recycle
AfT	aid for trade
APEC	Asia-Pacific Economic Cooperation
ASEAN	Association of South East Asian Nations
ASEM	Asia-Europe Meeting
BCBS	Basel Committee on Banking Supervision
BIS	Bank for International Settlements
CBD	Convention on Biological Diversity
CCS	carbon capture and sequestration
CFGS	Centre for Global Studies at the University of Victoria
CFSP	Common Foreign and Security Policy (of the European Union)
CIGI	Centre for International Governance Innovation
COREPER	Committee of Permanent Representatives to the European Union
DAC	Development Assistance Committee (of the Organisation for Economic Co-operation and Development)
ECB	European Central Bank
Ecofin	Economic and Financial Affairs Council of the Council of the European Union
EFTA	European Free Trade Association
ESDP	European Security and Defence Policy
EU	European Union
FATF	Financial Action Task Force
FSB	Financial Stability Board
FSF	Financial Stability Forum
G5	Group of Five: Brazil, China, India, Mexico, and South Africa
G7	Group of Seven: Canada, France, Germany, Italy, Japan, United Kingdom, United States, and the European Union
G8	Group of Seven plus Russia
G13	Group of Five plus the Group of Eight
G20	Group of Eight plus Argentina, Australia, Brazil, China, India, Indonesia, Korea, Mexico, Saudi Arabia, South Africa and Turkey
GAB	General Arrangements to Borrow
GAER	Council General Affairs and External Relations Council (of the Council of the European Union)
GDP	gross domestic product

GNI	gross national income
GTLP	Global Trade Liquidity Pool
	(of the International Financial Corporation)
HAP	Heiligendamm L'Aquila Process
HDP	Heiligendamm Dialogue Process
IASB	International Accounting Standards Board
IEA	International Energy Agency
IFC	International Finance Corporation
IFI	international financial institution
IGO	international government organization
IMF	International Monetary Fund
IMFC	International Monetary and Finance Committee
	(of the International Monetary Fund)
IOSCO	International Organization of Securities Commissions
IPR	intellectual property right
ITER	international thermonuclear experimental reactor
J8	Junior Eight
JODI	Joint Organisations Data Initiative
	(originally Joint Oil Data Initiative)
L20	Leaders' 20
LDC	least developed country
LTCM	Long-Term Capital Management
MDB	multilateral development bank
MDG	Millennium Development Goal
MEF	Major Economies Forum
MEM	Major Economies Meeting
NAB	New Arrangements to Borrow
NAFTA	North American Free Trade Agreement
NATO	North Atlantic Treaty Organization
NEPAD	New Partnership for Africa's Development
NGO	nongovernmental organization
O5	Outreach Five (see Group of Five)
ODA	official development assistance
OECD	Organisation for Economic Co-operation and Development
OPEC	Organization of Petroleum Exporting Countries
OSCE	Organization for Security and Co-operation in Europe
PSI	plurilateral summit institution
SDR	special drawing right
TARP	Troubled Asset Relief Program (in the United States)
TOES	The Other Economic Summit
UN	United Nations
UNFCCC	United Nations Framework Convention on Climate Change
UNGA	United Nations General Assembly
UNSC	United Nations Security Council

WEU   Western European Union
WTO   World Trade Organization

PART I
Introduction

Chapter 1

The European Union as a Global Player: Creating Global Public Goods through Partnerships and Multilateral Institutions

Marina Larionova

This book explores the role of the European Union in global governance with a focus on its evolving role in the Group of Eight since 2000. This evolution reflects the EU's growth in power and influence as well as its expanding competences and legal authority. This volume also analyses the EU's participation in the Group of Twenty, of which it has been a member since the group's finance ministers and central bank governors began meeting in 1999 – unlike the EU's gradual inclusion in G8 processes. The book traces the transformation of the EU's identity into a global actor, examining both how its participation in these institutions of global governance affects the EU and how the EU contributes to global governance as both an actor and a model.

Numerous definitions, many contested, of global governance reflect the complexity of this relationship. Governance involves 'setting goals and making decisions for an entire collectivity, including individuals or groups who have not explicitly agreed to them. It also involves a rather high level of intervention which may stabilize or alter a given status quo' (Jachtenfuchs and Kohler-Koch 2004). Global governance can be defined as 'rule making and power exercise at a global scale, but not necessarily by entities authorized by general agreement to act', steering the international order towards particular outcomes and values (Keohane 2003, 132).

Jan Aart Scholte (2011) highlights the planetary scope of the concept, identifying global governance as 'a complex of rules and regulatory institutions that apply to transplanetary jurisdictions and constituencies'. Global governance is exercised by states, formal and informal intergovernmental organizations, transnational networks, business corporations and nongovernmental organizations (NGOs). What emerges, according to Philippe Schmitter (2004), is multilevel governance that 'engages a multiplicity of politically independent, but otherwise interdependent actors – private and public – at different levels of territorial aggregation in more-or-less continuous negotiation/deliberation/implementation, and that does not assign exclusive policy *compétence* or assert a stable hierarchy of political authority to any of these levels'. Although this definition stresses the layered nature of EU governance, it captures the contemporary global governance features well. Moreover, the experience of operating in the multilevel governance system gives the EU a competitive advantage in fulfilling its objectives as a global actor – as they are stated in article 21 of the Treaty on European Union as amended by the Treaty of Lisbon.

The EU is a unique international entity in the process of 'creating an ever closer union among the peoples of Europe', which has entered a new stage since the Treaty of Lisbon came into force on 1 December 2009 ('Treaty on European Union' 1992). The EU, uniting 27 countries, is almost universal in scope of its policies and activities. It 'acts as a comprehensive institution in which the individual member state is embedded in a system of information and assessment in virtually every field of politics. As a result, member states mutually observe each other and constantly remind one another of their duties and obligations as members of a larger community' (Jachtenfuchs and Kohler-Koch 2004). The EU is a pre-eminent power mobilizing 'soft' power instruments of international influence such as economic and cultural capabilities, trade, institutional membership, aid, and diplomatic pressure (Moravcsik 2010).

Article 3 of the treaty states:

> In its relations with the wider world, the Union shall uphold and promote its values and interests and contribute to the protection of its citizens. It shall contribute to peace, security, the sustainable development of the Earth, solidarity and mutual respect among peoples, free and fair trade, eradication of poverty and the protection of human rights, in particular the rights of the child, as well as to the strict observance and the development of international law, including respect for the principles of the United Nations Charter.[1]

The treaty provides a legal and institutional framework for fulfilling these normative objectives through conferring on the EU a single legal personality, establishing the institution of a full-time president of the European Council with responsibility for external representation on issues relating to the Common Foreign and Security Policy (CFSP), and the institution of high representative for foreign affairs and security policy responsible for steering foreign policy and a common defence policy. These new arrangements have allowed the EU to 'upgrade its role as a global actor' (Emerson et al. 2011). They present both a baseline and a methodological framework for future comparative analysis. Indeed, the EU claims membership in both the G8 and the G20, where it is represented by the president of the European Council and the president of the European Commission.

The G8 and the G20, although different in their origins, membership, structure, mandate, and agenda, are both 'unorthodox' global governance institutions with informal modes of operation and capacities to respond flexibly to new and emerging challenges (Hajnal 2007). The G8 is an annual meeting of the leaders of

---

1   'Treaty on European Union.' (1992). Official Journal C 191, 29 July. <eur-lex.europa.eu/en/treaties/dat/11992M/htm/11992M.html> (July 2011).

Canada, France, Germany, Italy, Japan, Russia, the United Kingdom, the United States, and the European Union. First begun as the G7 in 1975, without Russia or the EU as members, it was envisaged by the founders as a forum for discussing world economic issues. Over time, the agenda broadened substantially, shifting from predominantly macroeconomic and trade issues to include a wide range of security, environment, energy, and development issues. The G20, first created by the G8 as a forum for finance ministers and central bankers as a result of the global financial crisis in 1999, began meeting at the leaders' level in response to another global financial crisis in 2008. It brings together advanced and emerging market economies. In 2009, the G20 leaders declared that their collective response 'helped stop the dangerous, sharp decline in global activity and stabilize financial markets' (G20 2009). They 'designated the G20 as the premier forum for our international economic cooperation'. The group continued to evolve. The G20 Seoul Summit agenda and the leaders' decision to move to an annual cycle marked the transition of the G20 from being a crisis committee to a steering committee. Since then, the G8 and G20 summits have worked together, bringing different configurations of leaders to deliberate on and direct global governance processes.

G8 performance can be explained by the 'concert equality' model, where the member states have equal capabilities, are equally vulnerable to external shocks, share common principles of democracy, and possess sufficient domestic control and political capital (Kirton 2005) (Kirton 2007).

Both the G8 and the G20 can be seen as based on a collective management model: their performance is increasingly effective due to global problems, the inadequacy of other global governance institutions, constraints imposed by globalization on independent actions by major powers, and the institutionalization of the leaders' format (Bayne 2005).

This volume follows a functional analytical paradigm to assess the effectiveness of international institutions in global governance. The paradigm has been used to explore the EU's contribution to the implementation of the main global governance functions of domestic (political) management, deliberation, direction setting, decision making, and the development of global governance itself. The concept of these six functions was adapted to reflect the special nature of the EU as a collective member of the G8, and also to allow the exploration of the extent to which the EU shapes G8 decisions and contributes to deliberation, direction setting, and decision making, and to assess the degree to which the EU and the G8 comply with their commitments.

The Structure of the Book

Part II, 'The Analytical Paradigm', provides an analytical framework for the study of the EU as a global transformative power. It opens up with 'The Concept and Definition of Global Public Goods', in which Sergey Medvedev and Igor Tomashov explore the definition and concept of global public goods. The key feature of global public goods is that their benefits and costs spread across borders, social groups, and generations. Citing examples of global public goods such as the atmosphere, climate, human rights, health, international peace, and others, the authors examine the history of the globalization of public goods and propose typologies and ways to solve the problem of international collective action.

In Chapter 3, 'Key Concepts for Exploring the Role of the European Union in the G8', John Kirton considers the main concepts of global governance that have been developed in international relations theory. Applying the concepts of soft power and soft law and the processes of membership, values, consensus, and compliance to the two institutions, Kirton shifts his analysis to other concepts of global governance and offers an assessment of EU and G8 contributions to global governance, their impact, and their relationship.

Part III, 'The Key Players', examines the transformation of G7/G8 system, the evolution of the EU as a global actor, and the emergence of G20 as a leaders' forum. It focuses on the EU as a member of these international institutions and its role in the institutional changes there over the past decade.

In Chapter 4, 'The G7/G8 System', Kirton explores the G8's core character, mission, capabilities, and governance. He considers how changes in outreach, in-reach, and down-reach have enhanced performance in the past and could do so in the years ahead. He finds that since its start in 1975, as a modern democratic concert the G8 has increasingly met its goals of producing a global democratic evolution and providing domestic political management, deliberation, direction setting, decision making, delivery, and the development of a new generation of global governance for itself and the world. The G8 has maintained its globally predominant capabilities, largely because it has broadened enormously in outreach embracing Japan, Italy, Canada, the EU, and Russia as full members, and also a wide array of multilateral organizations and rising or regional powers as participants in its annual summits and institutions.

In Chapter 5, 'The Future Role and Reform of the G8', Peter Hajnal and Victoria Panova focus on the period beginning in 1998, with only a brief reference to early reform initiatives of the G8. The chapter discusses reform proposals, as well as reforms already achieved or underway. It pays particular attention to the reform dimension of the evolving G20, the Group of Five (G5) countries (Brazil, China, India, Mexico, and South Africa) invited to G8 summits from 2005 to 2009, the Heiligendamm Dialogue Process (HDP) initiated at the 2007 Heiligendamm Summit, the summit of the BRICS (Brazil, Russia, India, China, and, since 2011, South Africa), and the Major Economies Forum on Energy and Climate, as well as to the G8's relationship to these structures. The chapter concludes with suggesting possible trajectories of G8 reform now that the G20 is firmly established at the leaders' level.

In Chapter 6, 'The European Union as a Leading International Player', Mark Entin presents his vision of the EU as a key global player. He explores it as a political institution, its internal structure, and its system of external relationships and mechanisms for cooperating with other global actors. The chapter focuses on factors underpinning the political cohesion of EU members such as the rule of law, a political culture of solidarity, and mechanisms for co-governing sovereignty. Entin evaluates the EU's future role and its rising influence in defining the global agenda, addressing global problems and needs, and promoting global development, based on an analysis of the EU's legal and institutional foundations for global policy practices and its ways of projecting them.

In Chapter 7, 'The Representation of the European Union in the G8', Judith Huigens and Arne Niemann discuss the multiple challenges involved in the representation of a regional organization in a concert of state powers. In assessing the evolution of the EU's role in the G8, they address several questions arising from its dual representation in the G8: What is the EU's status in the G8? In what capacity is the EU, a regional institution among states, present? How does this work, when there are also four EU members within the G8? What constitutes EU representation? They discuss two case studies of nuclear energy and development that illustrate the challenges that arise with such dual representation.

Chapter 8, 'The European Union in the G20,' by Marina Larionova and Thomas Renard, reviews the EU's input and impact on the first five summits of the G20 leaders. The analysis emphasizes institutional mechanisms that allow the EU to increase its influence within the G20 process through greater coordination (of European G20 members) and greater inclusion (of European non-G20 members). Indeed, the permanent presidency of the European Council has brought coherence and continuity, which are essential for forging consensus among the EU members in the G20 and internal consensus within the EU on effective common foreign policy. Larionova and Renard suggest that the EU could upgrade its status as an international actor within the G20 based on three factors: an established pattern of coordinating and agreeing language (or terms of reference) for G20 meetings, implementation of the commitments made at G20 summits for which the EU serves as a transmission mechanism, and a high level of compliance performance.

Part IV, 'Critical Case Studies', contains several critical examples of global governance and the EU's contribution to them. In Chapter 9, 'The G8, the European Union, Climate Change, and Energy', John Kirton and Victoria Panova look into the G8 and the HDP, which brought together the G8 and the G5 to analyze risks for sustainable world energy and economic development and propose improvements to the G8's energy-climate performance. Kirton then turns, in Chapter 10, 'G8 and G20 Financial Crisis Governance: The European Union Contribution', to an in-depth analysis of the contribution of the G8 and G20 to overcoming numerous regional-turned-global financial crises, as well as to the evolving the role of the EU in supporting G8 and G20 efforts as global players.

In Chapter 11, 'The European Union's Development Policy in the Context of the G8', Vitaliy Kartamyshev analyses the EU's leadership role over the past decade in providing multidimensional, high-quality, and predictable aid aimed at eradicating poverty and achieving the Millennium Development Goals (MDGs). He considers various aspects, including official development assistance (ODA), budget support, and aid for trade. He also identifies challenges for the EU in fulfilling this crucial role given the unfavourable economic environment that has prevailed since the financial crisis of 2008, and offers some recommendations for enhancing the efficiency of the EU's implementation of its development policy.

In Chapter 12, 'Security as a Global Public Good: Common Issues for the European Union and the G8', Sergey Medvedev and Igor Tomashov explore international peace and security as the most important global public goods, given their role in creating conditions for sustainable development. The chapter takes stock of the key problems and contradictions of safeguarding international peace and security and examines the history and future prospects of the EU's CFSP. Medvedev and Tomashov state that cooperation in this field is often constrained by the lowest common denominators of mutual deterrence and crisis management. They assert that new opportunities may be opened by a more active involvement in this process of the EU and the G8.

Medvedev and Tomashov also explore the growing role of knowledge as a factor for development of modern societies in Chapter 13, 'Knowledge and Education as Global Public Goods'. They examine the problems of international cooperation in the field, paying particular attention to initiatives of both the G8 and the EU. The authors posit that new solutions can be found by analyzing knowledge and education as global public goods.

Part V, 'Trends in Leadership and Models of Engagement', opens with Chapter 14, 'The European Union as a Model for Global Governance'. Vladimir Zuev explores the EU's decision-making models, reviews the key principles and possible options for integrating some aspects of the EU into the practice and functioning of contemporary global institutions. Both positive and negative consequences can emerge from strengthening the EU's supranational elements in international regulations, particularly in economic areas. Zuev also addresses such questions as whether international economic regulation should be international or supranational and why the EU model has enjoyed success and popularity among its members and neighbouring countries.

In the final chapter, 'The European Union and the G8: Priorities, Functions, Values', Marina Larionova and Mark Rakhmangulov present the findings of a study of the EU's contribution to global governance, focusing on its role in the G8. Using a qualitative and quantitative analysis, they compare the priorities, functions, and values of both institutions and examine the EU's contribution to defining the global agenda, the performance of global governance functions, the promotion of shared values, and engagement with international organizations. There is increasing congruence between the EU and G8 on their main priorities of political and security issues, economy and trade, energy, education, science, and innovation. The study finds that the EU's contribution to global governance is growing. The EU leads in influencing processes of forging consensus and compliance with commitments made at G8 summits. Its influence on direction setting and the development of global governance is increasing, although it varies depending on the policy sphere. Larionova and Rakhmangulov conclude that the EU contributes significantly to the consolidation and transformation of a shared system of values. Moreover, when the G8 is chaired by an EU member, it becomes an indisputable resource of EU influence on shaping the global discourse and implementation of global governance.

References

Bayne, Nicholas (2005). *Staying Together: The G8 Summit Confronts the 21st Century*. Aldershot: Ashgate.

Emerson, Michael, Rosa Balfour, Tim Corthaut, et al., eds (2011). *Upgrading the EU's Role as Global Actor: Institutions, Law and the Restructuring of European Diplomacy*. Brussels: Centre for European Policy Studies. <www. ceps.eu/ceps/download/4134> (July 2011).

G20 (2009). 'G20 Leaders Statement: The Pittsburgh Summit.' Pittsburgh, 25 September. <www.g20.utoronto.ca/2009/2009communique0925.html> (July 2011).

Hajnal, Peter I. (2007). *The G8 System and the G20: Evolution, Role, and Documentation*. Aldershot: Ashgate.

Jachtenfuchs, Markus, and Beate Kohler-Koch (2004). 'Governance and Institutional Development.' In *European Integration Theory*, edited by Antje Wiener and Thomas Diez. Oxford: Oxford University Press.

Keohane, Robert O. (2003). 'Global Governance and Democratic Accountability.' In *Taming Globalization: Frontiers of Governance*, edited by David Held and Mathias Koenig-Archibugi. Cambridge: Polity Press.

Kirton, John J. (2005). 'America at the G8: From Vulnerability to Victory at the Sea Island Summit.' In *New Perspectives on Global Governance: Why America Needs the G8*, edited by Michele Fratianni, John J. Kirton, Alan M. Rugman, et al., pp. 31–50. Aldershot: Ashgate.

Kirton, John J. (2007). *Canadian Foreign Policy in a Changing World*. Toronto: Thomson Nelson.

Moravcsik, Andrew (2010). 'Europe: Rising Superpower in a Bipolar World.' In *Rising States, Rising Institutions: Challenges for Global Governance*, edited by Alan S. Alexandroff and Andrew F. Cooper. Washington DC: Brookings Institution Press.

Schmitter, Philippe C. (2004). 'Neo-Neofunctionalism in European Integration Theory.' In *European Integration Theory*, edited by Antje Wiener and Thomas Diez. Oxford: Oxford University Press.

Scholte, Jan Aart (2011). 'Global governance, accountability, and civil society.' In *Building Global Democracy? Civil Society and Accountable Global Governance*, edited by Jan Aart Scholte. Cambridge: Cambridge University Press.

'Treaty on European Union.' (1992). Official Journal C 191, 29 July. <eur-lex. europa.eu/en/treaties/dat/11992M/htm/11992M.html> (July 2011).

PART II
The Analytical Paradigm

Chapter 2

The Concept and Definition of Global Public Goods

Sergey Medvedev and Igor Tomashov

The concept of global public goods is a useful tool for analysing the process of globalization from the point of view of the international community. This perspective reveals the growing interconnectedness of different trends and calls for greater responsibility and accountability on the part of key global actors. Rooted in the tradition of the political economy, it is still relatively new to the field of international relations. This chapter argues that the concept of global public goods should be taken up more actively by key international institutions, such as the European Union and the G8, in their practical policymaking.

The Role of the State in Providing Public Goods

The provision of public goods is one of the most important tasks of the modern state and, increasingly, of supranational and international organizations, such as the EU. Moreover, these institutions themselves may be seen as a 'public good' that should, according to institutional theory, establish clear 'rules of the game' and guarantee that every resident of a certain territory complies with them (North 1991). The importance of providing public goods has steadily grown as societies have evolved from agrarian to industrial and then from industrial to post-industrial.

In fact, in the Middle Ages rulers were concerned mainly with safeguarding the security of the inhabitants of their land and providing a minimum standard of medical care in case of epidemics (Desai 2003). Modernity brought significant growth in the amount and quality of state-provided public goods. The wealth of nations has increased with the development of capitalism, as citizens started to pay more taxes and demand more social services. The establishment of institutions and infrastructure necessary for economic growth became an immediate task for the states.

Adam Smith was one of the first who 'made a powerful plea for the state to provide education and training to overcome the debilitating effects of the division of labor in modern factories' (Desai 2003). In the 19th century the state began to regulate daily working hours. Added to these demands were calls to develop urban infrastructure and build roads and water systems as well as provide citizens with housing.

Another breakthrough, in the 20th century, was the welfare state, with its theoretical foundations based on the concept of global public goods: states should take responsibility for social welfare of citizens and for correcting the failures and negative externalities of the market. As a result, the provision of goods and services such as roads and primary education increased, and public health, housing, and higher education started to be seen as public goods. The amount of social payments and number of claimants have grown steadily (Desai 2003). The concept of public goods became one of the pillars of the science of economics.

Moreover, the issue of public goods delivery has gradually been internationalized, as states become more interconnected and interdependent through networks of supranational and international organizations and regimes that promote political, social, and economic cooperation. This list includes the World Trade Organization (WTO), the World Bank, the EU, and the G8. The massive changes of the late 20th and early 21st centuries have had a considerable influence. The collapse of communist regimes at the end of the 20th century necessitated new state institutions. The processes of globalization have eroded state sovereignty and a variety of new actors, namely transnational corporations, nongovernmental organizations (NGOs), and supranational structures have emerged. The expansion of capitalism and democracy and a qualitative leap in the development of technologies have raised the question of whether globalization provides new opportunities for reducing poverty and inequality or only widens social inequality. The concept of global public goods forms part of the answer to this question.

The Concept of Global Public Goods

Public goods are those goods and services that, being granted to one person, may be available to others without additional cost incurred to them (Block 2004). They are characterized by non-excludability and non-rivalry in both provision and consumption. Non-excludability means that the producer of a good cannot prevent other persons from enjoying it; non-rivalry assumes that consumption by one person does not diminish its availability for others (Afontsev 2003). National security, economic stability, social order, and the rule of law are public goods provided by government.

Few public goods are 'readymade'. On the contrary, the decision to make a certain good public or private is a result of social processes and political choices. The amount of financing allocated to providing public goods is defined through a process of political bargaining influenced by voters' choice of political parties. For example, public health and higher education vary in their extent of non-excludability and non-rivalry: they may be free or paid for; hospitals and universities may accommodate more or fewer patients and students, respectively. Television may be public and accessible to all who live in the broadcasting area, or it may be an excludable good as in the case of cable or private television.

The fact that some individuals and groups may benefit more than others from public goods does not change the main properties of those goods. However, it can determine voters' preferences and government policies. It can also increase the risk of free riding by avoiding the high costs of providing public goods (Afontsev 2003). The problem of distributing costs and benefits is especially sensitive with regard to global public goods.

Historically, one of the first global public goods was the principle of freedom on the high seas, which had been negotiated early in the 18th century (Gureev 1987). Later, the rules of international trade and travel between countries were established in the 19th century. Throughout the 20th century, further development of the principle was impossible because of the geopolitical and ideological rivalry among major powers – Germany, France, and Great Britain at the beginning of century; the USSR and the United States in its second half. The conditions re-emerged only at the end of the 20th century following the breakup of the Soviet bloc and the acceleration of globalization.

The benefits (and costs) of global public goods cut across state, social, and generational borders. They should extend to at least two countries, if not more, and should not discriminate against any population group or generation (Kaul and Mendoza 2003). Global public goods are characterized by the same features as national public goods, namely non-excludability and non-rivalry, seen from the standpoint of international actors. Examples of global public goods are the environment, communicable disease control, and financial stability.

Some public goods are invariably global in origin and characteristics (such as the ozone layer and climate); others emerge as a result of human activity (knowledge, human rights, cultural heritage, the internet) or represent a certain group of global policy outcomes and efforts aimed at guaranteeing peace and security, sustainable development, free trade, equality, and justice.

Different types of global public bads exist along with global public goods (Kaul, Grunberg, and Stern 1999). This term describes the opposite of global public goods: destruction of the environment, spread of infectious diseases, terrorism, the abuse of human rights, and so on. Global public bads emerge in the most cases as negative externalities when individuals, firms, or other actors undertake actions but do not bear the full costs, and usually attract more attention than global public goods.

Factors Contributing to Global Public Goods

National and global public goods do not contradict each other. On the contrary, in the globalized world, the creation of one contributes to the provision of others. Material welfare encourages people to take advantage of globalization more actively and leads to the spread of post-material values in developed societies. So the realization of humanitarian programmes in poor countries helps to reduce the global gap between the North and the South, which is why supranational and international organizations should implement such initiatives. In general, strengthening the interdependence between countries changes the perception of social reality and promotes the recognition of the importance of global public goods.

In recent decades, most global public goods are national public goods that have gone global (Kaul and Mendoza 2003). The doctrine of human rights, originally acknowledged only in some Western countries, became universal in 1948. At the end of the 20th century they became the ideological and institutional basis of a new world order (Medvedev 1999). The interdependence of economies has since grown to such an extent that financial stability and economic growth are impossible without coordination at the international level. People now understand that the environment is common to all the Earth's inhabitants and does not respect borders, so that environmental policy cannot be limited by the borders of individual states.

The development of new technologies is undoubtedly one of the greatest catalysts for change in lifestyles and world-views. First, new technologies have increased the quality of life and wealth of nations. Second, they lower transport and transaction costs, enhancing the mobility of goods, services, information, and people. Third, in conditions of decreasing economic and political barriers, global actors can use existing technology effectively, cooperating with each other, for example, in response to international political crises or in order to develop new production chains.

In many ways, the emerging international system is unique because its basic principle is not a balance of power or the doctrine of deterrence. The international system is built on 'network logic' that includes new members (Kaul, Grunberg, and Stern 1999). The larger the network, the greater the benefits to its members. The addition of new members, far from taking away from existing consumers (or members of the network), enhances the opportunities for all. States and actors tend to refuse non-cooperative strategies, understanding that such strategies may undermine the ability to respond to new systemic risks, such as climate change, excessive economic and financial volatility, or growing social inequality. Cooperation exists especially at the regional level.

Regional economic and political organizations tend to promote liberal world order and enhance the openness of states rather than divide the world into several 'protectionist fortresses' (Afontsev 2003). The best example here is the EU, an institution whose members have a long history of conflicts but realize the positive potential of collaborating on the provision of public goods. By this 'regionalization' of national public goods, member states have not only benefited economically themselves, but have also created a surplus product valuable for all in the world. New opportunities for cooperation with the EU were also opened up for other countries. The EU also had, at its disposal, more funds and other resources for increasing foreign assistance.

Types of Global Public Goods

Global public goods are a recent but highly important link in the chain of creation of public goods. Virtually all economic agents participate in their production and provision, namely producers and consumers of private goods, states, supranational and international organizations, and international political regimes (as in treaties and organizations). The producers pay taxes and can voluntarily help those NGOs that pursue transnational goals. The states provide public goods that benefit their citizens but are also used to create global public goods (for example, national air navigation systems). Most regional economic and political organizations aim at guaranteeing the conditions for peaceful development and sustainable economic growth in a particular territory that also benefit the entire international community. These organizations and the goods they provide can thus be characterized as 'intermediate' global public goods, which make possible the provision of 'final' ones (Afontsev 2003).

Global public goods may be divided into three classes according to the nature of their publicness and the conditions of their provision (Kaul and Mendoza 2003). The first class consists of global natural commons, such as the atmosphere and the high seas. As already mentioned, such global public goods are non-excludable and rival goods, although they are de facto available to all (Gardiner and Le Goulven 2002). This type of global public goods can be overused and abused, and may be difficult to renew.

The second class of global public goods consists of global human-made commons, such as theoretical and applied knowledge and global networks of information and transport communications (Kaul and Mendoza 2003). Access to such goods may be free or limited. For example, knowledge of the Pythagorean theorem cannot be limited, while access to the newest inventions is usually protected by patents and licences. Most of these goods are national public goods that become global and are non-excludable at the international level. However, it is difficult to guarantee their non-excludability to prevent underuse and illegitimate restricted access.

The third class of global public goods consists of global political outcomes (Kaul and Mendoza 2003). Unlike other goods, these are not material objects and cannot be created once and for all. Examples are international peace, free trade, the fight against infectious diseases, and environmental protection. These goods are non-excludable and non-rival, but the lack of institutional mechanisms and incentives to cooperate usually prevents key international actors from providing them.

Figure 2.1 illustrates how overuse, underuse, undersupply, and abuse of global public goods threaten humankind's well-being. The overexploitation of global natural commons leads to non-sustainability and consequently to possible natural catastrophes. The rapid spread of global human-made commons can have positive and negative effects. In fact, the promotion of human rights, knowledge, and new technologies contributes greatly to the development of human capital,

Figure 2.1   Typology of Global Public Goods

but may also increase the gap between those who are already enjoying these resultant benefits and those who lack resources for development. The domestic and international policy agenda of most countries should be oriented towards creating positive global political outcomes. It is the primary task of political leaders to ensure the peaceful development of the international community, stable economic growth, and social justice. It is thus important to classify different types of global public goods and design proper political strategies to tackle the existing problems of their supply.

Global public goods may be further divided into four categories: economic, social and political, infrastructural, and environmental global public goods (see Table 2.1).

Economic global public goods are liberal trade regime (free trade), financial and economic stability, sufficient supply of natural resources (for example, oil) critically important for the world's economy.

Social and political goods are safeguarding international peace and security, mediating conflicts, observing human rights, maintaining the rule of law and social order, fighting disease and improving medical standards. These goods cannot exist without effective institutions at different levels of global governance.

Table 2.1   Global Public Goods and Global Public Bads

Type of global public goods	Benefits		Nature of supply problem	Corresponding global public bads	Costs	
	Non-excludable	Non-rival			Non-excludable	Non-rival
Economic						
Liberal trade	+ (partly)	+	Undersupply	Fragmented markets	+	+
Financial and economic stability	+ (partly)	+	Undersupply	Financial crises, excessive volatility	+	+
Provision of the resources to the world economy	–	–	Undersupply	Lack of resources	+	+
Social and political						
Peace and security	+	+	Undersupply	Wars, conflicts, terrorism	+ (partly)	+
Human rights	+ (partly)	+	Underuse, lack of access	Human rights abuse, discrimination	+ (partly)	+
Rule of law and social order	+ (partly)	+	Undersupply	Social conflicts, injustice, corruption	+ (partly)	+
Fighting disease	+	+	Undersupply	Infectious diseases (AIDS, malaria)	+	+
Infrastructural						
Global system of air navigation	+	+	Underuse	Incompatibility of standards	+	+
Internet	+ (partly)	+	Underuse, lack of access	Barriers to the internet (censorship, absence of physical infrastructure)	+ (partly)	+
Knowledge	+ (partly)	+	Underuse	Barriers to information	+ (partly)	+
Environmental						
Ocean	+	–	Overuse	Contamination of the ocean	+ (partly)	+
Atmosphere, climate stability	+	–	Overuse	Global warming	+	+
Biodiversity	+	+	Overuse	Disruption of ecosystems	+	+

Source: Gardiner and Le Goulven (2002).

Infrastructural goods are the result of cooperation among different countries and the standardization of goods provided by them. Examples include global air navigation systems, the physical and virtual infrastructure of the internet, and knowledge in its broadest sense.

Ecological goods are the ocean, atmosphere, biological diversity, climate stability, and so on.

Global Public Bads

Global public bads are phenomena and processes opposite to global public goods: international crime, terrorism, poverty and inequality, the spread of communicable diseases, the abuse of human rights, and environmental degradation (Gardiner and Le Goulven 2002). Despite considerable progress in recent years in overcoming political and financial gaps, global public bads are often a higher global priority, for developed and developing states as well as for supranational and international organizations, than global public goods.

Global bads are more public than global goods. They attract the attention of the public, mass media, and politicians. While the creation and provision of goods are usually perceived as a routine process, public bads appear in concrete forms that threaten people's lives and well-being daily, and thus provoke a wide public response. In an ideal model, the provision of global public goods should lead to the eradication of bads and vice versa. In reality, however global public policy is based on other principles, being accountable to citizens of democratic countries and to mass media.

Investment in providing global public goods does not usually generate immediate effect. The benefits cannot always be calculated in terms of economic efficiency and should be directed to the poorest areas of the world. Consequently, it is difficult to move beyond the rhetoric on the common challenges of globalization to real action. The United States spends around 20 percent of its federal budget on defence, which is approximately 16 times more than its foreign policy spending (Nye 2002). In sum, the country spends only 0.1 percent of its gross domestic product (GDP) on aid to foreign countries, which is three times less than the EU and seven times less than the level of spending on official development assistance recommended by the UN (0.7 percent GDP) (Nye 2002; Gates 2010).

The international agenda is oriented towards the struggle with global public bads rather than the provision of global public goods. Rich countries have enough knowledge, technologies, and resources to protect against global threats – and sometimes prefer to distance themselves from the instability and conflict areas. On the one hand, the September 11 attacks showed the futility of such a strategy and the need for a global security system. On the other hand, the consequences of subsequent invasions into Afghanistan and Iraq revealed the inadequate legitimacy of 'liberal imperialism' and exposed rifts within the West.

In the modern world, public bads arise because nation-states and international organizations do not produce enough global public goods. Moreover, differing definitions of good and bad, global inequality, and lack of cooperation among states make it difficult to formulate clear strategies. International cooperation is often restricted by the lowest common denominator, which is the struggle with existing problems, but does not lead to reduced costs. On the contrary, spending on defence, conflict management, the establishment of new international institutions, the response to natural disasters (which are all measures to counter global bads) may considerably exceed the long-term investment in the provision of global public goods. In the long run, providing global public goods is more cost-effective than fighting global public bads. There is thus a demand for new approaches to the problem of international collective action.

Global Public Goods and the Problem of Collective Action

The deep transformation of the last 20 years, since the end of the Cold War, has radically changed the global geopolitical landscape. The erosion of state sovereignty, growing interdependence among key international actors, and the emergence of new actors (such as transnational corporations and international NGOs) have led to the 'globalization' of the concept of public goods. Global public goods should produced and provided at the international level, rather than the national level, and key international organizations and forums should drive positive change. Another shift is the widening of the range and scope of problems facing the international community. Human rights abuse as well as social and ethnic conflicts with regional and global impacts (such as political destabilization and migration) are no longer restricted to a country's domestic affairs. Moreover, the global economy has reached an unprecedented level of integration, as demonstrated by the financial crisis of 2008.

However, this globalized world is not becoming any more equal. The US and the EU maintain the lead in global politics, economy, and culture. In the final analysis, the prospect of fighting global public bads boils down to the ability of Western countries to respond to external threats and overcome their self-interest. The provision of global public goods is impossible without the commitment of those countries to make long-term investments and to give up voluntarily some of their super-profits in favour of the 'black hole' of developing countries. The rise of China and the realization of the principle of sharing global responsibility has led to some hope of revising the global agenda (Lomanov 2008). However, since its economic development is to a large extent the result of the wealth of the key consumers of Chinese goods – in the US and Europe – China's position has been undermined by the global financial crisis.

The lack of international collective action is one of the main obstacles to creating stable mechanisms for providing global public goods. The common aims of international actors are vague; they lack the understanding and vision of collective action and coordination. There is no clear solution to the problem of distributing the costs of providing of global public goods, and the temptation of free riding is too strong. Traditional and rational thinking is sometimes not able to understand the stimulus of those who engage in humanitarian activities. However, the number of transnational NGOs that address global humanitarian concerns is growing, and this is an encouraging fact.

There are three main strategies for creating global public goods: summation, weakest link and best practice (Kaul, Grunberg, and Stern 1999). Summation aims at pooling the efforts of all stakeholders, but carries the greatest risk of free riding. Its essence is simple: everyone contributes to the creation of the global public good, for example, trying to reduce carbon dioxide emissions. An overall reduction of emissions is a result of actions of all the participants irrespective their size, status, and geographical location.

In the weakest link strategy, the provision of the global public good is measured by the effort of the weakest member. Most developed countries will make considerable progress in their fight against infectious diseases or terrorism, but the creation of the final good – that is, the eradication of these public bads – is impossible without involving every country in the world. Cooperation with the weakest links in the chain is thus critical to the provision of global public goods.

Best practice is the most promising method for creating global public goods. It is best suited to the current deep social and technological gap between the North and the South. The provision of global public goods in these conditions is a prerogative of developed countries, which have considerable knowledge and opportunities to develop environmentally friendly technologies, overcome infectious diseases, and respond to emergencies. There is, however, a question about whether these public goods are truly global or whether they deepen the gap between the richest and poorest parts of humanity.

Multidimensional international cooperation is undoubtedly the main prerequisite for progress in providing global public goods. The foundation has been laid since the 1990s. Much depends on the strategies of countries in managing the global financial and globalization crisis that began in 2008. The first steps must be taken by the Western countries and their multilateral institutions. The future of the humanity depends on the resolve of the EU, the G8, and the G20 to create and provide global public goods in a proactive and preventive manner, as these groups and their members have both the influence and the resources to bring about the necessary positive changes in international cooperation.

References

Afontsev, Sergey (2003). 'Ot bor'by k rynky: economicheskaya kooperativnost' v miropoliticheskom vsaimodeistvii.' ['From Struggle to Market: An Economic Cooperation in International Political Interaction.'] *International Trends* 1(2). <www.intertrends.ru/two/002.htm> (July 2011).

Block, Fred (2004). 'Roli gosudarstva v ekonomike ' ['The Role of the State in the Economy.'] *Ekonomicheskaya Sociologia* 5(2): 37–56. <ecsoc.hse.ru/data/178/588/1234/ecsoc_t5_n2.pdf> (July 2011).

Desai, Meghnad (2003). 'Public Goods: A Historical Perspective.' In *Providing Global Public Goods: Managing Globalization*, edited by Inge Kaul, Pedro Conceição, Katell Le Goulven, et al., pp. 63–77. New York: Oxford University Press. <www.undp.org/globalpublicgoods/globalization/pdfs/Desai.pdf> (July 2011).

Gardiner, Rosalie, and Katell Le Goulven (2002). 'Sustaining Our Global Public Goods.' Briefing paper prepared for the World Summit on Sustainable Development, Heinrich Böll Foundation. <www.worldsummit2002.org/texts/Globalpublicgoods-briefing.pdf> (July 2011).

Gates, Bill (2010). '2010 Annual Letter from Bill Gates: Rich Countries' Aid Generosity.' Bill and Melinda Gates Foundation. <www.gatesfoundation.org/annual-letter/2010/Pages/rich-countries-foreign-aid.aspx> (July 2011).

Gureev, S.A. (1987). 'Princip svobody otkrytogo morya v sovremennykh usloviyakh.' ['The Principle of the Freedom of the High Seas in Contemporary Conditions.'] *Pravovedeniye* 1. <www.law.edu.ru/article/article.asp?articleID=178124> (July 2011).

Kaul, Inge, Isabelle Grunberg, and Marc A. Stern, eds. (1999). *Global Public Goods: International Cooperation in the 21st Century*. New York: Oxford University Press.

Kaul, Inge, and Ronald U. Mendoza (2003). 'Advancing the Concept of Public Goods.' In *Providing Global Public Goods: Managing Globalization*, edited by Inge Kaul, Pedro Conceição, Katell Le Goulven, et al., pp. 78–111. New York: Oxford University Press. <www.undp.org/globalpublicgoods/globalization/pdfs/KaulMendoza.pdf> (July 2011).

Lomanov, Alexander (2008). 'Mnogopolyarnaya gegemoniya.' ['Multipolar Hegemony.'] *Rossia v Global'noy Politike* 5. <www.globalaffairs.ru/numbers/34/10441.html> (July 2011).

Medvedev, Sergey (1999). 'Kosovo: A European Fin-de-Siècle.' *CTheory*. <www.ctheory.net/articles.aspx?id=117> (July 2011).

North, Douglass (1991). *Institutions, Institutional Change, and Economic Performance*. Cambridge: Cambridge University Press.

Nye, Joseph S. (2002). *The Paradox of American Power: Why the World's Only Superpower Can't Go It Alone*. Oxford: Oxford University Press.

Chapter 3

Key Concepts for Exploring the Role of the European Union in the G8

John J. Kirton

In order to explore the present and future role of the European Union in the G8, it is important to invoke, develop, and apply several key concepts from contemporary international relations theory. This chapter thus focuses in turn on soft power and soft law, concerts, vulnerability and shocks, globalization and complex adaptive systems, and multilateral governance and networks.

Soft Power and Soft Law

Soft power is a key concept for exploring the dynamics of the EU-G8 relationship. Whereas the term 'global public goods' refers primarily to the products of the EU and G8's global governance, as the two entities operate both alone and together, soft power refers to the influence those products exert, and to the diplomatic and political process by which such products arise. Soft power is therefore a form of national power or relative capability mobilized by EU and G8 members to conduct their EU/G8 diplomacy, a process of influence within these international institutions as members try to shape them to their preferred ends, and a type of impact that the institutions as collective actors have on their members and outsiders, on international relations, and on global order as a whole. It is power, process, and product alike.

Soft power in its key components has long had a legitimate, indeed central, place in the mainstream realist repertoire. Hans Morgenthau (1948) specified the soft, essentially non-material ideational capabilities of 'national will' and 'quality of diplomacy' as having a multiplicative rather than merely additive importance among the relevant material factors of national power he identified. Subsequent realists in this tradition have been faithful to the calculus set by Morgenthau (see Cline 1975, 1978).

The modern conception of soft power is pre-eminently the one introduced in 2002 by Joseph Nye (2002). It offered a third form of power and diplomacy, beyond coercion ('sticks') or payment ('carrots'). It added the distinctive power of attraction that could equally be used to influence the 'minds of men' through active persuasion efforts or even without any conscious or active effort on the attractors' part. Its sheer magnetic pull could work all alone.

A closely related concept, operating at the level of the international institution rather than its state members (as soft power primarily does), is that of soft law and the principles and norms it embeds (Abbott et al. 2000). Hard law – soft law's opposite on an ideal type spectrum – flows from the hierarchy within sovereign, territorial, exclusive Hobbesian or Westphalian states. It refers to 'legally binding obligations that are precise (or can be made precise through adjudication or the issuance of detailed regulations) and that delegate authority for interpreting and implementing the law' (Abbott and Snidal 2000). Hard law often comes in the form of a treaty. It is restrictive and can be judged when necessary.

Soft law, in contrast, is not legislatively entrenched. But it is far more than pure politics, where power and fixed interest and preferences are fully present and legalization entirely absent (Meyer 2009). Soft law is flexible but binding in a political, sociological, psychological, and personal sense rather than a legal one. It is still results oriented, as the actors that make commitments do so with the intention of complying with them. The type of soft law applied, among the many forms available, often reflects the problem being addressed (Chinkin 1989). Soft law covers a wide spectrum of intergovernmental behaviour.

The distinction between hard and soft law points to a defining difference between the EU and the G8 (Bayne 2011). Virtually since its start, what is now the EU has been the world's premier hard law international institution, wielding in some respects supranational authority over its member states. This authority is legally entrenched internationally and domestically, exercised by the European Commission as the regional civil service, adjudicated by the European Court of Justice, and overseen by the European Parliament. In sharp contrast, the G8 is a quintessential soft law institution, with no legal agreement or charter, and no executive, judiciary, legislature, or secretariat of any form. Indeed, it has no permanent physical embodiment at all.

Yet beyond this stark central distinction, two important complexities exist. First, the EU is also an informal soft law institution, both in the form of its intergovernmental summit-level European Council and also in the many non-legally mandated instruments and actions (from moral suasion onwards) that its agents wield to get their way. Second, the G8 contains as a member the EU with its ever expanding membership and the ever greater hard law and international organizational capacity that this supranational entity brings. Both the EU and G8 are thus both hard law and soft law bodies, if in different degrees and ways. Together they produce multilevel governance, with the four countries of Germany, France, Italy, and the United Kingdom serving as G8 members in their own right and also serving as core members of an EU that is a member of the G8 in its own right. The stark Westphalian formula of self-contained, territorially exclusive sovereign states operating in an anarchic system is compromised in these ways.

Membership

If both the EU and the G8 are thus soft law institutions, they also exercise soft power in consequential ways. The first and perhaps the greatest power of attraction they wield is the pull of potential membership, which powerfully influences the otherwise autonomous behaviour of sovereign states that are not yet a member of the club. It has long been known how powerfully the EU attracts would-be applicants to alter their internal policies, political affairs, and even constitutional structure to make them more EU-like and thus more likely to be accepted into the EU club (Checkel 2001). To a large degree these potential applicants are pulled by the promise of 'payment', in the form of subsidies or protection from potential predators outside. But the prestige of membership in such an elite club and the allure of being accepted as a modern, like-minded polity and as an equal have an additional, autonomous effect.

The highly informal G8 also exercises a similar power of potential membership attraction. A large number of consequential countries have wanted to join the club, since the leaders of the United Kingdom, Germany, France, and the United States met as the G4 at the British embassy in Helsinki in July 1975, followed by the first stand-alone G6 summit (which added Japan and Italy) at Rambouillet in France in November that year. While many have sought admission, including the original EU members of the Netherlands and Belgium as well as the EU itself from the outset and, subsequently, Australia, enough have succeeded to keep the promise and, from this, the power of potential membership attraction alive (Hajnal 2007). Immediately after the G8 started with six members in 1975, it added Canada in 1976. One year later it expanded again to include the EU as a member of the club, although not a member-state. EU accession confirmed the G8's character as having an open and expansionist membership, as being democratically devoted, and being an informational institution where other international institutions had an integral place. In the cases of both Canada's accession and the EU's, as well the case of Russia's admission in 1998, securing full membership was an incremental process, with the effect that the power of potential full membership was reinforced. To this day, the EU is not yet a member of all G8 institutions and has never hosted a summit at its own. Yet it increasingly sends two leaders to the annual G8 summit (the head of the commission and the rotating head of the council and presidency of the European Council assuming that state is not a member of the G8). Moreover, as early as 1982, in the trade ministers Quadrilateral composed of the US, Japan, Canada, and the EU, the EU itself extinguished the very existence of G8 members and major EU powers Germany, France, the UK, and Italy as separate actors in the club.

The would-be members of the G8 have been driven not only by a desire for payment. It is often more costly to be a member of the G8 club, which is counted on to finance and otherwise provide very expensive global public goods, rather than to remain a free-riding state on the outside. Nor have claimants and candidates been driven only by a defensive positionalist desire to prevent, through a de facto veto, any collective G8 club action that can do them harm or by an offensive hope of mobilizing members to reinforce their preferred preference in the world. Rather, they have also been driven by a desire for the prestige – at home and abroad – that sheer membership or participation in this small, elite, exclusive club of the world's major powers confers.

In this latter desire, states are pursuing what Morgenthau, that foundational World War Two realist, and, later, Robert Gilpin (1989) termed a foreign policy of 'prestige'. Such states are rational in their behaviour from the standpoint of their domestic policies as well. Indeed, the first of the six key dimensions of G8 governance performance is domestic political management – the way leaders use their membership and involvement in the G8 summit to help get what they want in politics and policy back home. The remaining dimensions, all internationally oriented, are of a more rational, instrumentalist nature: deliberation, direction setting, decision making, delivery, and the development of global governance.

Values

A second form of soft power, wielded by both the EU and the G8, exists in the shared values they and their members embody, espouse, and radiate outwards to a wanting world. Probably the most powerful of these values are open democracy and individual liberty, the core mission of both the EU and G8 as international institutions and – if more in principle that in practice – of all member states in each club. The expanding membership of both the G8 and the EU has reinforced rather than diminished this soft power pull. Another powerful value is the acceptance as equal allies of former enemies with unequal relative capabilities. Here both the EU and G8 have included countries on both the decline and rise. Both the EU and the G8 have included from the start the 1945 vanquished powers of Germany and Japan, as the Permanent Five members of the United Nations Security Council (UNSC) have not. The G8 accepted Russia before its material defeat as a Cold War power. The EU for more than six decades and even the G8 for four decades have helped end the interstate war in Europe that erupted recurrently for centuries before 1945.

Consensus

If potential membership and shared values are sources of soft power for the G8 and EU, consensus is the decision-making procedure by which unequal material capabilities are translated into outcomes that reflect the preferences of all members more equally. Both the European Council and the G8 depend on consensus, not in the latter case in the hard law form of a unit veto system but in a flexible exchange in which reluctant members, even the most powerful, adjust and even acquiesce in light of the overwhelming desire of the other members of the club. The resistant are thus attracted into the consensus of the club. This soft decision-making process can lead to hard commitments, replete with high levels of precision and obligation, if not necessarily delegation to others to put the consensus and commitment into effect. Although the EU, with its array of organizations, has many such opportunities for delegation, it also relies on the soft law alternatives on which the G8 entirely depends. It is also worth asking whether the dense conversation that leads to consensus, together with the prestige of membership in these elite clubs, reconstructs the conceptions of interest and identities of the members in ways that ease the task of delegation.

Compliance

Another soft power process within both the European Council and G8 concerns implementation, starting with the compliance with the consensus and the commitments of the club.

In the case of the informal, soft law G8, the compliance of member states with their commitments has always been positive overall, and has been steadily rising to rather high levels, especially since 1991. As an example, compliance has been high in the critical field of the environment, including climate change. Between 1975 and 1989, compliance with G7 commitments in energy – the closest cognate field assessed – was the highest of any issue area, at +0.73, relative to an overall all-issue area average of +0.30, measured on a scale from –1.00 to +1.00 (von Furstenberg and Daniels 1991). (Russia was not included in any compliance assessments until 1998.) Between 1988 and 1995, compliance with all climate change and biodiversity commitments rose to substantial levels, on the part of both the weakest member, Canada, and the most powerful member, the US (Kokotsis 1999). On climate change, from 1985 to 2007 compliance with the 45 measured priority commitments (out of a total of 166) produced an average compliance score of +0.50. During this time, compliance on climate change was as follows: the EU (+0.78), UK (+0.67), Japan (+0.63), Germany (+0.60), Canada (+0.51), France (+0.47), US (+0.39), Russia (+0.29), and Italy (+0.23) (see Table 3.1). All these major powers were in the positive range, with the world's second and third most powerful countries (Japan and Germany) achieving substantial compliance and the US also scoring well. The EU as a separate actor scored the highest compliance. Since 1987, particularly since 2002, compliance has generally risen, with a big dip between 1999 and 2001 and another brief dip in 2006. This record suggests that global, plurilateral summit institutions (PSIs), using soft law instruments, are effective in binding the world's most powerful states and above all one of its most powerful international institutions, the EU.

Within the EU, compliance comes from processes both hard and soft (Checkel 2001). An analysis of the implementation of EU environmental directives – a hard law instrument – from 1998 to 2000, as measured by the number of official infringements received by the 15 member states for non-implementation, suggests that the most faithful implementation comes from the smaller EU members (Denmark 5, Sweden 8, Netherlands 8), while the greatest violators include the larger members (Portugal 46, Italy 42, Belgium 40, Ireland 36, France 32, UK and

Table 3.1   G8 Compliance Scores on Climate Change and European Union Infringements on Implementation of Environmental Directives

G8 Compliance on Climate Change		European Union Implementation of Environmental Directives	
1985–2007	**Compliance Score**	**1998–2000**	**Number of Infringements**
European Union	+0.78	Denmark	5
United Kingdom	+0.67	Sweden	8
Japan	+0.63	Netherlands	8
Germany	+0.60	Germany	22
Canada	+0.51	Greece	26
France	+0.47	United Kingdom	28
United States	+0.39	Spain	28
Russia	+0.29	France	32
Italy	+0.23	Ireland	36
Average	+0.51	Belgium	40
		Italy	42
		Portugal	46

Source: Kokotsis (1999) and Perkins and Neumayer (Perkins and Neumayer 2007).

Spain 28, Greece 26, Germany 22, Austria 19, Luxembourg 16, and Finland 11) (Perkins and Neumayer 2007). In addition, members often implement directives late. This suggests that regional organizations, using hard law instruments, are not notably effective in binding the most powerful states that will have the biggest impact.

In addition to this comparative record on compliance, the EU's performance within the G8 stands out. The EU has consistently proven to be one of the highest complying members of the G8 club. One possible explanation – that it has bureaucracy of its own to implement – seems unlikely, because other members such as the US have large national organizations of their own to do such work. This performance points to the potential potency of soft power instruments – notably the skill the EU has acquired in forging meaningful, workable consensus among its members states and its desire to comply in order to strengthen its still fragile credentials within the prestigious G8 club.

Two other elements of the G8's compliance record illustrate the autonomous impact of soft power. First, the fact that compliance can be higher in regard to welfare objectives than it is for implementing instruments or actions used by member governments suggests that moral suasion works: if G8 governors collectively declare they want something, they will tend to get it, even though their own legal, organized governments do nothing to put it into effect (von Furstenberg and Daniels 1991). The second is the accumulating evidence on the catalysts of compliance contained within G8 commitments. While a few hard law instruments matter – notably reference to the functionally core international organization, many others including money mobilized (payment) do not (Kirton et al. 2010; Kirton, Roudev, and Sunderland 2010). At the same time, some soft law catalysts – notably priority placement – work in exerting a compliance creating effect.

Concerts

A second core concept is the classic one of the concert, drawn from the realist tradition in international political theory. Present in Morgenthau's (1948) compilation, it acquired further prominence with Henry Kissinger's (1957) classic, *A World Restored: Metternich, Casterleagh, and the Problems of Peace, 1812–1822*, and Hedley Bull's (1995) *The Anarchical Society: A Study of Order in World Politics*. It has since been theoretically developed by several leading scholars, and applied to G8 governance, starting with William Wallace (1984) and John Kirton (1989) and continuing with Richard Rosecrance (2001), Risto Penttilä (2003), and others.

The concept of concert is reliably realist in that it focuses on great power governance. Indeed, it highlights great power dominance of the system and their individual and collective provision of global order and global public goods. It identifies a concert as a distinctive form of international institution, and shows how it operates and what its systemic function and impact are. A concert is a club that includes all the great powers in the system, and only those powers. It meets at the summit or ministerial level, to decide collectively, by consensus, on all the major systemic issues of the day, including the existential questions of the states' territorial boundaries and even what states should exist. A concert's systemic power arises from its collective predominance, systemic reach, prestige, and internal diversity and from the absence of any outside great power rivals to form a counter-coalition to challenge concert governance or contain its systemic effect.

Both the EU and the G8 are, increasingly, global concerts. The EU, after Britain's accession, contains all the European great powers and historical imperial powers of regional and global relevance and reach, including such contenders for top-tier status as contemporary Spain. Its institutional embodiment as a concert comes in the increasingly frequent summits of the European Council. However, the presence of non-great powers as equal members of the Council erodes its claim to be a concert in pure form. Moreover, the absence of Russia as a full member limits its claim to be a pan-European global concert, relative to other Euro-centric PSIs (but not concerts) such as the Organization of Security and Co-operation in Europe (OSCE). It may even limit its claim to be a regional, European concert, depending on how Europe is defined. But it is clear that the admission of Russia as a full member of the European Council would make the council a genuinely global concert, given Russia's continuing status as a superpower, classically defined (Fox

1944). The admission of Canada, another Arctic, Pacific and Atlantic power that borders on two European states (France and Denmark) as well as Russia, would help as well.

The G8 began life in 1975–76 as a global democratic concert containing all and only the major powers that were democracies from around the world. The admission of Russia as a permanent member in 1998 transformed it into a more global concert while maintaining its core character and soft power as a democratic one. At present, the rise of China, India, and Brazil as first-tier powers of actual or potential global relevance and reach raises the question of the imminent need or desirability for the G8 to admit them as permanent members, if the G8's character as a global (and still overwhelmingly democratic) concert is to be maintained (Alexandroff 2008; Cooper and Antkiewicz 2008). There is a credible case to make that India and even Brazil currently meet the criteria for inclusion in the democratic, major power G8 concert, and even that China someday will.

As a permanent and virtually full member of the G8 concert, the EU is far better positioned to exert global influence and shape world order in the G8 than in any other global institution (such as the UNSC and the executive boards of the International Monetary Fund and the World Bank). While the expansion of the G8 to include Russia, as a democratizing major European power, was easy for the EU to encourage and accept, any expansion of the G8 to embrace the very different and more distant China, India, and Brazil has not been. Yet the EU's secure place in an expanded G8 global concert would multiply its global impact even if it would potentially dilute its influence within the club. Moreover, the EU's role in shepherding Russia's inclusion could give the EU an important role in bringing in multilingual and federal India, China, and Brazil too.

Vulnerability and Shocks

The third important concept is vulnerability, first introduced to international relations theory by Robert Keohane and Joseph Nye (1977) in *Power and Interdependence: World Politics in Transition*. It distinguished between mere sensitivity, where changes in one polity are felt instantly within another in an increasingly interdependent system, and vulnerability, where the negative (and positive) societal impacts are still felt by and within the receiving polity even after it unilaterally changes its national policy (through protectionist, isolationist, or other substantive policy adjustments) to offset the impacts. After the advent of interdependence, this vulnerability unfolded within the Westphalian world dominated by self-contained, rational states. The oil supply shock experienced by America in 1973 due to the embargo by the Organization of Petroleum Exporting Countries (OPEC) was the paradigmatic empirical case that brought to life this concept of classic state-to-state controlled vulnerability.

The new vulnerability set this state-centric world aside to focus on the unintended, even unconscious, or invisible threats, arising from non-state or even non-human sources or processes arising anywhere, which could flow in an untargeted and uncontrolled fashion to attack any other state and its citizens, in ways that the receiving government, even if aware, was unable to prevent (Kirton 2007). Another oil shock experienced by America – the world's most powerful country – in 1979, due to the Iranian fundamentalist revolution using terrorist tactics to assault the sanctity of diplomatic establishments, moved the world into the age of new vulnerability. A succession of compounding vulnerabilities in finance, terrorism, nuclear energy, crime, health, the environment, and cyberspace have become a recurrent feature of American and global life today (Nye 2011).

These new vulnerabilities can be chronic, incremental, cumulative, and invisible; they can exact severe damage and death, even if they never erupt into a single geographically and temporally concentrated catastrophic event. But they are more likely to have political global governance impacts if they are activated and brought to the attention of major power governors by shocks. Shocks are sudden, severe, surprising events that cause exceptional, abnormal, outlier damage and death. They are distinct from the classic acute international crisis, defined by high threat, high surprise, and low time to respond, in that they are real rather than potential impacts and can be responded to over a longer period of time in order to reduce the underlying vulnerability that they reveal to all.

The members of both the EU and the G8, and hence their institutions, are increasingly afflicted by the new vulnerability and the shocks that they generate, and thus are also driven by the processes that arise. The members of both the EU and the G8 have moved from being interdependent at their start to being increasingly inter-vulnerable not only to processes or events that occur in another member (no matter how geographically distant) but in the global community as a whole. As a result both the EU and the G8 have been drawn into global governance, as opposed to intra-regional or intra-G8 governance. Both the EU and the G8 – notably the EU Council and the G8 summits – have agendas dominated by these new vulnerabilities even if the old threats and crises – such as the nuclear explosions in India and North Korea – remain on the agenda as well.

Both the EU and the G8 increasingly respond to the shocks that show such new vulnerability, particularly to second and subsequent shocks and even to the accumulating, non-shocking evidence that identifies chronic, compounding vulnerabilities approaching critical thresholds, as in the case of climate change. Moreover, the increase in these new vulnerabilities is moving the EU and the G8 from being institutions-as-forums dominated by competition based on relative capability among their autonomous members with distinct preferences, interests, and values towards being clubs or even communities with a common responsibility to provide global public goods to prevent damage and even extinction to themselves and those outside. This thrust towards community takes place largely apart from any periodic moves or controversies about hard law being taken to higher-level, more supranational constitutions in the EU's case. In both the EU and the G8, this creation of community and consolidation is a one-way ratchet-like street with virtually no retreats, even if there are many detours, delays, and gridlocks, which might last for a long time, along the route.

Globalization and Complex Adaptive Systems

The next core concept is the movement driven in part by the systemic process of regionally concentrated and system-wide globalization (as in communications, transportation, and trade). More importantly, it is also driven by the processes where complex adaptive systems are at work, notably the natural environment, health, and contemporary finance (Holling 2001; Jervis 1997; Rosenau 1997). Globalization refers to the increasing speed, scope, scale, and penetrative impact of trans-border flows. Complex adaptive systems are, distinctly, processes characterized by non-linearity, uncertainty, complexity, and unpredictability. The former leads countries to calculate how they can and do act to win a game they all accurately understand, so they will not fall behind their competitors and may even move ahead. The latter leads all to come together to discover the way things now work in a world no one understands, to prevent each and all from going down for good. Constructing not only national interests and identities, but the connections that define how the system works, is the task at hand.

Multilevel Governance and Networks

The final pair of useful concepts are the concepts of multilevel governance and networks. Multilevel governance directs attention vertically to the way in which actors at several levels of analysis, from supranational entities such as the EU to local governments, act simultaneously across national borders horizontally, and within and across their own polities hierarchically, in order to achieve their intended results. Such multilevel dynamics are fuelled by the fact that the legal and actual hierarchical division of authority and jurisdiction is not symmetrical across all state members of the EU and the G8 (especially with the EU as a member), and by the openness of all states within each club. Such multilevel governance can be seen as an extension of the transnational relations or two-level games, concepts developed in the 1970s and '80s to explain G8 governance (Evans, Jacobson, and Putnam 1993).

The newer concept of networks for global governance focuses horizontally on the flow of politically relevant communication and interaction of state and non-state actors of all sorts (Slaughter 2009). Horizontal flows, rather than the hierarchical legal or capability-based authority, determine outcomes. This concept captures the character of the G8 at the levels of leaders, ministers, and officials, as a club and concert of equals, especially as it has extended to link with the Group of Five (G5) of China, India, Brazil, Mexico, and South Africa, the Group of Twenty (G20) systemically significant states, many other participating countries

Table 3.2   The G8/G20 Summit Network through Plurilateral Summit Institutions

G20	G8+ G5	MEM	CMW	FRA	ASEM	OSCE	APEC	SOA	SCO	NATO	Total
United States	+	+	-	-	-	+	+	+	-	-	+	6
Japan	+	+	-	-	-	+	-	+	-	-	-	4
Germany	+	+	-	-	-	+	+	-	-	-	+	5
United Kingdom	+	+	+	-	+	+	-	-	-	-	+	6
France	+	+	-	+	+	+	-	-	-	-	+	6
Italy	+	+	-	-	-	+	+	-	-	-	+	5
Canada	+	+	+	+	-	+	+	+	-	-	+	8
Russia	+	+	-	-	-	-	+	+	-	+	-	5
European Union	+	+	-	-	-	+	-	-	-	-	-	3
China	+	+	+	-	-	+	-	+	-	+	-	5
India	+	+	+	-	-	+	-	-	-	Observer	-	5
Brazil	+	+	-	-	-	-	-	-	+	-	-	3
Mexico	+	+	-	-	-	-	-	+	+	-	-	4
South Africa	+	+	+	-	-	-	-	-	-	-	-	3
Indonesia	-	+	-	-	-	+	-	+	-	-	-	3
Korea	-	+	-	-	-	+	-	+	-	-	-	3
Australia	-	+	+	-	-	-	-	+	+	-	-	3
Argentina	-	-	-	-	-	-	-	-	+	-	-	1
Saudi Arabia	-	+	-	-	-	-	-	-	-	-	-	2
Turkey	-	-	-	-	-	+	+	-	-	-	+	3
Spain	-	-	-	-	-	+	+	-	-	-	+	3
Netherlands	-	-	-	-	-	+	+	-	-	-	+	3

Notes: APEC = Asia Pacific Economic Cooperation; ASEM = Asia–European Union meeting; CMW = Commonwealth; FRA = Francophonie; G5 = Group of Five; MEM-16 = Major Economies Meeting; NATO = North Atlantic Treaty Organization; OSCE = Organization for Security and Co-operation in Europe; SCO = Shanghai Co-operation Organization; SOA = Summit of the Americas.

Includes only plurilateral summit institutions of trans-regional reach containing members from the developed and emerging and developing worlds. Spain and the Netherlands are included because they have been invited to participate in G20 summits. G8 members are indicated in bold.

and international organizations, and a growing dense array of civil society groups. It similarly captures the character of the energetically expanding EU, with the supranational European Commission added as an actor in the net.

Of particular importance for global governance is the global network of PSIs and the countries or other actors, inside or outside the EU and the G8, that constitute the most well-connected hubs. Table 3.2 reports a preliminary mapping of those major PSIs of global membership to which at least one member of the G20 belongs. It shows that European Council members Britain and France stand second (along with the US), as the most well-connected countries in the overlapping global PSI network. All G8 members (save Japan, but including Russia equally with Germany and Italy) are in the most well-connected top tier. The one anomaly is the EU itself as a G8 member. This points to the need to consider why the EU ranks relatively low, and what the advantages would be for EU, the G8, and global governance of making the EU a member of more global PSIs.

References

Abbott, Kenneth W., Robert Keohane, Andrew Moravcsik, et al. (2000). 'The Concept of Legalization.' *International Organization* 54(3): 401–20.

Abbott, Kenneth W., and Duncan Snidal (2000). 'Hard and Soft Law in International Governance.' *International Organization* 54(3): 421–56.

Alexandroff, Alan S., ed. (2008). *Can the World Be Governed? Possibilities for Effective Multilateralism.* Waterloo ON: Wilfrid Laurier University Press.

Bayne, Nicholas (2011). 'Challenge and Response in the New Economic Diplomacy.' In *The New Economic Diplomacy*, edited by Nicholas Bayne and Stephen Woolcock, pp. 59–79. Farnham: Ashgate.

Bull, Hedley (1995). *The Anarchical Society: A Study of Order in World Politics.* New York: Columbia University Press.

Checkel, Jeffrey T. (2001). 'Why Comply? Social Learning and European Identity Change.' *International Organization* 55(3): 553–88.

Chinkin, Christine M. (1989). 'The Challenge of Soft Law: Development and Change in International Law.' *International and Comparative Law Quarterly* 38(4): 850–66.

Cline, Ray S. (1975). *World Power Assessment: A Calculus of Strategic Shift.* Washington DC: Center for Strategic and International Studies.

Cline, Ray S. (1978). *World Power Trends and U.S. Foreign Policy in the 1980s.* Boulder CO: Westview.

Cooper, Andrew F., and Agata Antkiewicz, eds (2008). *Emerging Powers in Global Governance: Lessons from the Heiligendamm Process.* Waterloo ON: Wilfrid Laurier University Press.

Evans, Peter B., Harold K. Jacobson, and Robert D. Putnam, eds (1993). *Double-Edged Diplomacy: International Bargaining and Domestic Politics.* Berkeley: University of California Press.

Fox, William T. R. (1944). *The Super-Powers: The United States, Britain, and the Soviet Union – Their Responsibility for Peace*. New York: Harcourt, Brace.

Gilpin, Robert (1989). *War and Change in World Politics*. Cambridge UK: Cambridge University Press.

Hajnal, Peter I. (2007). *The G8 System and the G20: Evolution, Role, and Documentation*. Aldershot: Ashgate.

Holling, Crawford (2001). 'Understanding the Complexity of Economic, Ecological, and Social Systems.' *Ecosystems* 4(5): 390–405.

Jervis, Robert (1997). *System Effects: Complexity in Political and Social Life*. Princeton: Princeton University Press.

Keohane, Robert, and Joseph Nye (1977). *Power and Interdependence: World Politics in Transition*. Boston: Little, Brown.

Kirton, John J. (1989). 'Contemporary Concert Diplomacy: The Seven-Power Summit and the Management of International Order.' Paper presented at the annual convention of the International Studies Association, 29 March–1 April, London. <www.g8.utoronto.ca/scholar/kirton198901> (July 2010).

Kirton, John J. (2007). *Canadian Foreign Policy in a Changing World*. Toronto: Thomson Nelson.

Kirton, John J., Nikolai Roudev, and Laura Sunderland (2010). 'Finance and Development Compliance in the G8: The IMF and World Bank Role.' In *Making Global Economic Governance Effective*, edited by John J. Kirton, Marina Larionova and Paolo Savona. Farnham: Ashgate.

Kirton, John J., Nikolai Roudev, Laura Sunderland, et al. (2010). 'Health Compliance in the G8 and APEC: The World Health Organization's Role.' In *Making Global Economic Governance Effective*, edited by John J. Kirton, Marina Larionova and Paolo Savona. Farnham: Ashgate.

Kissinger, Henry (1957). *A World Restored: Metternich, Castlereagh, and the Problems of Peace, 1812–1822*. Boston: Houghton Mifflin.

Kokotsis, Eleanore (1999). *Keeping International Commitments: Compliance, Credibility, and the G7, 1988–1995*. New York: Garland.

Meyer, Timothy (2009). 'Soft Law as Delegation.' *Fordham International Law Journal* 32(3). <papers.ssrn.com/sol3/papers.cfm?abstract_id=1214422> (July 2010).

Morgenthau, Hans Joachim (1948). *Politics among Nations: The Struggle for Power and Peace*. New York: Knopf.

Nye, Joseph S. (2002). *The Paradox of American Power: Why the World's Only Superpower Can't Go It Alone*. Oxford: Oxford University Press.

Nye, Joseph S. (2011). *The Future of Power*. New York: PublicAffairs.

Penttilä, Risto E.J. (2003). *The Role of the G8 in International Peace and Security*. Oxford: Oxford University Press.

Perkins, Richard, and Eric Neumayer (2007). 'Implementing Multilateral Environmental Agreements: An Analysis of EU Directives.' *Global Environmental Politics* 7(3): 13–31.

Rosecrance, Richard, ed. (2001). *The New Great Power Coalition: Toward a Concert of Nations*. New York: Rowman and Littlefield.

Rosenau, James N. (1997). 'Many Damn Things Simultaneously: Complexity Theory and World Affairs.' In *Complexity, Global Politics, and National Security*, edited by David S. Alberts and Thomas J. Czerwinski. Washington DC: National Defense University.

Slaughter, Anne-Marie (2009). 'America's Edge: Power in the Networked Century.' *Foreign Affairs* 88(1): 94–113.

von Furstenberg, George M., and Joseph P. Daniels (1991). 'Policy Undertakings by the Seven "Summit" Countries: Ascertaining the Degree of Compliance.' *Carnegie-Rochester Conference Series on Public Policy* 35: 267–308.

Wallace, William (1984). 'Political Issues at the Summits: A New Concert of Powers?' In *Economic Summits and Western Decisionmaking*, edited by Cesare Merlini. London: St. Martin's Press.

PART III
The Key Players

Chapter 4

The G7/G8 System

John J. Kirton

An assessment of the G8's relevance to the European Union and their relationship requires a careful charting of the development of the G8 system as an international institution since its 1975 start, in the context of the many recent moves toward and proposals for often far-reaching G8 reform.

Such calls are driven by an emerging consensus that the G8 is rapidly losing its relevance in a world where power is shifting to the many emerging economies outside the established club (Fues 2007; Ikenberry 2008; Payne 2008). The central claim is that the G8 as the centre of global governance is declining in effectiveness, responsiveness, representativeness, and legitimacy largely because it no longer commands the globally predominant capability it once did. The primary prescription is that the G8 should reach out to include as full members the rapidly rising powers of China, India, Brazil, Mexico, South Africa, and perhaps others or it will soon be replaced by broader bodies such as a G20 finance ministers' forum now elevated to a summit-level club (Martin 2006; Cooper and Jackson 2007; Gnath 2007; Lesage 2007a). Countering this consensus are the G8 governors themselves, who have largely resisted this analysis and advice (Edwards 2011; Harper 2011). However, in the scholarly world, defenders of the current G8 configuration and the global governance status quo are very few indeed (Payne 2008; Uda 2008).

Reform proposals, such as the G8's need for a secretariat and a council of ministers, are sometimes borrowed with little thought from very different institutions, including the regional semi-supranational EU, or deduced from liberal institutionalist assumptions that more legalized formality is a good thing (Ikenberry 1993; Abbott et al. 2000). Rarely are they accompanied by any detailed analysis showing that the proposed changes – often already instituted in some form during the G8's four decades – would credibly cause the enhanced performance that the advocate seeks. This is despite the wealth of serious scholarly works now available on how well, how, and why the G8 actually works (Putnam and Bayne 1987, 1984; Bergsten and Henning 1996; Bayne 2000, 2005; Dobson 2004a, 2004b, 2006; Bailin 2005; Baker 2006; Hajnal 2007b).

This chapter explores the G8's core character, mission, capabilities, and governance. It assesses on this basis how changes in the G8's outreach, in-reach, and down-reach have enhanced its performance in the past and could do so in the years ahead. The analysis finds that since the start in 1975, the G8 as a modern democratic concert has increasingly met its central goal of producing a global democratic revolution and providing domestic political management, deliberation, direction setting, decision making, delivery, and the development of a new generation of global governance for itself and the world.[1] During this time, the G8 has maintained many of its globally predominant capabilities, largely because it has broadened enormously in outreach, embracing Japan, Italy, Canada, an EU expanding to 27 states and a now-reviving Russia as full members. It has also embraced a wide array of multilateral organizations and rising or regional powers as participants in its annual summit and institutions. It has thickened its own structure through in-reach by developing a dozen ministerial and more than 80 official-level institutions across many policy fields, if not yet ministerial forums for health, agriculture, industry, investment, and defence. It has deepened civil society participation through down-reach to involve at the G8 level the legislative speakers of its members, nongovernmental organizations (NGOs), religious leaders, the media, youth, and universities, but not yet parliamentarians, judiciaries, business, and labour as a whole. The G8's greatest failure has been its refusal to accept as new full members the rapidly rising democratic powers of the 21st century, as the G20 summit has done since its start in 2008 (Kirton 2010).

The G8 as a Democratic Concert

The G8 was consciously conceived and crafted as a global democratic concert by its leading visionary and architect, Henry Kissinger (1957, 1975). It was first recognized as such by British scholar William Wallace (1984), soon joined by others when the post-Cold War world dawned (Kirton 1989; Lewis 1991–92; Odom 1995). The concept of the G8 as a concert has now been accepted and applied by several leading international relations scholars and other analysts (Kibbe, Rosecrance and Stein 2001; Rasmussen 2001; Rosecrance and Stein 2001; Stein 2001; Alexandroff 2008, 2001; Fearon 2008).

The core characteristics of a concert are well known (Elrod 1976; Jervis 1986; Kupchan and Kupchan 1991, 1995; Bull 1995; Held 1995). Concerts must include only major powers. Decisions on the key questions of war, peace, territorial adjustment, and state creation must be made through consultation, conversation, and consensus, rather than the unilateralism, balancing, and bandwagoning that prevailed before the searing memory of Napoleon's revolutionary devastation brought the Concert of Europe to life in 1815. And great powers must not be humiliated, especially when their ultimate agents, namely their leaders, meet face to face, as the whole world looks on.

From the start, the G8 was a modern democratic concert (Kirton 1989; Dewitt, Haglund and Kirton 1993). As the G8 itself explicitly stated at the start of its communiqué from its first summit in November 1975, its central purpose, indeed

---

1   For the purposes of this chapter, the term 'G8' includes the G7 period of 1975–97, before Russia became a member.

its very *raison d'être*, was to protect within its own members and promote globally the values of 'open democracy, individual liberty, and social advance'. To be sure, among its founding and newer members there is a considerable divergence in the philosophy and practice of open democracy at home, starting with the great divide between presidential and parliamentary systems, the political party system, and how often the party in power has changed. Moreover, all members have been slow to approach the shared standard of democratic ideals, and some have suffered severe setbacks along the way. America, Britain, and Canada, whose democratic journey dates from the Magna Carta of 1215, have been travelling toward the ideal for the better part of a millennium, and have suffered such traumas as slavery, civil war, civil strife, and the Watergate constitutional crisis along the way. Nonetheless, open democracy is a sufficiently foundational, strong, shared standard that it is the second core criterion (after major power inclusion) by which the G8's composition, performance, and reform should be judged.

Concert and democracy form the foundation on which the subsequent and subordinate criteria of effectiveness, responsiveness, representativeness, and legitimacy are built. Effectiveness refers to the capacity of the club to solve the problems at hand, ideally in the most efficient and desirable way. It can be charted across the six basic dimensions of global governance that most international institutions perform. The first is domestic political management, where G8 governors give their own citizens as well as the world's the confidence that open democratic societies can overcome the many profound challenges they face. The second is deliberation, where G8 governors meet face to face to foster transparency, understanding, trust, and the priority for particular problems that require solutions from global governors in a globalizing world. The third is direction setting, by defining on democratic foundation new principles of fact, causation, rectitude, and new norms for proscribing, permitting, and prescribing what states and other actors should, may, and should not do as a result (Krasner 1982). The fourth is decision making, by collectively committing to specific, future-oriented actions, often replete with precision, obligation, and delegation, to put the consensus on these principles and norms into practical effect (Abbott et al. 2000). The fifth is delivering these commitments by having the members individually comply with what they have collectively committed to, and do so not only in their converging expectations but in their observed behaviour as well. The sixth is developing global governance, by generating a new system of international institutions to meet the changing needs of the global community in a rapidly globalizing age, and doing so by incremental improvement and prescient action as well as through the 'big bangs' that come only after destructive global wars (Ikenberry 2001).

Responsiveness refers to the fast-moving flexibility of an institution in recognizing new problems and addressing them in a timely and well-tailored way. It also extends to proactively and preventatively addressing them up before they break out in big and much more costly forms. To be sure, concerts – the ultimate form of collective great power governance – are inherently conservative, consultative, and slow-moving creatures. The leaders of their member states as individuals cannot be expected or asked to see and shape the future more clearly and wisely than anyone else (Bayne 1999). But because they have at their call the great capabilities of their states and societies, they can be expected and asked to identify and project critical global trends and challenges before others do. And with their great global reach, responsibilities, and roles, and their basic rule of collective decision making with no surprises, they can be expected and asked to see, prevent, and respond to crises sooner and better than other classes of countries, and other kinds of international institutions do.

Representativeness is highly problematic, as the endless debate and impasse about reform of the Permanent Five of the United Nations Security Council (UNSC) attest. In virtually all cases, effective forums for global governance are created as self-selected clubs of victor powers, with the great powers most responsible for the victory at the centre of the creation and cabal (Ikenberry 2001). Today's UN was born in 1945, and its predecessor the League of Nations was born in 1919, very much this way. For concerts, the relevant criterion of representativeness is whether all the great powers – victor and vanquished – are included in the club. They were in 1815 and in the post–Cold War G8 in 1998, but not in the League in 1919 or the UN in 1945.

The tendency to define representativeness in geographic terms has little relevance for the G8 concert, especially in today's world. The G8 is composed of only and all of the world's major powers that, by definition, are those that affect, consider, and have a sense of individual and collective responsibility for the entire world all the time (Bull 1995). Given intensifying globalization, defined by the decline and death of distance, geographical or regional representation matters much less today than it may have mattered in the brief interlude after the empires of Europe's great global powers faded away and before today's post–Cold War globalization arrived. On the other dimensions of representativeness – race, religion, language, level of development, and a broader array of 'civilizational' criteria – the G8 has always possessed sufficient diversity among its existing members, and with their largely open societies, multicultural demography and mobile diasporas as well (Huntington 1996). It is only on the gender dimension where, with only three women ever attending the summit, G8 leadership – if not their states and societies below – is egregiously flawed, although less at this level than the UN, the International Monetary Fund, or the World Bank have been with their executive heads (Dobson 2008). Adding most of the favourite country candidates, apart from a democratic India once led by Indira Gandhi, and a democratic Brazil now led by Dilma Rousseff, would do relatively more harm than good here.

Legitimacy is not primarily about 'being there' to be seen, to watch, or to speak. Every individual on the planet reserves the right in his or her professional or private life to have meetings at which not everyone in some larger group or the entire world has a natural, human, or socially constructed right to be present. In the political world of global governance, the Permanent Five is a particular case in point. Such exclusive meetings are not illegitimate as a result. Nor does legitimacy arise only when some outside analysts' arbitrary and rather perfectionist concepts of procedure and performance are applied ex post (Sohn 2005).

Legitimacy, defined as 'right rule', is seen in the voluntary participation, consent, deference, or acquiescence of the governed, in the absence of coercion, intimidation, or bribery by the governors. It has several dimensions. One is input legitimacy – whether the right number and set of views and actors are consulted, responded to, or otherwise have their inputs fed in. A second is throughput legitimacy – how well and how fairly the right process deals with all relevant views in a respectful, equal, and balanced way. The third is output legitimacy, or whether the right decisions are made to solve the problem in the interests of the club and the broader community of which it is a part. The fourth is 'within-put' legitimacy – whether the right values propel the governance system throughout. On this last dimension, the G8, as a club devoted to open democracy, individual liberty, and social advance, has a powerful, built-in legitimacy as a centre of global governance for a world where these values are increasingly cherished by many and shared by most (Buchanan and Keohane 2006). Indeed, when all the members of the UN unanimously endorsed the principle of an international 'responsibility to protect' at their World Summit in September 2005, they abandoned the UN's old constitutional charter principle of non-interference in the internal affairs of sovereign states to accept the core principle of the G8 since its start. The G8 led the use of force to protect civilians in Kosovo in 1999 and Libya in 2011, approved respectively by UNSC resolutions 1244 and 1973, thus putting this principle into effect.

Finally, the field of global governance innovation and reform is one that has long attracted idealists (Held 2004, 1995). They sometimes operate with admirable normative inspiration but less practical restraint on what they calculate and propose. While such an approach is appropriate for some purposes, it is more useful to consider G8 reform in the real world with reference to how comparable centres of global governance, over several centuries, have operated and evolved, and the results of the innovations, reforms, and architecture attempted and achieved there. For some purposes the G8 can be assessed against the other plurilateral summit institutions (PSIs) relevant to global governance, since they first arose with the British Empire-turned-Commonwealth about a century ago (Dunn 1996; Kirton 2008a). However, since the 1975 emergence of the G8, its prime competitor and thus comparator, as a comprehensive centre of global governance, is the Bretton Woods–UN system born out of war and victory in 1944–45.

The G8's Rising Relative Capabilities, 1975–2008

If the G8's claim to be an effective centre of global governance rests ultimately on its members' combined capabilities, it does not face an urgent need to add more members to maintain its global collective predominance in the face of any declining relative capability possessed by its current permanent members. This is due above all to the progressive incorporation of now rising Russia and an expanding EU. A close look at relative capability – measured by the real world of internationally transacted gross domestic product (GDP) at market exchange rates – reveals that the G8 has remained relatively constant in collective predominance since its start.

When today's G8 was founded in 1975 with its seven members (United States, Japan, Germany, Britain, France, and Italy, as well as Canada, promised a place by Kissinger from the start), the group commanded 69.01 percent of the world's capabilities as measured by GDP in the market exchange rates at the time. In 2008, the G8's eight country members plus the EU with its 27 members, contained 72.55 percent of the world's capabilities. If the G8's origin at the summit level is dated back to the July 1975 lunch at the British embassy in Helsinki of the 'Berlin Dinner' big four of the United States, Germany, Britain, and France, the rise is even stronger.

Since 1975 the G8 has kept pace with the rise of outside powers by adding as permanent members Canada, an ever expanding EU, East Germany as part of today's united Germany, and the Russian Federation. During this time, the expanding policy competence and supranational features of the EU have increasingly brought the G8 toward resembling a regular federal state (see Appendix 4.1) (Ruggie 1993). More specialized concepts of capability confirm this conclusion (Fox 1944; Morgenthau 1948; Keohane and Nye 1977). For example, G8 members still account for most official development assistance and the military missions protecting civilians in Libya in 2011.

The G8's Rising Performance, 1975–2008

With these predominant capabilities, the G8 has put in a robust and rising performance as a centre of global governance over its four-decade life (Rosenau 1995, 1997; Murphy 2000; Payne 2005). It has done so, first, by protecting within its members and promoting globally the values and practice of open democracy, individual liberty, and social advance. By this ultimate standard it has been strikingly successful in producing the global democratic revolution still unfolding throughout the world with the post-Cold War victory starting in 1989, and the Arab awakening starting in 2011 constituting its two greatest surges.

The G8 started defensively, by bringing democrats in and keeping communists out of a new post-Franco Spain in 1975, an embattled Italy in 1976, and a France with home-grown communists in its coalition government as the new cold war of the 1980s began (Hajnal 2007b). In 1989 the G8 sparked and shaped the second Russian revolution – the largely peaceful destruction of the Soviet Union, bloc, and system and the rise of largely democratic polities in their place. It later helped bring democracy to the Balkans and Indonesia, protect it in the Americas, and support it in Africa as the new millennium dawned. These successes were brought by the G8 acting as a concert of all the world major power democracies, delivered by popularly elected leaders deeply committed to democracy, through a club they considered their own. Strengthening these fundamental foundations for proven performance is the standard by which any G8 reform proposals should be judged and by which any G8 reform programme should unfold.

Across all the six dimensions of global governance, the G8 performed well during its first 37 years (Kirton 2008c). As Appendix 4.2 shows, from 1975 to 2011, it held 108 days of leaders' discussions whose outcomes were recorded in 206 public documents. These contained 3,479 collective commitments, which were complied with by G8 members in the following year at an average level of +0.41 on a scale ranging from –1 to +1. Over this time G8 performance rose. Although performance has varied from year to year, there was a general ratchet-like rise, with two notable jumps. The first came as the Cold War ended in 1989 and the second as globalization took hold when the 21st century dawned. As all these achievements took place without the addition of any G8, EU- or UN-like legal charter, council of ministers, secretariat, or stand-alone bureaucracy, the value of many of the standard liberal institutionalist, legalized, hard law proposals for G8 reform are cast into considerable doubt (Abbott et al. 2000; Kirton and Trebilcock 2004). At the same time, this robust and rising record allows for evidence-based assessments of the current proposals for outreach, in-reach, and down-reach to improve performance even further in the years ahead.

Outreach: Membership and Participation

The first component, outreach, has long received most of the attention in the G8 reform debate (Kirton 2005; Martin 2006; Cooper and Jackson 2007; Lesage 2007b; McCain 2007; Bergsten 2008; Cooper and Antkiewicz 2008; Holbrooke 2008; Kirton 2008b). As Appendix 4.3 shows, the G8 has already more than doubled its membership as measured by the number of countries whose leaders came to the summit every year. Its first major expansion from the 'Berlin Dinner' four – the United States, Britain, France, and Germany, whose leaders had lunch at the British embassy in Helsinki in July 1975 – to the six at the first regular summit at Rambouillet a few months later in November was a 50 percent advance. Adding Japan and Italy brought the world's second and fifth ranking powers in, turned a Euro-Atlantic club into a Mediterranean, Asia-Pacific, and thus global one. It substantially expanded the G8's geographical, linguistic, and religious diversity. Adding Canada, a transcontinental country with the second largest territory in the world, in 1976 made the G8 more of a Pacific and Arctic club as well as an Atlantic and Americas club. The addition of the expanding multicultural EU, with its reunified Germany and now 27 members, reinforced the power, geographical reach, and diversity of the club, especially later by bringing in less economically developed Russia, which is not a member of the Organisation for Economic Co-operation and Development (OECD).

Throughout all this membership expansion, the G8 never removed a member, in keeping with the rules of a concert (but not of collective security). Its only two moves – both minor – in this direction came in 1985 when France refused to attend the first special summit on East-West nuclear arms control and in August 2008 when G7 foreign ministers and finance ministers held conference calls to discuss Russia's invasion of democratic Georgia and issued statements in response. The G8 has happily included the four European powers alongside the EU as members since 1977. It has always expanded by adding one member at a time. It has done so increasingly slowly and incrementally, with Russia and the EU still not full members of all ministerial forums.

Turning the G8 into a G13 by adding five full members all at once would thus be an unprecedented step. Nor is it clear why such a move would be needed. With the ever expanding EU included, the G8 now has 32 states as permanent members involved at first or second hand. The inclusion of a now rapidly rising Russia has enormously increased the G8's diversity on many dimensions, including level of development, as well as increasing the G8's predominant capability and internal equality. The EU does the same. The G8 thus stands in sharp contrast with a UNSC that has been frozen with the same permanent five members for almost 70 years, and with an IMF and World Bank whose executive boards have remained largely unchanged since 1944.

In terms of partial participation, as Appendix 4.4 shows, since 1996 a total of 17 different multilateral organizations have had their executive heads invited to the G8 summit and have come. The UN, representing virtually all the global community, has come to all but two since 2001. To be sure, the UN-G8 connection could be strengthened. But the best way to do so is by having the UN invite the G8, represented by its annual chair, to its inner management clubs such as the UNSC's Permanent Five. For those who argue, in formulaic realist fashion, that multilateral organizations do not matter and that only countries count, Appendix 4.5 shows that 44 countries have participated in the summit since 2001. They are led by members of the New Partnership for Africa's Development (NEPAD) and the emerging economies of the Group of Five (Brazil, China, India, Mexico, and South Africa), and include a wide range of democratic powers from all regions of the world.

In-Reach: The Institutionalization of Leaders, Ministers, and Officials

The G8's own institutionalization assumes even more importance as the leaders' time together at their regular annual summit has dwindled to one working day. At the leaders' level, in 2008 and 2009 the G8 successfully had the recently formed Major Economies Meeting/Forum (MEM/MEF) as a summit-level institution become an integral part of the annual G8 summit itself. Moreover, the G8 members have served as the core of the G20 summit, which started meeting in November 2008.

At the ministerial level, the G8 has developed a dozen ministerial institutions, with Japan in 2008 reinforcing the ones for energy, environment, development, and science and technology, while creating the one for agriculture that held its first meeting in 2009 (see Appendix 4.6). The G8 body for trade (where Europe was combined into one actor represented by the EU in the Trade Ministers Quadrilateral) has fallen into disuse at the ministerial level, if not at the deputies' level, even as the prospects for successfully concluding the long overdue Doha Development Agenda have declined. G8 ministerial institutions for investment, innovation, health, food and agriculture, transportation, communication, and defence have not emerged, despite the prominence that these matters have assumed on the summit agenda. As globalization has made many local and national issues now a matter for global governance, more portfolio ministries in G8 governments could benefit from having a G8 institution of their own.

At the official level, the G8 has created 97 bodies with 51 of them born since 2003 (see Appendix 4.7). They have been produced by all countries hosting the summit during the current cycle. The allegedly unilateralist United States of President George Bush in 2004 was particularly energetic in such international institution building. The official bodies, which come in diverse forms, are concentrated in policy areas that reflect the summit priority subjects at the time they are formed and in fields, such as energy and terrorism, where UN bodies are non-existent or weak. They have come to cover a wide range of fields. They are usually short-lived, although since the start a few such as the Nuclear Suppliers Group have continued. There has been a post–Cold War tendency to make them continuing bodies, as with the Financial Action Task Force (FATF) of 1989, and the Roma and Lyon Groups on crime and terrorism (Scherrer 2008, 2009). They have also expanded to include many other countries, with the first body – the London Nuclear Suppliers Group that coalesced in 1975 – now having 45 members in its club by 2008.

Institutionalization at the official level has tended to preserve the leaders' flexibility to start and stop such bodies as they wish, and thus keep their direct relationship with the leaders themselves. There has thus never been a G8 secretariat, beyond short-lived, issue-specific, selective steps such as the Support Implementation Group and Heiligendamm Dialogue Process platform that G8 governors have invented to assist with particular tasks (Cooper and Antkiewicz 2008).

Down-Reach: Civil Society Inclusion

The third component – down-reach for civil society inclusion – is where the G8 system expanded the least until 1998 (Hajnal 2007b, 2007a, 2008). Civil society started to connect with the G8 at the annual summit in 1984, when The Other Economic Summit (TOES) held a conference for oppositional NGO activists near the summit's time and place (see Appendix 4.8). In 1998 civil society became much more organized, connected, and influential, as the ad hoc coalition of religious, labour, and NGO groups in Jubilee 2000 mounted a multi-year campaign, met with G8 host Tony Blair at and during the G8's 1998 Birmingham Summit, and pushed the G8 to go further and faster on debt relief for the poorest. At Okinawa in 2000 such civil society groups were granted space on the summit site to hold briefings and met with the host prime minister of Japan, Yoshiro Mori, during the summit itself.

In the 21st century the G8 began to institutionalize its connection with civil society. In 2002, when Canada hosted the Kananaskis Summit, the Forum International de Montréal organized a meeting of global civil society leaders with G8 sherpas (the leaders' personal representatives), starting an engagement that continued and strengthened in subsequent years. Also in 2002, at the initiative of the speaker of the US House of Representatives, the speakers of the lower houses of G8 legislatures began to meet and continue to do so annually. However, compared to the degree of legislative involvement in other similar PSIs, starting with the venerable Commonwealth, which is almost a century old, the G8's legislative institutionalization is very late and still very light (Kirton 2008a).

The 2005 Gleneagles Summit inspired the creation of the multi-stakeholder Commission for Africa to support the work of British host Tony Blair and some summit colleagues on this priority (Wickstead 2007). The Make Poverty History campaign mobilized many across Britain. Through its Live 8 concert on the eve of the summit, it connected with up to a billion citizens around the world (Cooper 2007). There was also a Junior Eight (J8), during which secondary school students from G8 countries met briefly with the G8 leaders at the summit itself.

The next major step in forging the connection between the G8 and civil society came in 2006 when Russia hosted the G8 for the first time. The Russians created a formal year-long institution and process of Civil G8. It culminated with a meeting of 700 global civil society leaders with host Vladimir Putin in a freewheeling, public session on the eve of the St Petersburg Summit. That year G8 religious leaders also gathered for the first time, creating a process that continued to grow (Hamilton 2011). The year 2006 also marked the first meeting of the Moscow Club, where representatives of G8 news agencies began their annual meeting with G8 governors just before the summit's start. There has also arisen the University Eight, where leaders of universities from G8 countries meet. A process for their national academies of science to gather is developing as well.

References

Abbott, Kenneth W., Robert Keohane, Andrew Moravcsik, et al. (2000). 'The Concept of Legalization.' *International Organization* 54(3): 401–20.

Alexandroff, Alan S. (2001). 'China and the World Trade Organization: Can Economic Engagement Triumph over Containment?' In *The New Great Power*

Coalition: Toward a Concert of Nations, edited by Richard Rosecrance, pp. 345–66. New York: Rowman and Littlefield.

Alexandroff, Alan S. (2008). 'Introduction.' In *Can the World Be Governed? Possibilities for Effective Multilateralism*, edited by Alan S. Alexandroff, pp. 1–16. Waterloo ON: Wilfrid Laurier University Press.

Bailin, Alison (2005). *From Traditional to Group Hegemony: The G7, the Liberal Economic Order, and the Core-Periphery Gap*. Aldershot: Ashgate.

Baker, Andrew (2006). *The Group of Seven: Finance Ministries, Central Banks, and Global Financial Governance*. London: Routledge.

Bayne, Nicholas (1999). 'Continuity and Leadership in an Age of Globalisation.' In *The G8's Role in the New Millennium*, edited by Michael R. Hodges, John J. Kirton and Joseph P. Daniels, pp. 21–44. Aldershot: Ashgate.

Bayne, Nicholas (2000). *Hanging In There: The G7 and G8 Summit in Maturity and Renewal*. Aldershot: Ashgate.

Bayne, Nicholas (2005). *Staying Together: The G8 Summit Confronts the 21st Century*. Aldershot: Ashgate.

Bergsten, C. Fred (2008). 'A Call for an "Asian Plaza".' *International Economy* 22(2 (Spring)): 12–15, 70. <www.iie.com/publications/papers/bergsten0508. pdf> (July 2011).

Bergsten, C. Fred, and C. Randall Henning (1996). *Global Economic Leadership and the Group of Seven*. Washington DC: Institute for International Economics.

Buchanan, Allen, and Robert O. Keohane (2006). 'The Legitimacy of Global Governance Institutions.' *Ethics and International Affairs* 20(4): 405–37.

Bull, Hedley (1995). *The Anarchical Society: A Study of Order in World Politics*. New York: Columbia University Press.

Cooper, Andrew F. (2007). *Celebrity Diplomacy*. Boulder: Paradigm Publishers.

Cooper, Andrew F., and Agata Antkiewicz, eds. (2008). *Emerging Powers in Global Governance: Lessons from the Heiligendamm Process*. Waterloo ON: Wilfrid Laurier University Press.

Cooper, Andrew F., and Kelly Jackson (2007). 'Regaining Legitimacy: The G8 and the "Heiligendamm Process".' *International Insights* 4(10). <www. cigionline.org/articles/2007/07/regaining-legitimacy-g8-and-heiligendamm-process> (July 2011).

Dewitt, David, David Haglund, and John J. Kirton, eds (1993). *Building a New Global Order: Emerging Trends in International Security*. Toronto: Oxford University Press.

Dobson, Hugo (2004a). *Japan and the G7/8, 1975–2002*. London: RoutledgeCurzon.

Dobson, Hugo (2004b). 'Japan and the G8 Evian Summit: Bilateralism, East Asianism, and Multilateralism.' *G8 Governance* 9. <www.g8.utoronto.ca/ governance/dobson_g8g.pdf> (July 2011).

Dobson, Hugo (2006). *Group of 7/8*. London: Routledge.

Dobson, Hugo (2008). 'Where Are the Women at the G8?' G8 Information Centre, 9 July. <www.g8.utoronto.ca/scholar/dobson-2008.html> (July 2011).

Dunn, David H. (1996). *Diplomacy at the Highest Level: The Evolution of International Summitry*. New York: St. Martin's Press.

Edwards, Leonard (2011). 'Keeping the G8 Relevant: From Muskoka to Deauville.' In *The 2011 G8 Deauville Summit: New World, New Ideas*, edited by John J. Kirton and Madeline Koch, pp. 178–79. London: Newsdesk. <www.g8.utoronto.ca/newsdesk/g8deauville2011.pdf> (July 2011).

Elrod, Richard B. (1976). 'The Concert of Europe: A Fresh Look at an International System.' *World Politics* 28(2): 159–74.

Fearon, James D. (2008). 'International Institutions and Collective Authorization of the Use of Force.' In *Can the World Be Governed? Possibilities for Effective Multilateralism*, edited by Alan S. Alexandroff, pp. 160–95. Waterloo ON: Wilfrid Laurier University Press.

Fox, William T.R. (1944). *The Super-Powers: The United States, Britain, and the Soviet Union – Their Responsibility for Peace*. New York: Harcourt, Brace.

Fues, Thomas (2007). 'Global Governance Beyond the G8: Reform Prospects for the Summit Architecture.' *Internationale Politik und Gesellschaft* 2: 11–24. <www.fes.de/ipg/inhalt_d/pdf/03_Fues_US.pdf> (July 2011).

Gnath, Katharina (2007). 'Beyond Heiligendamm: The G8 and Its Dialogue with Emerging Countries.' *Internationale Politik* 8(3). <www.g8.utoronto.ca/scholar/IPGE_3_Gnath.pdf> (July 2011).

Hajnal, Peter I. (2007a). 'Civil Society's Long Road to Heiligendamm.' In *G8 Summit 2007: Growth and Responsibility*, edited by Maurice Fraser, pp. 207–01. London: Newsdesk.

Hajnal, Peter I. (2007b). *The G8 System and the G20: Evolution, Role, and Documentation*. Aldershot: Ashgate.

Hajnal, Peter I. (2008). 'Meaningful Relations: The G8 and Civil Society.' In *G8: Hokkaido Toyako Summit 2008*, edited by Maurice Fraser, pp. 206–08. London: Newsdesk.

Hamilton, Karen (2011). 'Faith Forum Calls for Inspired Leadership.' In *The 2011 G8 Deauville Summit: New World, New Ideas*, edited by John J. Kirton and Madeline Koch, pp. 184–85. London: Newsdesk. <www.g8.utoronto.ca/newsdesk/g8deauville2011.pdf> (July 2011).

Harper, Stephen (2011). 'A "New" G8: Building on Muskoka's Foundations.' In *The 2011 G8 Deauville Summit: New World, New Ideas*, edited by John J. Kirton and Madeline Koch, pp. 12–13. London: Newsdesk. <www.g8.utoronto.ca/newsdesk/deauville/g8deauville2011-harper-en.html> (July 2011).

Held, David (1995). *Democracy and the Global Order: From the Modern State to Cosmopolitan Governance*. Stanford: Stanford University Press.

Held, David (2004). *A Globalizing World? Culture, Economics, Politics*. 2nd ed. New York: Routledge.

Holbrooke, Richard (2008). 'The Next President: Mastering a Daunting Agenda.' *Foreign Affairs* 87(5): 2–24.

Huntington, Samuel P. (1996). *The Clash of Civilizations and the Remaking of World Order*. New York: Simon and Schuster.

Ikenberry, G. John (1993). 'Salvaging the G7.' *Foreign Affairs* 72(2): 132–39.

Ikenberry, G. John (2001). *After Victory: Institutions, Strategic Restraint, and the Rebuilding of Order after Major Wars*. Princeton: Princeton University Press.

Ikenberry, G. John (2008). 'The Rise of China and the Future of the West: Can the Liberal System Survive.' *Foreign Affairs* 87(1): 23–37.

Jervis, Robert (1986). 'From Balance to Concert: A Study of International Security Cooperation.' In *Cooperation under Anarchy*, edited by Kenneth A. Oye, pp. 58–79. Princeton: Princeton University Press.

Keohane, Robert, and Joseph Nye (1977). *Power and Interdependence: World Politics in Transition*. Boston: Little, Brown.

Kibbe, Jennifer, Richard Rosecrance, and Arthur A. Stein (2001). 'Conclusion.' In *The New Great Power Coalition: Toward a Concert of Nations*, edited by Richard Rosecrance, pp. 367–79. New York: Rowman and Littlefield.

Kirton, John J. (1989). 'Contemporary Concert Diplomacy: The Seven-Power Summit and the Management of International Order.' Paper presented at the annual convention of the International Studies Association, 29 March–1 April, London. <www.g8.utoronto.ca/scholar/kirton198901> (July 2010).

Kirton, John J. (2005). 'Toward Multilateral Reform: The G20's Contribution.' In *Reforming from the Top: A Leaders' 20 Summit*, edited by John English, Ramesh Thakur and Andrew F. Cooper, pp. 141–68. Tokyo: United Nations University.

Kirton, John J. (2008a). 'Enlarged Directorates as Effective Global Governance for All.' In *Lessons from the Past, Solutions for the Future*, edited by Kimon Valaskakis. Athens: New School of Athens.

Kirton, John J. (2008b). 'From G8 2003 to G13 2010? The Heiligendamm Process's Past, Present, and Future.' In *Emerging Powers in Global Governance: Lessons from the Heiligendamm Process*, edited by Andrew F. Cooper and Agata Antkiewicz, pp. 45–79. Waterloo ON: Wilfrid Laurier University Press.

Kirton, John J. (2008c). 'The G8 and Global Governance: An Architectural Review.' Paper prepared for the conference on 'Opportunities and Challenges for the G8: Lessons for the UK and Japan', Sheffield, 29 February–1 March.

Kirton, John J. (2010). 'The Group of Eight's Legacy, Limitations, and Lessons.' In *The New Dynamics of Summitry: Innovations for G20 Summits*, edited by Colin I. Bradford and Wonhyuk Lim, pp. 17–60. Washington DC and Seoul: Brookings Institution Press and Korea Development Institute.

Kirton, John J., and Michael J. Trebilcock, eds. (2004). *Hard Choices, Soft Law: Voluntary Standards in Global Trade, Environment, and Social Governance*. Aldershot: Ashgate.

Kissinger, Henry (1957). *A World Restored: Metternich, Castlereagh, and the Problems of Peace, 1812–1822*. Boston: Houghton Mifflin.

Kissinger, Henry (1975). 'The Industrial Democracies and the Future.' Address to the Pittsburgh World Affairs Council, 11 November. *Department of State Bulletin* 73(1901): 757–64.

Kokotsis, Eleanore (1999). *Keeping International Commitments: Compliance, Credibility, and the G7, 1988–1995*. New York: Garland.

Krasner, Stephen (1982). 'American Power and Global Economic Stability.' In *America in a Changing World Political Economy*, edited by William Avery and David Rapkin. New York: Longman.

Kupchan, Charles, and Clifford Kupchan (1991). 'Concerts, Collective Security, and the Future of Europe.' *International Security* 16 (Summer): 114–61.

Kupchan, Charles, and Clifford Kupchan (1995). 'The Promise of Collective Security.' *International Security* 20: 52–61.

Lesage, Dries (2007a). 'Globalisation, Multipolarity, and the L20 as an Alternative to the G8.' *Global Society* 21(3): 343–61.

Lesage, Dries (2007b). 'Is the World Imaginable without the G8?' *Internationale Politik und Gesellschaft* 4: 107–16. <www.g8.utoronto.ca/scholar/lesage_IPG.pdf> (July 2011).

Lewis, Flora (1991–92). 'The G7 1/2 Directorate.' *Foreign Policy*, pp. 25–40.

Martin, Paul (2006). 'Annual Meeting of the Development and Peace Foundation.' Speaking notes, Dresden, 8 June. <www.paulmartin.ca/20060608-annual-meeting-of-the> (July 2011).

McCain, John (2007). 'An Enduring Peace Built on Freedom: Securing America's Future.' *Foreign Affairs* 86(6): 19–34.

Morgenthau, Hans Joachim (1948). *Politics among Nations: The Struggle for Power and Peace*. New York: Knopf.

Murphy, Craig N. (2000). 'Global Governance: Poorly Done and Poorly Understand.' *International Affairs* 76(4): 789–803.

Odom, William (1995). 'How to Create a True World Order.' *Orbis* 39(2): 155–72.

Payne, Anthony (2005). 'The Study of Governance in a Global Political Economy.' In *Globalizing International Political Economy*, edited by Nicola Phillips. Houndmills, Basingstoke: Palgrave Macmillan.

Payne, Anthony (2008). 'The G8 in a Changing Global Economic Order.' *International Affairs* 84(3): 519–33.

Putnam, Robert, and Nicholas Bayne (1984). *Hanging Together: Co-operation and Conflict in the Seven-Power Summit*. 1st ed. Cambridge MA: Harvard University Press.

Putnam, Robert, and Nicholas Bayne (1987). *Hanging Together: Co-operation and Conflict in the Seven-Power Summit*. 2nd ed. London: Sage Publications.

Rasmussen, Greg (2001). 'Great Power Concerts in Historical Perspective.' In *The New Great Power Coalition: Toward a Concert of Nations*, edited by Richard Rosecrance, pp. 203–20. New York: Rowman and Littlefield.

Rosecrance, Richard, and Arthur A. Stein (2001). 'The Theory of Overlapping Clubs.' In *The New Great Power Coalition: Toward a Concert of Nations*, edited by Richard Rosecrance, pp. 221–34. New York: Rowman and Littlefield.

Rosenau, James N. (1995). 'Governance in the Twenty-First Century.' *Global Governance* 1(1): 13–43.

Rosenau, James N. (1997). *Along the Domestic-Foreign Frontier: Exploring Governance in a Turbulent World.* Cambridge: Cambridge University Press.

Ruggie, John G. (1993). 'Territoriality and Beyond: Problematizing Modernity in International Relations.' *International Organization* 47(1): 139–74.

Scherrer, Amandine (2008). 'The G8 Facing Organized Crime.' Paper prepared for the International Studies Association convention, Honolulu, 1–5 March.

Scherrer, Amandine (2009). *G8 versus Transnational Organized Crime.* Aldershot: Ashgate.

Sohn, Injoo (2005). 'Asian Financial Cooperation: The Problem of Legitimacy in Global Financial Governance.' *Global Governance* 11(4): 487–504.

Stein, Arthur A. (2001). 'Constrained Sovereignty: The Growth of Intrusiveness.' In *The New Great Power Coalition: Toward a Concert of Nations*, edited by Richard Rosecrance, pp. 261–82. New York: Rowman and Littlefield.

Uda, Shinichiro (2008). 'The Policy of Outreach and Expanding for the G8: Beyond the Eight.' Paper prepared for the conference on 'Opportunities and Challenges for the G8: Lessons for the UK and Japan', Sheffield, 29 February–1 March.

von Furstenberg, George M., and Joseph P. Daniels (1991). 'Policy Undertakings by the Seven "Summit" Countries: Ascertaining the Degree of Compliance.' *Carnegie-Rochester Conference Series on Public Policy* 35: 267–308.

Wallace, William (1984). 'Political Issues at the Summits: A New Concert of Powers?' In *Economic Summits and Western Decisionmaking*, edited by Cesare Merlini. London: St. Martin's Press.

Wickstead, Myles (2007). 'Where To From Here?' In *Biotechnology and Health: South Africa's Aspirations in Health-Related Biotechnology*, edited by Joanna Chataway and Wilmot Godfrey James. Pretoria: Van Schaik.

Appendix 4.1   European Union Legal Policy Competence

	Of all	Trade	Environment	Economics and money	Foreign policy	Security and defence	Employment and social affairs	Education	Customs union	Immigration policy	Justice	Culture	Development, human resources and aid	Health	Consumer protection and food safety	Fisheries	International Agreements	Welfare state	Corporate tax rates	Agriculture	Space	Energy
1975	22	4[a]	0	0	0	0	0	0	4[b]	0	0	0	0	0	0	4[c]	0	0	0	4[d]	3[e]	3[f]
1976	22	4	0	0	0	0	0	0	4	0	0	0	0	0	0	4	0	0	0	4	3	3
1977	22	4	0	0	0	0	0	0	4	0	0	0	0	0	0	4	0	0	0	4	3	3
1978	22	4	0	0	0	0	0	0	4	0	0	0	0	0	0	4	0	0	0	4	3	3
1979	22	4[g]	0	0	0	0	0	0	4	0	0	0	0	0	0	4	0	0	0	4	3	3
1980	22	4	0	0	0	0	0	0	4	0	0	0	0	0	0	4	0	0	0	4	3	3
1981	22	4	0	0	0	0	0	0	4	0	0	0	0	0	0	4	0	0	0	4	3	3
1982	22	4	0	0	0	0	0	0	4	0	0	0	0	0	0	4	0	0	0	4	3	3
1983	22	4	0	0	0	0	0	0	4	0	0	0	0	0	0	4	0	0	0	4	3	3
1984	22	4	0	0	0	0	0	0	4	0	0	0	0	0	0	4	0	0	0	4	3	3
1985	22	4	0	0	0	0	0	0	4	0	0	0	0	0	0	4	0	0	0	4	3	3
1986	25	4[h]	3	0	0	0	0	0	4	0	0	0	0	0	0	4	0	0	0	4	3	3
1987	25	4	3	0	0	0	0	0	4	0	0	0	0	0	0	4	0	0	0	4	3	3
1988	25	4	3	0	0	0	0	0	4	0	0	0	0	0	0	4	0	0	0	4	3	3
1989	25	4	3	0	0	0	0	0	4	0	0	0	0	0	0	4	0	0	0	4	3	3
1990	29	4	3	4[i]	0	0	0	0	4	0	0	0	0	0	0	4	0	0	0	4	3	3

1991	29	4	3	4	0	2	0	0	0	4	3	0	0	0	0	0	4	0	0	4	3	3
1992	45	4ʲ	3	4	0	2	0	0	0	4	3	0	0	2	0	0	4	0	0	4	3	3
1993	47	4	3	4	2	2	0	0	0	4	3	0	2	2	0	0	4	0	0	4	3	3
1994	47	4	3	4	2	2	0	0	0	4	3	0	2	2	0	0	4	0	0	4	3	3
1995	47	4	3	4	2	2	0	0	0	4	3	0	2	2	0	0	4	0	0	4	3	3
1996	47	4	3	4	2	2	0	0	0	4	3	0	2	2	0	0	4	0	0	4	3	3
1997	52	4	3	4	2	2	2	2	0	4	3	2	2	2	0	3	4	0	0	4	3	3
1998	52	4	3	4	2	2	2	2	0	4	3	2	2	2	0	3	4	0	0	4	3	3
1999	52	4	3	4ᵏ	2	2	2	2	0	4	3	2	2	2	0	3	4	0	0	4	3	3
2000	54	4	3	4	2	2	2	2	2	4	3	2	2	2	0	3	4	0	0	4	3	3
2001	54	4	3	4	2	2	2	2	2	4	3	2	2	2	0	3	4	0	0	4	3	3
2002	54	4	3	4ˡ	2	2	2	2	2	4	3	2	2	2	0	3	4	0	0	4	3	3
2003	54	4	3	4	2	2	2	2	2	4	3	2	2	2	0	3	4	0	0	4	3	3
2004	54	4	3	4	2	2	2	2	2	4	3	2	2	2	0	3	4	0	0	4	3	3
2005	54	4	3	4	2	2	2	2	2	4	3	2	2	2	0	3	4	0	0	4	3	3
2006	54	4	3	4	2	2	2	2	2	4	3	2	2	2	0	3	4	0	0	4	3	3
2007	54	4	3	4	2	2	2	2	2	4	3	2	2	2	0	3	4	0	0	4	3	3
2008	54	4	3	4	2	2	2	2	2	4	3	2	2	2	0	3	4	0	0	4	3	3

Notes: 0 = no competence, 5 = full compliance. 2 = complementary competence (action by European Union limited to supporting, encouraging, and coordinating action taken by members and union-level action cannot supersede competence of member); 3 = shared competence (provisions by EU may limit action of member states, and the members cannot implement measures that are not in accordance with EU provisions); 4 = full competence. a. Since 1957, common external tariff since 1968; b. Since 1968; c. Since 1970; d. Since 1960; e. Since 1975: European Space Agency; f. Since 1951; g. European Monetary System; h. Single European Act; i. Start development; j. Maastricht Treaty; k. Implementation of the euro; l. Introduction of the euro.

Source: Compiled by Judith Huigens.

Appendix 4.2   G8 Performance, 1975–2011

Year	Domestic political management	Deliberation			Direction setting	Decisional	Delivery	Development of global governance	
	Communiqué compliment	Days	Statements	Words	Core values			Ministerials created	G8 bodies created
1975	2	3	1	1,129	5	14	0.57	0	1
1976	0	2	1	1,624	0	7	0.09	0	0
1977	1	2	6	2,669	0	29	0.08	0	1
1978	1	2	2	2,999	0	35	0.36	1	0
1979	0	2	2	2,102	0	34	0.82	1	2
1980	0	2	5	3,996	3	55	0.08	0	1
1981	1	2	3	3,165	0	40	0.27	1	0
1982	0	3	2	1,796	0	23	0.84	0	3
1983	0	3	2	2,156	7	38	-0.11	0	0
1984	1	3	5	3,261	0	31	0.49	1	0
1985	4	3	2	3,127	1	24	0.01	0	2
1986	3	3	4	3,582	1	39	0.58	1	1
1987	2	3	7	5,064	0	53	0.93	0	2
1988	3	3	3	4,872	0	27	-0.48	0	0
1989	3	3	11	7,125	1	61	0.08	0	1
1990	3	3	3	7,601	10	78	-0.14	0	3
1991	1	3	3	8,099	8	53	0.00	0	0
1992	1	3	4	7,528	5	41	0.64	1	1
1993	0	3	2	3,398	2	29	0.75	0	2
1994	1	3	2	4,123	5	53	1.00	1	0
1995	3	3	3	7,250	0	78	1.00	2	2
1996	1	3	5	15,289	6	128	0.41	0	3
1997	16	3	4	12,994	6	145	0.13	1	3
1998	0	3	4	6,092	5	73	0.32	0	0
1999	4	3	4	10,019	4	46	0.38	1	5
2000	1	3	5	13,596	6	105	0.81	0	4
2001	1	3	7	6,214	3	58	0.55	1	2
2002	0	2	18	11,959	10	187	0.35	1	8

2003	0	3	14	16,889	17	206	0.66	0	5
2004	0	3	16	38,517	11	245	0.54	0	15
2005	8	3	16	22,286	29	212	0.65	0	5
2006	6	3	15	30,695	256	317	0.47	0	4
2007	12	3	8	25,857	651	329	0.51	0	4
2008	8	3	6	16,842	33	296	0.48	1	4
2009	13	3	10	31,167	62	254	0.33	2	9
2010	8	2	1	6,102	32	36	0.46	0	0
2011	7	2	3	15,458	172	120	NA	0	1
Total	108	102	206	351,184	1179	3479	–	16	94
Average	3.0	2.76	5.72	9,755.11	8.36	96.64	0.41	0.43	2.54

Notes: NA = not available. Delivery scores from 1975 to 1989 measure compliance with commitments selected by George von Furstenberg and Joseph Daniels (1991). Compliance scores from 1990 to 1995 measure compliance with commitments selected by Ella Kokotsis (1999). Compliance scores from 1996 to 2010 measure compliance with the G8 Research Group's selected commitments (see <www.g8.utoronto.ca/compliance>).

Appendix 4.3   Membership in G8 Summits

1975   United States, Britain, France, Germany
1975   Japan, Italy
1976   Canada
1977   European Community (9 members)
1981   European Community (10 members)
1982   Belgium* (also in 1987, 1993, 2001)
1986   European Community (12 members), Netherlands* (also 1991, 1997)
1995   European Union (15 members)
1998   Russia
2002   Spain* (also 2010)
2003   Greece*
2004   European Union (25 members), Ireland*
2006   Finland*
2007   European Union (27 members)
2009   Sweden
2010   European Council President (Belgium) (also 2011)

Note: * Leader participate in the G8 summit as the head of the rotating presidency of the European Council.

Appendix 4.4   Participating Multilateral Organizations in G8 Summits

Multilateral Organization	Total	1996	2000	2001	2002	2003	2004	2005	2006	2007	2008	2009	2010	2011
United Nations	11	1a	1a	1	1	1		1	1	1	1	1		1
World Bank	9	1a	1a	1		1		1		1	1	1		1
World Trade Organization	8	1a	1a	1		1		1		1	1	1		
International Monetary Fund	7	1a				1		1		1	1	1		1
International Energy Agency	5							1	1	1	1	1		
African Union	7							1	1	1	1	1	1	1
World Health Organization	3		1a						1	1				
OECD	3			1					1			1		
Food and Agriculture Organization	2			1								1		
International Atomic Energy Agency	2								1			1		
UNESCO	1								1					
Commonwealth of Independent States	1								1					
International Labour Organization	1											1		
International Fund for Agriculture and Development	1											1		
World Food Programme	1											1		
NEPAD	3											1	1	1
Arab League	1													1
Total	66	4	4	5	1	4	0	6	8	7	6	13	2	6

Note: Executive heads of secretariat or organization only. Excludes country chairs. a. Multilateral organizations participated only in sideline events. UNESCO = United Nations Educational, Social, and Cultural Organization; NEPAD = New Partnership for Africa's Development; OECD = Organisation for Economic Co-operation and Development.

Appendix 4.5   Participating Countries in G8 Summits

Country		2000	2001	2002	2003	2004	2005	2006	2007	2008	2009	2010	2011
South Africa	12	2000	2001	2002	2003	2004	2005	2006	2007	2008	2009	2010	2011
Nigeria	11	2000	2001	2002	2003	2004	2005		2007	2008	2009	2010	2011
Algeria	11	2000	2001	2002	2003	2004	2005		2007	2008	2009	2010	2011
Senegal	11	2000	2001	2002	2003	2004	2005		2007	2008	2009	2010	2011
China	6				2003		2005	2006	2007	2008	2009		
India	6				2003		2005	2006	2007	2008	2009		
Brazil	6				2003		2005	2006	2007	2008	2009		
Mexico	6				2003		2005	2006	2007	2008	2009		
Ghana	4					2004	2005		2007	2008			
Egypt	5				2003				2007		2009	2010	2011
Ethiopia	4						2005			2008	2009	2010	
Tanzania	2						2005			2008			
Turkey	2					2004					2009		
Australia	2									2008	2009		
Indonesia	2									2008	2009		
Korea	2									2008	2009		
Bangladesh	1		2001										
Mali	1		2001										
El Salvador	1		2001										
Moroccoa	1				2003								
Saudi Arabia	1				2003								
Malaysia	1				2003								
Switzerland	1				2003								
Afghanistan	1					2004							
Bahrain	1					2004							
Iraq	1					2004							
Jordan	1					2004							
Yemen	1					2004							
Uganda	1					2004							
Congob	1							2006					
Kazakhstanc	1							2006					
Angola	1										2009		
Denmark	1										2009		
Libyad	1										2009		
Netherlands	1										2009		
Spain	1										2009		
Malawi	1											2010	
Colombia	1											2010	
Jamaica	1											2010	
Haiti	1											2010	
Guinea	1												2011
Niger	1												2011
Cote d'Ivoire	1												2011
Tunisia	1												2011
Total	49	4	7	4	9	12	11	7	10	14	19	10	9

Note: a. Representing the G77; b. Representing the African Union; c. Representing the Commonwealth of Independent States; d. Representing the African Union; e. Does not include outside presidencies of the European Union.

Appendix 4.6   G8 Ministerial Institutions

Recurrent
1973   Finance, 1975, 1986–
1975   Foreign affairs, 1984–
1979   Energy, 1998, 2002, 2005–
1981   Trade until about 2000
1992   Environment
1994   Employment and labour
1995   Information to 1996
1995   Terrorism
1997   Justice and home affairs (crime)
2000   Education, 2006
2002   Development, 2003, 2005, 2007, 2008
2002   Research/Science and technology 2008
Total = 12

One Time Only
1997   Small and medium-sized enterprises
2006   Health
2009   Agriculture

G8-Centric Ministerial Institutions from Start
1999   G20 finance ministers and central bank governors
2001   Global Health Security Initiative (without Russia, with Mexico)
2005   Gleneagles Dialogue on Energy and Climate

Official-Level Bodies
1975–1981   8
1982–1988   9
1989–1995   14
1996–2002   16
2003–2010   50
2011   1
Total   97

Appendix 4.7   Civil Society Involvement in G8 Summits

1984   The Other Economic Summit near summit site
1988   G8 Research Group: conferences, website (1996–),
        compliance reports (1996–)
1998   Jubilee 2000 ad hoc coalition meets Tony Blair as host during summit
2001   Genoa Social Forum
2002   Forum International de Montréal starts global civil society–G8 sherpa
        meetings
2002   Legislative lower house speakers annual meeting starts
2005   Commission for Africa with multi-stakeholder membership
2005   Make Poverty History Campaign, Live 8 Concert engage 1 billion
        citizens
2005   Junior 8 (J8) secondary school students meet leaders during summit
2005   Religious leaders summit starts
2006   Civil 8 formed to advise Russian presidency
2006   Media news agencies form Moscow Club to meet with G8 minister
        annually
2006   G8 Youth Summit
2008   G8 University Summit
2008   G8 Business Summit
2008   Indigenous Leaders Summit
2008   Nongovernmental organizations invited to participate at the
        International Media Centre during the summit
2009   Roma Civil G8
2009   NGOs participate in media centre at summit
2010   Civil-G8 Dialogue

Chapter 5

The Future Role and Reform of the G8

Peter I. Hajnal and Victoria Panova

This chapter analyses proposals to reform the G8, as well as reforms already achieved or underway. It focuses on the period beginning with 1998, with only brief references to early reform initiatives. It pays particular attention to the reform dimension of the evolving G20 systemically significant countries (including the G8 members), the Group of Five (G5) countries invited to several G8 summits (Brazil, China, India, Mexico, and South Africa), the Heiligendamm process that evolved out of the G8 and G5 meetings, the BRICS (Brazil, Russia, India, China, and, since 2011, South Africa), and the Major Economies Forum on Energy and Climate (MEF), as well as to the G8's relationship to these groups. The chapter concludes with outlining possible trajectories of G8 reform now that the G20 is firmly established at leaders' level.

Calls for Reform

There is widespread and growing recognition of structural, procedural, and other shortcomings of the G8 as it currently exists and the need to reform or replace it. This sentiment has been expressed in the media, academia, and civil society and, increasingly and significantly, by several present and former leaders and other high-level officials of G8 countries. These voices include, among others, those of former Canadian prime minister Paul Martin (2007), French president Nicolas Sarkozy (2008), former British prime minister Gordon Brown, and even former German chancellor Helmut Schmidt (2007), who was one of the founding fathers of the original G7 in 1975 (Parker 2009). They have called for G8's transformation into a different institution so that all significant actors could play their full role in addressing global challenges.

Despite its proven flexibility and significant achievements over its four-decade history, the G8 remains rooted in an earlier era, and has not adequately responded to changing political and economic realities. The most pressing issue has been the emergence of crucial new actors outside the G8 framework and their significance in global governance. Without the full participation of major emerging economies that are systemically important countries, satisfactory initiatives and action in response to global problems cannot be taken. Even wider participation is necessary to address global challenges of climate change, poverty, health, and financial architecture.

Over the years there has been a plethora of reform proposals, ranging from abolishing the G8 altogether to expanding or reducing its membership, rationalizing its agenda and processes, increasing its legitimacy and representativeness, replacing it with a new body, or supplementing it with additional bodies or a permanent secretariat. Leaders of the G7, the predecessor of the G8, have expressed their wish to stage smaller, more intimate, and more focused summit meetings with fewer officials in attendance and fewer media correspondents. Others, too, have proposed various courses of action, ranging from abolition to institutional strengthening of the G8 (Hajnal 2007a, 2007b; Kirton 2008).

Many of these proposals have merit and some have had high-level advocates, notably Paul Martin, who for several years pressed for the establishment of the 'Leaders' 20' (L20), perhaps with the same initial membership as the G20 finance ministers' forum, which has been meeting since 1999. The complete integration of the G5 members with the G8 to form a G13 was another proposal that gained currency. However, for such far-reaching reform to become reality, it must be not only promoted by the advocates of change, but also agreed upon and endorsed by consensus of the G8 leaders. This remains true with the emergence in November 2008 of the G20 leaders' forum alongside with the continuing G20 finance ministers' and various sub-groups. In their first two years, the G20 leaders met on 2 April 2009 in London, on 24–25 September 2009 in Pittsburgh, on 26–27 June 2010 in Toronto, and on 11–12 November 2010 in Seoul, with the Seoul Summit launching an annual schedule so that the next summit would be held in Cannes on 3–4 November 2011.

The 1998 Birmingham Reforms and their Aftermath

The Birmingham Summit on 15–17 May 1998 undertook major reform of the G7, producing several innovations in participation, format, and agenda. Birmingham officially integrated Russia into the club, turning it into the G8. It was a leaders-only summit, with foreign and finance ministers meeting separately in London a week earlier, on 8–9 May, to prepare for the summit and to deal with issues not on the leaders' agenda. This made it possible to achieve greater informality than had been the case at previous summits and enabled the leaders to spend considerable time together to discuss the issues they wanted to cover. As well, Birmingham had a more focused agenda than previous summits. The more limited agenda also reduced the volume of documentation, although this effect proved to be rather inconsistent at subsequent summits (Bayne 2005).

This internal reform became established practice. However, it did not satisfy critics. Shortly after the Birmingham Summit, Jeffrey Sachs (1998) proposed transforming the G8 into a G16 comprising the present G8 plus eight developing countries. For this expanded club, Sachs placed democratic governance as the major criterion of membership, arguing that the core candidates should be Brazil, India, Korea, and South Africa, to be joined 'soon [by] a democratic Nigeria'. In his view, a 'development agenda' should guide this new body, including global financial markets and international financial reform, conditionality and foreign aid, reform of the international assistance programmes, and an end to the debt crisis. Once Birmingham opened the door to summit reform, post-summit assessments and proposals have proliferated.

In July 2001, just after the tumultuous Genoa Summit on 20–22 July, a lead article in the *Financial Times* (2001) questioned 'whether G8 summits should exist and, if so, in what form', and noted that 'summits have worked best when the leaders have had a chance to be separate from their national entourages ... and when there has been a crisis to try to sort out'. The piece concluded that there should have been 'a commitment to hold the next G8 only when there is a burning topic to discuss'. The terrorist attacks of 11 September 2001, mere months later, thrust such a topic into the international consciousness, placing security at the top of the agenda. In the post-9/11 era, security for the leaders became, if anything, even more paramount for summit host countries. Therefore, since Kananaskis in 2002 most G8 summits have been held at remote places. This has had the advantage of easier security for the G8 leaders but also the disadvantage of the leaders meeting far from the media, the public, and civil society. Furthermore, the remote locale does not necessarily prevent protestors, rock stars, or civil society campaigns like Make Poverty History from making their presence felt.

The Shadow G8 (formerly called G8 Preparatory Conference) was launched in 2000. A think tank of distinguished individuals with high-level previous summit experience, led by C. Fred Bergsten of the Peter G. Peterson Institute of International Economics, it was based on the premise that 'recent G8 summits have not fulfilled their potential. [Its members believed] that summits should reform their methodology and adopt agendas that effectively address the sweeping changes in global economic and security affairs that characterize the early years of the new century' (Bergsten and de Montbrial 2003). Given that the G8 leaders have had a hard time reforming themselves (although the Birmingham reforms were worthwhile), the question can be asked whether it was time to start a new group in which the heads of systemically important countries could meet and get to know one another. The Shadow G8 functioned until 2006; in 2007 a different 'Shadow G8' appeared briefly under the leadership of Joseph E. Stiglitz.

The L20 Initiative

One of the most interesting reform ideas to expand the leaders' forum was the proposal to turn the G20 finance ministers' forum into a leaders-level group of 20, or L20. As early as 2001, Shadow G8 member Wendy Dobson noted that the challenges to leaders had changed since the Cold War days when the G7 was first established. She asserted that a 'G3' or G7 'directorate' [was] no longer acceptable ... [What was required was] consensus among a wider group' (Dobson 2001). She envisioned two scenarios to build on the precedent of the G20 finance ministers' forum: convening functional groups of ministers from G20 countries on systemic problems such as climate change, North-South issues, trade, and poverty alleviation and expanding leaders' meetings to include all G20 countries. In the interest of efficient management, this body would require a steering committee with revolving membership. In Dobson's view, it would not replace the G8, but would meet periodically before or after G7/8 summits.

The L20 idea was taken up enthusiastically by Canadian prime minister Paul Martin who, in his previous post as finance minister, had been the first chair of the finance ministers' G20. In a 2005 issue of *Foreign Affairs*, he made the case for an expanded leaders' level forum and introduced the term 'L20' (Martin 2005). He reviewed and analysed the circumstances of the emergence and functioning of the finance ministers' G20, discussed the need for a similar forum for political leaders, and outlined the L20's possible composition, initial agenda, potential role, and relations with existing multilateral organizations. Martin's choice of publishing in this influential journal reflected his recognition that summit reform was not possible without the support of the United States.

Building on this framework to examine the ramifications of a potential transformation from the ministerial level to the leaders' level, the Centre for International Governance Innovation (CIGI) and the University of Victoria's Centre for Global Studies (CFGS), both in Canada, sought to answer a number of questions: What are the issues? What would be the appropriate design for a successful L20 acceptable to the leaders? And what was the best route to attaining consensus to establish the L20 process? Such a new summit-level grouping, if successful, would be more broadly representative than the G8, bringing to the table systemically important developing countries (notably China, India, and Brazil) and countries with emerging economies. It would focus on priorities at the highest level, transcending national bureaucracies, and would be an institution enjoying legitimacy in promoting fiscal, social, and environmentally responsible policies. It would also address the efficiency gap and would catalyse and guide broader reforms of global governance. One of the aims of the CIGI/CFGS project was to broaden the understanding of the initiative among the G8 members and prospective L20 members by including academics and practitioners from each member. CIGI, with the involvement of CFGS, examined the receptivity of the South to the idea of the L20 and the modalities of achieving such a grouping: having an L20 replace the G7/8 through a 'giant leap', incrementally increasing the membership of the G8 through a G9 and G10 to an eventual L20, and creating an L20 that would operate alongside a continuing G8 (see English, Thakur, and Cooper 2005; see also Heap 2008, for another account of such proposals).

Other Reform Proposals

Another initiative was introduced and explained by Peter Kenen, Jeffrey Shafer, Nigel Wicks, and Charles Wyplosz (2004). They trace the evolution of international economic and financial cooperation and conclude that its machinery was becoming obsolete, notwithstanding the G7's record of negotiating joint positions and exerting its influence in the Bretton Woods institutions (the International Monetary Fund and the World Bank). They recommend the creation of new structures: making room for new players (for example, by streamlining European representation in the G7 and in the IMF's Executive Board); establishing a new 'G4' comprising the United States, the eurozone, Japan, and China to deal with exchange rate problems and adjustments; and convening an 'Independent Wise Persons Review Group' to examine existing institutions and groups including the G7. They also propose establishing a new 'Council for International Financial and Economic Cooperation' with 15 or fewer members to set the agenda and provide strategic direction for the international financial system and to oversee multilateral institutions of international economic cooperation. This council would include the systemically important countries represented at the finance ministers' level. The heads of the United Nations, the IMF, World Bank, and the World Trade Organization (WTO) would be invited to the council's meetings. Commenting on this book, *The Economist* (2004) agreed that the G7 was no longer what it had been and had become only one of an 'alphanumeric panoply of bodies' attempting to coordinate economic policies. *The Economist* noted with approval the book's proposal to give China its rightful place in the structure of macroeconomic diplomacy, stating that without China, 'the G7 cannot hope to achieve much'.

In a somewhat similar vein, Stephen Roach (2004) recommends a new architecture for economic policy coordination, remarking that the global economy was in need of rebalancing. One step toward that would be to replace the G7 with a new G5 consisting of the US, the eurozone, Japan, the United Kingdom, and China. Roach argues that the G7 is a creature of a different era. He finds it particularly odd that it excludes China while giving the European Union's eurozone three votes (Germany, France, and Italy). His G5 would be a full-fledged organization based on a charter embracing in its mandate all aspects of global economic imbalances. It would have a permanent staff and would hold semi-annual meetings based on consultations between the finance ministries and central banks of the members and the G5's staff of experts. The staff would produce semi-annual reports to serve as agenda for the formal meetings. Like the proposal by Kenen at al. (2004), Roach's ideas do not account for the non-economic agenda of the G8: the environment, security, health, and other transnational issues.

Colin I. Bradford (2005) argues that the existing 'institutional framework for dealing with contemporary global challenges does not match the scope, scale and nature of the challenges themselves'. One aspect of this mismatch is the G8 and the broader G8 system as it is now constituted. Given considerable reluctance to instituting major reform and expansion of the G8 into a true L20, Bradford suggests adding a few regular core members (China, India, Brazil, and South Africa being the leading candidates) to the G8, turning it into a G12, and allocating six additional places to other countries that would participate on a rotating basis depending on particular issues on the agenda. This formula would enhance both the representativeness and the legitimacy of the summit mechanism and would provide top-level strategic leadership to the whole international system.

Edwin Truman (2004) suggested disbanding the G7/8 and moving many of its policy coordination functions to the G20. He argued that this strengthening of the G20 would be a major step in rationalizing the institutions of international economic cooperation. He called for ad hoc working groups in addition to representation at the level of leaders, ministers of finance, and central bank governors. He saw the United States and the eurozone as leaders of this strengthened G20. At the same time, he also envisioned the policy coordination of the US and the eurozone as an 'informal G2'. This 'finance G2' concept is also explored by C. Fred Bergsten (Bergsten 2004; Bergsten and Koch-Weser 2004), who argues that 'Euroland' and the US need a new G2 mechanism not only to monitor and consult on the evolution of the dollar-euro exchange rate but also, more ambitiously, to develop a new G2 monetary regime. This G2 would not be a substitute for the G7 and would function informally and without even public announcement of its existence and activities.

George Haynal (2005) makes the case for a 'G-xx' – a more comprehensive and representative summit process, where xx does not necessarily stand for 20 but suggests that the number of members is an open question. He argues that such a more inclusive summit 'would express the changing nature and balance of power in the world and assist our shared institutions to function better by providing them with the appropriate political direction'. Haynal outlines the weaknesses of the existing international system of institutions: the UN Security Council (UNSC) and General Assembly (UNGA), specialized agencies including the Bretton Woods institutions, and the WTO. He suggests that new global issues, as well as linkages among international institutions now missing, could be addressed by a G-xx. He identifies a core membership of the G-xx: the existing G8; China, India, South Africa, Brazil, and, possibly, Mexico; and representation from Africa, the Middle East, Southeast Asia, the Americas, and the former Soviet bloc. He envisions the G-xx as functioning alongside the G8, not replacing it. Differing from the L20 initiative, he considers that transforming the G20 finance ministers' forum into a leaders-level summit would overburden the G20; nonetheless, he would proceed from the existing composition of the G20. Finally, he recommends starting with a 'one-off' process of the leaders, meeting perhaps on the margins of UNGA, and focusing on global security as the initial agenda.

Media comments around the time of the 2005 Gleneagles Summit reflected increasing frustration with the current membership of the G8. Richard Haass (2005) called the G8 'increasingly an anachronism' and added: 'No one today would propose an annual meeting that includes Canada (population of 31m [million], gross domestic product of $870bn [billion] [£485bn]), Italy (58m and $1,200bn) and Russia (144m and $615bn) but not China (1.3bn and $1,650bn) and India (1.1bn and $650bn).' He argued: 'The G8 needs to become the G10. Both China and India deserve a seat … It would be a concession to reality that would benefit everyone.'

The concept of expanding the G8 was raised again in early 2006 by Anders Åslund (2006), who proposed that China, India, Brazil, and South Africa be invited as full members to transform the G8 into a more representative G12. More significantly, because it concerns the view of a key G8 leader, just two days before the 2006 St. Petersburg Summit British prime minister Tony Blair planned to call for making China, India, Brazil, South Africa, and Mexico full-fledged members of the G8, turning it into the G13 (Elliott and Wintour 2006). This would build on the 'G8+5' formula established at Gleneagles. Focusing on a successor to the Kyoto Protocol, Blair stated: 'There is no way we can deal with climate change unless we get an agreement that binds in the US, China and India ... We have got to get an agreement with a binding framework – of that I am in no doubt at all.' Blair was pushing the need to make the G8+5 arrangement more formal in part because Brazil and India are principal players in trade negotiations.

Following the election of Barack Obama as president of the United States, Zbigniew Brzezinski (2009) suggested the creation of two informal groupings: an expanded G8 alongside a G2 of the US and China, the G2 being the most relevant mechanism to deal best with world issues. 'We certainly need to collaborate closely in expanding the current Group of Eight ... to a G14 or G16, in order to widen the global circle of decision-makers and to develop a more inclusive response to the economic crisis', wrote Brzezinski. 'But to promote all that we need an informal G2. The relationship between the US and China has to be a comprehensive partnership, paralleling our relations with Europe and Japan. Our top leaders should therefore meet informally on a regular schedule for personal in-depth discussions not just about our bilateral relations but about the world in general.'

British prime minister Gordon Brown, host of the G20 London Summit on 2 April 2009, was 'a leading advocate of the G20 format, arguing that the old G8 club of rich, industrial countries was no longer acceptable for directing world affairs' (Parker 2009). He thus added his voice to those of several fellow G8 leaders in calling for a more representative forum of global governance. Even earlier, shortly after the first G20 summit in November 2008, some said the G20 'summit effectively sounded the death knell for the exclusive club of rich nations represented by the G8' (Elliott 2008). Paul Martin (2009) went so far as to say that the London Summit confirmed 'that the G8's days as the world's steering committee have drawn to a close. Yet the world cannot afford a vacuum. Only a successful G20 will fill the void.'

As the L20 project evolved, an agenda that might be appropriate for the new leaders' forum was carefully considered. The various potential topics foreseen by the L20 think tanks, as well as in other proposals for a G20, included global health and global security. In the end, what sparked the convening of the first G20 summit was the financial crisis that erupted in 2008. As of the 2009 London Summit, there were already signs of agenda expansion in view of trade, development, and other linkages to the core financial and economic issues.

To cite one more example of recent reform proposals, in October 2008 the Commission of Experts of the President of the UN General Assembly on Reforms of the International Monetary and Financial System was appointed, headed by Joseph Stiglitz and comprising 18 senior international economists, former and current government ministers, as well as central bank officials from Japan, Africa, Europe, Latin America and Asia. Its mandate was to study the reform of international financial institutions and to create a coordinated approach to global financial structures that were seen as needing a drastic overhaul. In March 2009 the commission recommended the creation of a new elected 'Global Economic Coordination Council' that would be part of the UN, would meet annually at the head-of-state level, and would be a 'democratically representative alternative to the G-20' (Commission of Experts of the President of the UN General Assembly on Reforms of the International Monetary and Financial System 2009). The proposed council would be independent of the Security Council and would have 20 to 25 members (Morris 2009; UN News Centre 2009). Following this initiative, UNGA convened the United Nations Conference on the World Financial and Economic Crisis and its Impact on Development on 24–26 June 2009 in New York, which produced a set of proposals accepted by consensus and later endorsed by UNGA (UNGA 2009).

Russia's Position

Interestingly, and in contrast with the broad range of proposals and deliberations on the reform of the G8 mechanism originating in Europe and North America, not much is found on the Russian side. The G8's newest member has taken a variety of approaches to what the G8 is, what its role should be, and – the major part of deliberations – the place and role of Russia within it. At the same time, Russian academia, government, and civil society do not seem to pay as much attention to the reform of the so-called club mechanisms. It is widely perceived within Russia that the UN structure should remain the principal actor in the field, with other mechanisms – the G8 and G20 included – taking a secondary and supportive role *vis-à-vis* the leading organization.

Moreover, with the ups and downs in the relationship between Russia and the West, it has become more relevant for Russia not to pay much attention to G8 solidarity and ways to strengthen it, but rather for Russia to concentrate on the bilateral approach and focus on its common interests with the former 'Outreach' countries, primarily within the BRICS grouping. This preference is clear from intensified cooperation among the BRICS members, whether on the side-lines of a G8 or G20 summit or independently (the BRIC leaders – that is, Brazil, Russia, India, and China – met for the first time in Yekaterinburg, Russia, in June 2009, then in Brasilia in April 2010, and in Sanya, China, in April 2011 when they invited South Africa to become a member; BRIC ministers had already been meeting since 2006). BRICS collaboration was evident at the meeting of G20 finance ministers and central bank governors in February 2011, when the BRICS members elaborated a position on a new system of indicators for macroeconomic policy. Furthermore, it was a joint Russian-Chinese initiative to raise the possibility of introducing the more reliable global currency (the special drawing right [SDR]) to guarantee against the periodic rise and fall of the US dollar.

The G5 and the Heiligendamm L'Aquila Process

Brazil, China, India, Mexico, and South Africa have frequently been invited to attend specific parts of G8 summit meetings since 2005. First referred to as the 'G8+5' at Gleneagles in 2005, in the run-up to the Heiligendamm Summit in 2007, the German hosts preferred the designation of 'Outreach 5' (O5). The five countries formed their own 'G5' around the time of the 2008 Hokkaido Summit. Both the German hosts at Heiligendamm and the Japanese at Hokkaido accepted the G5 designation.

German chancellor Angela Merkel, in preparing for Heiligendamm, announced at the World Economic Forum in Davos in January 2007 the wish to deepen the integration of the O5 into the summit process. That summit created the so-called Heiligendamm Dialogue Process (HDP), and then, in 2009, the Heiligendamm L'Aquila Process (HAP), which, however, coexisted for a time with the G5. The G5, however, has faded from the G8 scene with the growing importance of the G20, where those five countries perform as initial participants and equal players, as well as the continuing BRICS group. Both the G8 and the G20 are likely to remain, at least for the time being. But the example and experience of the HDP/ HAP are helpful in the examining the further evolution of ideas for the structure of global governance.

How did the HDP/HAP work? Merkel recognized the need to involve the most important developing countries in the decision-making process, or at least to get the G5 countries' consent to the decisions of the 'geriatric' developed countries. She suggested a structured, topic-driven dialogue of the G8 members with Brazil, China, India, Mexico, and South Africa, which was announced in the G8's declaration on 'Growth and Responsibility in the World Economy' issued at the Heiligendamm Summit (G8 2007). However, because the G5 members were discontent with the non-consultative nature of the documents, a more elaborate declaration was issued (G8 et al. 2007).The HDP rested on four main pillars: promoting and protecting innovation; enhancing the freedom of investments through transparency, including socially responsible behaviour of business; energy, especially through increasing energy efficiency and fostering technological cooperation in order to reduce carbon dioxide admissions; and better cooperation and coordination in the field of sustainable development, particularly in Africa. It was originally scheduled to continue for two years, with an interim report to be submitted to the 2008 Hokkaido summit and the final results to be reported at the

G8 L'Aquila Summit in 2009. Germany, having initiated the process, allocated €5.5 million to the project (Cooper and Antkiewicz 2008).

In the discussions on investment, G5 members opposed any discussion of the concept of 'equal conditions', on which there was no consensus among the participants. The G5 view was that, apart from protecting the investors' interests, the interests of the countries that receive investments should be taken into account. The G5 also argued that developing countries often run into limitations on investments in western markets.

The G5 also took great interest in the issue of corporate social responsibility. They preferred the United Nations initiatives, such as the Global Compact Governance Framework issued in 2005 and the Ten Principles of the Global Compact issued in 2004, as well as the 2003 Norms on the Responsibilities of Transnational Corporations and Other Business Enterprises with regard to Human Rights, rather than the Guidelines for Multinational Enterprises produced by the Organisation for Economic Co-operation and Development (OECD). It is to the OECD's guidelines that the G8 turns for the elaboration of those principles.

With regard to innovation, the G5 countries did not believe that market mechanisms constitute a panacea for the development of innovation processes. The positions outlined in the Heiligendamm documents on intellectual property rights (IPRs) were inherently opposed to their interests. They wanted attention to be shifted to the issues of strengthening institutional capacities, undertaking explanatory work, and preparing qualified personnel in this field. As well, discussions on IPR protection should be balanced by commitments by the developed countries to transfer technologies and services to the developing countries at reasonable prices.

The G5 countries wanted energy security to be included in the discussion. They proposed a Chinese initiative formulated on the side-lines of the 2006 St. Petersburg Summit. The issue of energy efficiency could thus be complemented by the use of alternative and renewable sources of energy, such as wind, solar, geothermal, tidal, hydro, photovoltaic, and biofuel. This suggestion was supported by Russia, which in turn put forward the idea that energy security issues be discussed based on the provisions outlined in the G8 St Petersburg declaration on Global Energy Security (G8 2006). It was one among several instances when Moscow identified its interests as aligned more with the emerging economies rather with the developed G7 (Panova 2008). As a result, the HDP partners decided to discuss aspects of energy security as described in the St. Petersburg declaration as well as those proposed by the G5, focusing on cooperation on energy development and utilization, as well as capacity building for demand-side management of energy systems. The HDP's energy working group was supported by the International Energy Agency (IEA), particularly with regard to sustainable building networks, energy efficiency in power generation, alternative sources of energy, and renewable energy.

At the heart of the discussion on sustainable development lay the Millennium Development Goals (MDGs), particularly with regard to Africa. The major focus was on increasing the efficiency of aid to Africa in order to advance its sustainable development and eradicate poverty. All the participants supported the OECD's Paris Declaration on Aid Effectiveness adopted in 2005 and reiterated the commitments it contained. The G5 partners, committed to fulfilling MDGs, believed that the list of topics for discussion should be expanded to include new sources of financing development, debt write-offs, and the creation of a unified policy on trade, investment, and the international financial system.

The EU-G8 Relationship

The European Union's relationship with the G8 has had a complicated history that goes back before the G7 itself was formed in 1975. During the years 1973–75 when the finance ministers of France, Germany, Japan, the UK, and the US held a series of secret meetings, the European Community expressed its discontent at being excluded as a single body, rather than being represented separately by only three of its member states. Italy's last-minute admission as member of the G6 club of leaders starting with the 1975 Rambouillet Summit offered a partial solution (Canada did not participate in the 1975 summit).

A fuller remedy was obtained with the official participation of the European Community beginning with the 1977 G7 London Summit. At every summit since then, the European Community (later the EU) was present at the leaders' table (Hainsworth 1990). The EU occupies an unusual position in the G7/8: it is a member but not a member state (although some analysts consider it an observer). The EU does not host a summit, and therefore cannot directly shape the agenda. In all other respects the EU is a full member, with a sherpa and full participation in the preparation and conduct of the summits. It also participates in the ministerial meetings and other subsidiary G7 and G8 bodies (but it was absent from the G7 finance ministerials before 1998). The EU is particularly active on issues where its members act collectively. It is represented at G8 summits by the president of the European Commission; when the European Council was chaired by a country that was not a G8 member, the Council president was also present. Since the Lisbon Treaty entered into force at the end of 2009, the president of the Council is a regular participant along with the Commission president.

The EU has been a full member of the G20 since the finance ministers and central bank governors began meeting in 1999. This applies both to the G20 finance forum and now to the G20 leaders' summits and other G20 bodies.

Many G8 reform proposals involve the EU, particularly those that call for a single representation for the EU as a whole, or for the eurozone.

What Next?

Clearly, the world faces several possible choices in reforming the global governance system. The reform proposals analyzed in this chapter offer several alternative scenarios.

- *Expansion of the G8.* The many proposals to expand the G8 include, among others, Sachs's (1998) G16 formula incorporating the G8 plus eight developing countries with democratic governance. Brzezinski (2009) also calls for an expanded G8 that, however, would coexist with a G2 of the US and China as most relevant to geopolitical realities. Many others have called on the G8 absorb the G5 as full members. Silvio Berlusconi, the host of the 2009 L'Aquila Summit, also invited Egypt to participate in the G8+G5 part of the discussions, and even characterized the result as the G14. It is not certain whether G5 members appreciated this addition.
- *Survival of the G8+G5 Formula.* The G5 countries have always been rather dubious of their relationship with the G8. The fading engagement of the G5 since 2010 with the G8 shows members' preference for the G20, in which they are full members and which accommodates diverse systems of government among its members. The G5 faced a dilemma between the attraction of membership in the powerful G8 club on the one hand and, on the other hand, problems associated with the possible association with the rich 'Western' or 'Northern' G8. For the G5 members, this raised issues about their identity as developing countries. With the growing importance of the G20 and BRICS, the G5 countries' connection with the G8 has lost relevance. But should the G20 summit prove inefficient, then a G8+G5 formula, or even G13 format, could prove attractive and beneficial for the same reasons for which half of the G8's members are fond of their forum: with UN reform stalled, the 'G8+' formula offers a unique opportunity for those without a permanent seat on the UNSC to increase their power significantly and have a strong say in shaping the architecture of world governance. The 'G8+' formula is increasingly considered the most important mechanism of global governance, albeit complementary to the UN.
- *Coexistence of the G8 and the G20.* A joint article by Britain's Gordon Brown and Italy's Silvio Berlusconi, written just before the G20 London Summit, suggests the two bodies continuing to exist, as similarly described by Dobson (Berlusconi and Brown 2009; Dobson 2001). Some leaders who were previously sceptical of the G8 in favour of the G20, notably America's Barack Obama and France's Nicolas Sarkozy, came to accept the advantages of both forums continuing.
- *The Replacement of the G8 by the G20.* The L20 project preferred replacing the G8 with the G20, although it acknowledged two other possible

trajectories: the incremental expansion of the G8 and coexistence of the G8 and the L20. Truman's (2004) formulation also advocates such an outcome.

- *Replacement of the G8 by or Coexistence of the G8 with a Different Group.* Among the most interesting proposals along these lines is that of Kenen and colleagues (2004) calling for the streamlining of European representation in the G7 by establishing a G4 of the US, the eurozone, China, and Japan. This would include a substantial part of the G7 but leave out Canada, Russia, and the UK – hardly an outcome that would be acceptable to those omitted. Roach's (2004) proposal is a variation on this theme: it would establish a new G5 with the US, the eurozone, China, and the UK, thus leaving out Canada, Japan and Russia. Other variations include Bradford's (2005) G12 or G18 and Åslund's (2006) G13 (the G8+G5) or G12, without Mexico. Haynal's (2005) 'G-xx' posits the current G8 plus the G5 (possibly without Mexico) as well as an indeterminate number of others from Africa, the Middle East, Southeast Asia, and so forth. This body would coexist with the G8. An interesting variation on this theme is the 2009 proposal of the Stiglitz panel that would establish a council of 20 to 25 members under the aegis of the UN (Commission of Experts 2009).

- *The G2 Concept.* The concept of the G2 has been suggested in various proposals over the years. For example, Truman (2004) would want a G2 of the US and the eurozone to coexist with the G20. Bergsten and Koch-Weser (2004) argue the same way. More recently, the US and China have been mentioned as a G2 configuration (Brzezinski 2009). These proposals imply an acknowledgement of a long-established process of bilateral and plurilateral negotiations that have become routine, often around the G8, and now the G20, summits.

- *Variable Geometry.* The G8 could continue as the core of discussions while leaving appropriate room for wider participation, depending on the topic on the agenda and involving various combinations of the G8, the G5, the MEF, HAP, the BRICS, and other groupings. On the occasion of the G20 London Summit, Italian foreign minister Franco Frattini (2009) wrote an open letter to the Rome newspaper *Il Messaggero* advocating just such a process, arguing that 'thanks both to its format and to its method, the structure of the G8 summit is still extremely valid today and that its flexibility will allow it to spawn an advanced and strategic model in support of world governance'. He said the 2009 G8 summit would 'be a clear illustration of a variable geometry structure based on the dossiers under consideration'. As an example, he suggested the summit would include a meeting of the 'historic core' of countries, a joint discussion by the G8 with the G5 members as well as Egypt, and a meeting that would include a 'representative group of African countries'. According to Frattini, the format should be dictated by the policy goals, so it could 'respond to real political-economic needs in a rapidly changing world'.

The question of efficiency versus representativeness is a constant in reform-oriented debates: the smaller the group, the more efficient it is likely to be – but smaller groups lack adequate representativeness. Some might consider that the G20 summit is too unwieldy to be efficient, although it is unquestionably much more representative of geopolitical realities than the G8. Of course, even the G20 is not completely representative; to achieve that, it would, at the extreme, have to grow to the universality of the UN with its 193 members ('G193').

A final thought: history does not repeat itself the same way twice, but there are apparent parallels between recent developments in the G8/G20 and the early history of the G7. The latter started with a series of finance ministers' meetings among five countries, then evolved into leaders' summits, first as G6 in 1975, then as G7 from 1976 to 1997, and, finally, as G8, with Russia starting in 1998. The original five leaders met on the margins of the 1976 G7 Puerto Rico Summit. The finance ministers' forum of the five countries survived in parallel with the G7 summits until 1987 when it faded away, yielding to the G7 finance ministers' forum. The G7 leaders continued to meet on the side-lines of the G8 summits until the 2002 Kananaskis Summit. The G20 finance ministers began meeting first in 1999, and the leaders began meeting in 2008. It is possible that some version of this progression will once again play itself out.

References

Åslund, Anders (2006). 'Russia's Challenges as Chair of the G8.' Policy Brief No. 06-3, March, Institute for International Economics, Washington DC. <www.iie.com/publications/pb/pb06-3.pdf> (July 2011).

Bayne, Nicholas (2005). *Staying Together: The G8 Summit Confronts the 21st Century*. Aldershot: Ashgate.

Bergsten, C. Fred (2004). 'The Euro and the Dollar: Toward a "Finance G2".' Paper prepared for 'The Euro at Five: Ready for a Global Role?', 26 February. <www.iie.com/publications/papers/bergsten0204.pdf> (July 2011).

Bergsten, C. Fred, and Thierry de Montbrial (2003). 'Letter of Transmittal to the Leaders of the G8 Member Countries.' In *Restoring G8 Leadership of the World Economy: Recommendations for the Evian Summit from the Shadow G8*, pp. 4–5. Institut Français des Relations Internationales, Institute for International Economics, and the Charles Stewart Mott Foundation. <www.iie.com/publications/papers/g8-2003.pdf> (July 2011).

Bergsten, C. Fred, and Caio Koch-Weser (2004). 'The G2: A New Conceptual Basis and Operating Modality for Transatlantic Economic Relations.' In *From Alliance to Coalitions: The Future of Transatlantic Relations*, edited by Werner Weidenfeld, Caio Koch-Weser, C. Fred Bergsten, et al., pp. 237–49. Gütersloh: Bertelsmann Foundation Publishers. <www.voltairenet.org/IMG/pdf/From_alliance_to_coalitions.pdf> (July 2011).

Berlusconi, Silvio, and Gordon Brown (2009). 'Joint Article by President of the Council Berlusconi and British Prime Minister Brown.' 19 February. <www.g8italia2009.it/G8/Home/News/G8-G8_Layout_locale-1199882116809_InterventoBerlusconi.htm> (July 2011).

Bradford, Colin I. (2005). 'Global Governance for the 21st Century.' Paper prepared as part of the G20 and Global Governance project, Brookings Institution, Washington DC. <www.brookings.edu/views/Papers/20051024bradford.pdf> (July 2011).

Brzezinski, Zbigniew (2009). 'The Group of Two That Could Change the World.' *Financial Times*, 13 January.

Commission of Experts of the President of the UN General Assembly on Reforms of the International Monetary and Financial System (2009). 'Recommendations.' 19 March, United Nations. <www.un.org/ga/president/63/letters/recommendationExperts200309.pdf> (July 2011).

Cooper, Andrew F., and Agata Antkiewicz, eds. (2008). *Emerging Powers in Global Governance: Lessons from the Heiligendamm Process*. Waterloo ON: Wilfrid Laurier University Press.

Dobson, Wendy (2001). 'Broadening Participation in G7 Summits.' Toward Shared Responsibility and Global Leadership: Recommendations for the G8 Genoa Summit from the G8 Preparatory Conference, Turin, 21–22 January. <www.iie.com/publications/papers/g8-2001.pdf> (July 2011).

Economist (2004). 'G-Force.' 7 October. <www.economist.com/node/3262467> (July 2011).

Elliott, Larry (2008). 'This Summit Signalled the Passing of the Exclusive Club of Wealthy Nations.' *Observer*, 16 November, p. 6. <www.guardian.co.uk/business/2008/nov/16/global-economy-global-recession> (July 2011).

Elliott, Larry, and Patrick Wintour (2006). 'Blair Wants Developing Nations in New G13 to Help Secure Key Deals.' *Guardian*, 13 July. <www.guardian.co.uk/politics/2006/jul/13/uk.topstories3> (July 2011).

English, John, Ramesh Thakur, and Andrew F. Cooper, eds (2005). *Reforming from the Top: A Leaders' 20 Summit*. Tokyo: United Nations University.

Financial Times (2001). 'For Slimmer and Sporadic Summits.' 23 July, p. 10.

Frattini, Franco (2009). 'The G8's Strategic Function in the Future.' 2 April. <www.g8italia2009.it/G8/Home/News/G8-G8_Layout_locale-1199882116809_1199893538098.htm> (June 2011).

G8 (2006). 'Global Energy Security.' St. Petersburg, 16 July. <www.g8.utoronto.ca/summit/2006stpetersburg/energy.html> (January 2011).

G8 (2007). 'Growth and Responsibility in the World Economy.' Heiligendamm, 7 June. <www.g8.utoronto.ca/summit/2007heiligendamm/g8-2007-economy.html> (July 2011).

G8, Brazil, China, et al. (2007). 'Joint Statement by the German G8 Presidency and the Heads of State and/or Government of Brazil, China, India, Mexico, and South Africa on the Occasion of the G8 Summit in Heiligendamm.'

Heiligendamm, 8 June. <www.g8.utoronto.ca/summit/2007heiligendamm/g8-2007-joint.html> (July 2011).

Haass, Richard (2005). 'Leaders Have a Flawed Gleneagles Agenda.' *Financial Times*, 1 July. <www.cfr.org/us-strategy-and-politics/leaders-have-flawed-gleneagles-agenda/p8238> (July 2011).

Hainsworth, Susan (1990). 'Coming of Age: The European Community and the Economic Summit.' Country Study No. 7, G7 Research Group. <www.g8.utoronto.ca/scholar/hainsworth1990/index.html> (July 2011).

Hajnal, Peter I. (2007a). *The G8 System and the G20: Evolution, Role, and Documentation*. Aldershot: Ashgate.

Hajnal, Peter I. (2007b). 'Summitry from G5 to L20: A Review of Reform Initiatives.' CIGI Working Paper No. 20, March, Centre for International Governance Innovation, Waterloo ON. <www.cigionline.org/publications/2007/3/summitry-g5-l20-review-reform-initiatives> (July 2011).

Haynal, George (2005). 'Summitry and Governance: The Case for a G-xx.' In *Canada Among Nations 2004: Setting Priorities Straight*, edited by David Carment, Fen Osler Hampson and Norman Hillmer, pp. 261–74. Montreal: McGill-Queen's University Press.

Heap, Peter C. (2008). *Globalization and Summit Reform: An Experiment in International Governance*. New York: Springer.

Kenen, Peter B., Jeffrey R. Shafer, Nigel L. Wicks, et al. (2004). *International Economic and Financial Cooperation: New Issues, New Actors, New Responses*. London: Centre for Economic and Policy Research.

Kirton, John J. (2008). 'The Case for G8 Reform.' Lecture delivered at Chuo University, Tokyo, 26 June. <www.g8.utoronto.ca/scholar/kirton_reform_080629.pdf> (July 2011).

Martin, Paul (2005). 'A Global Answer to Global Problems.' *Foreign Affairs* 84(3): 2–6.

Martin, Paul (2007). 'Breaking Deadlocks in Global Governance: The L20 Proposal.' *Global Governance* 13(3): 301–05.

Martin, Paul (2009). 'Key Challenges.' In *The G20 London Summit: Growth, Stability, Jobs*, edited by John J. Kirton and Madeline Koch, pp. 24–25. London: Newsdesk. <www.g8.utoronto.ca/newsdesk/g20london2009.pdf> (July 2011).

Morris, Harvey (2009). 'Call for Council to Replace G20.' *Financial Times*, 23 March.

Panova, Victoria (2008). 'Russia and Evolution of the Heiligendamm Process.' In *Emerging Powers in Global Governance: Lessons from the Heiligendamm Process*, edited by Andrew F. Cooper and Agata Antkiewicz, pp. 285–306. Waterloo ON: Wilfrid Laurier University Press.

Parker, George (2009). 'Heads Agree to New York Reunion.' *Financial Times*, 3 April.

Roach, Stephen (2004). 'How to Fix the World.' Global Economic Forum, Morgan Stanley, 17 December. <www.morganstanley.com/GEFdata/digests/20041217-fri.html> (June 2011).

Sachs, Jeffrey (1998). 'Global Capitalism: Making It Work.' *Economist*, 12 September, pp. 23–25.

Sarkozy, Nicolas (2008). 'Conférence de presse.' Paris, 8 January. <www.sarkozynicolas.com/nicolas-sarkozy-conference-de-presse-8-janvier-2008-texte-integral> (July 2011).

Schmidt, Helmut (2007). 'Observations on the Present State of the World.' Address at the opening ceremony of the 25th annual plenary session of the InterAction Council, Vienna, 21 May. <www.interactioncouncil.org/keynote-speech-observations-on-the-present-state-of-the-world> (July 2011).

Truman, Edwin M. (2004). 'The Euro and Prospects for Policy Coordination.' Paper prepared for 'The Euro at Five: Ready for a Global Role?', 26 February. <www.iie.com/publications/papers/truman0204-3.pdf> (July 2011).

UN News Centre (2009). 'Global Finance Structures Must Be Revamped, Says UN Expert Panel.' 26 March. <www.un.org/apps/news/story.asp?NewsID=30 309&Cr=financial+crisis&Cr1> (July 2011).

United Nations General Assembly (2009). 'Outcome of the Conference on the World Financial and Economic Crisis and Its Impact on Development.' A/RES/63/303, New York, 13 May. <www.un.org/ga/search/view_doc.asp?symbol=A/RES/63/303&Lang=E> (July 2011).

Chapter 6

The European Union as a Leading International Player

Mark Entin

The European Union is a new and unique player on the international scene. There has never been anything similar in human history. Applying traditional approaches to it does not make sense, nor does doing so help to understand its role in international affairs and its conduct in the international arena. However, until recently, most politicians and international experts were doing just that, and the results are well known. A number of catch phrases and bywords have enriched world folklore and serious studies, reflecting an utter lack of understanding of the essence of the phenomenon and unwillingness to sort things out.

There are two somewhat popular jokes that usually travel from one presentation to another. The first is said to belong to Henry Kissinger. As the US Secretary of State, he asked for a telephone number to be used in case of emergency or crisis for contacting the European Community.

The second is rather a collective creative product that claims, quite seriously though somewhat teasingly, that the EU, having long become a world economic giant, has nonetheless remained a political dwarf. And its common foreign and security policy is neither common, nor foreign, nor even a policy at all. In all major international developments, crucial for the world at large, the EU played a secondary role and revealed a conspicuous inability to act. It happened so always, starting with the Suez crisis and the EU's predecessor, the European Coal and Steel Community, up to the recent wars in the Balkans and the Middle East. But this has not been true for some time as many things have changed. Yet these disrespectful characteristics of the EU linger.

In fact, the strange situation in which the EU has found itself may be better described by the following simple story. Imagine a race like the Tour de France or the Girga d'Italia. Some strongest and toughest racers are breaking away from the peloton. It is not far from the finish. Suddenly one of them (wearing the EU flag) can go no further: he is breathless, exhausted, on the verge of collapsing right on the road. But the rider knows that the others have covertly taken some 'bio-stimulants'. So he begs for help, and someone gives him a pill. He swallows it, and it works a miracle! In a minute, he is back to life and off he goes, twice as fast as before. He overtakes the others and finishes first. After the award ceremony he runs up to the person who gave him the drug, asking for more to be used in future.

The person laughs, saying: 'It's just a matter of your mental state! We gave you a placebo. It had an impact not on your muscles, which are fine, but on your brain!'

The placebo that Brussels invented for itself at the beginning of the 21st century, and on the eve of an ill-prepared and hasty expansion, was a constitutional process with its unclear goals. The old EU members placed their stakes on designing and accepting a treaty that would lay down a constitution for Europe (i.e., for the European Union). But it was a miscalculation. The idea was rejected at the referendums in France and the Netherlands. The Lisbon Treaty that entered into force in 2009 has become a second, more humble and less ambitious attempt.

The EU drastically needed reforms. Its institutions should be better adapted to new conditions. New realities should be taken into account and the entire integration mechanism needs readjustment. But Brussels wanted more. It became convinced that all the problems could be resolved at once (like in the 1950s, when a failed defence and political union was rushed into). It wanted to launch a constitutional revolution and to proclaim a post-modern super-state with all the appropriate attributes in order to act less conspicuously but more efficiently, instead of making a standard choice in favour of the policy of 'small things', introducing small, consistent, and interrelated changes, at which it has been much more successful.

The truth is that the European Union does not require deep transformation. It does not need any basic restructuring or inventing a new philosophy of integration, or changing the principles of its functioning. What it does need is shifting priorities, modernizing the current policies, and adapting itself to tougher and merciless rules of globalization. In other words, it is high time to give up demagogy. It is necessary to learn to understand and defend its own interests, which means using its enormous inherent potential and natural advantages more efficiently.

The European Union has long become a super-powerful entity. The attempts to call it, or compare it to, a super-state or an empire can only create confusion and are, in fact, pointless. The EU is entirely different, and it has no analogies, which does not make it weaker or helpless. As to self-identification, there is a long way to go. The same is true of realizing its responsibility for expressing common and global, and not private and sometimes vested, interests. Brussels is not yet mature for this.

And there are no guarantees that it will cope with the intrinsic and complex contradictions and will survive in the struggle for global competitiveness. The problems to be addressed by the EU are different in principle from those of other leading world players. And Brussels often views itself in a distorted way. Neither does it succeed in viewing itself extrinsically.

However, such a look at the European Union as a leading international player from outside is particularly needed. It is indispensable, therefore, to analyse the specific features of the EU, step by step, in order to understand its legal framework for its external economic and political functioning, to study major directions of its external activities and policies, and to get a glimpse of the future of this unique integrated entity.

EU Special Features

The European Union, in fact, defines itself as a strange and incomprehensible political creature. It consists of thousands of contradictions. None of its features can be assessed unequivocally as negative or positive. They should merely be diagnosed correctly.

The EU has a very complicated internal structure. Its process of generating ideas, preparing and making decisions, and implementing and reviewing decisions is different from other major international players, be it states or international organizations. The rational and the irrational reveal themselves in various ways. Many processes are hidden from observation and take place at the levels of governance that are actually monitoring them. They may also be caused by the factors that are not obvious at all.

This creates problems for the European Union itself, as well as for its partners. They do not have a clear idea of whom they are dealing with or what they have agreed upon, who is responsible and for what, what can be expected in future, etc. Thus, an indispensable feature of the EU conduct, as well as of the structure of its ties with the rest of the world and major international players, is its variability. It is difficult to predict EU actions and to forecast how relations with the EU will develop. The EU conduct internationally is consistently aimed at promoting its interests and is rarely counted among its merits.

EU without Borders

Strange things are evident right from the start, or from what other leading international players take for granted and as a strictly defined constant, namely certainty about the borders and basic importance of state sovereignty.

Formally, the European Union consists of 27 sovereign states. They are all full-fledged members of the union. Their total territory makes up a single territory. Citizens of member states are EU citizens and have additional rights granted by EU citizenship. The external borders of member states make up the common EU border with the rest of the world. The internal borders have mostly been done away with.

However, it is not that simple. The political and geographical borders of the EU are not stable. They may change further. The EU has not yet finalized the area of its living space. No one can known how far the external expansion may stretch. The final decision has not yet been taken by Brussels and by the 27 capitals. Some states would like to proceed further, while others would rather draw a line somewhere. Some believe that the European Union has gone too far with the integration. Others would like even more. The signals sent by various inner forces are contradictory.

Thus, the Balkan policy has long been considered as internal. The absorption of the sub-region is just a matter of time. It will start with Croatia and will proceed until all the Balkan countries become members of the European community. In April 2009, accordingly, Albania submitted an application for accession.

Brussels is already actively approaching the political elites in Moldavia, Ukraine, Belorussia and even the Transcaucasia, skilfully encouraging their dreams of joining the EU. Under the Lisbon Treaty any of them can claim membership if the political and economic criteria are met. The neighbourhood and eastern partnership policies take care of the compliance with these criteria. Being European countries, they conform to the legal and geographical criteria a priori. As to Turkey, the Rubicon has been crossed. The country has been given a candidate status. However, at the current pace, the negotiations may last endlessly.

The EU southern borders present few problems. Israel has been dissuaded from acceding. The most developed countries of Northern Africa, which took the risk of applying or preparing for it, have been recommended to withdraw. But it is not that simple, and there are some subtleties.

The EU seeks to involve the entire Mediterranean region, including the Black Sea basin, and to impose its values and standards throughout. Historically, the former colonial states, now EU members, used to dominate there and still have great cultural and political influence in the region, regarded by the EU as a natural ally. It is a source of raw materials and cheap labour, also making the EU younger. The sustainability and accelerated development of the Mediterranean region are vitally important for the EU.

All recent EU initiatives to create a Mediterranean union are imbued with such considerations. In principle, such plans may considered utopian. Yet there is still unrealized potential. The EU can use its natural advantages, such as a large set of integration measures that are easy to use and at its disposal.

The belt of stability and the neighbourhood that the EU is seeking to create is not the only goal of integration. The EU is positioning itself as far as it can reach, proposing its own patterns of state and law and an established model of social and economic development to individual countries and groups of countries that tend to 'flock together'.

After the alternative offered by the Soviet Union had vanished and the US messianism had been seriously discredited through excessive use of force, it seemed that the future of the world was to be European. However, an unexpected and smart rival to the EU recently emerged in the competition for becoming a role model and in the fight for markets, as well as for economic and political influence. In terms of soft force, the EU started yielding not to Washington but to the Shanghai consensus.

Lack of Internal Uniformity

When the Cold War ended, the European Union made a difficult political choice in favour of external expansion. Thus, it actually gave up, for the time being, hopes for further integration. Brussels did not reject it but it just did not succeed in it. And it started along the avenue of extensive development, postponing other more ambitious plans for future. The expansion was fruitful on the one hand, but, on the other, much has been lost.

The EU received extraordinary political dividends and won the gratitude of many people, having completed the mission of uniting Europe. It extended the space of individual freedom, stability, and prosperity as far as Central, East and Southeast Europe. In return, it got access to enormous and underestimated assets, a new endless area for safe capital investment, and cheap, culturally similar, and skilled labour force. The common market expanded widely and the EU population reached 450 million people. Brussels received an enormous, valuable prize.

But the integration community lost its major value. It was no longer uniform and cohesive. It absorbed nations with almost non-compatible historical backgrounds. Now it unites people who have different values and behavioural attitudes.

The 27 is no longer what the original 6 or 15 used to be. It is an entirely new political and economic space that is much more difficult to organize and to manage as there are too many member states.

All member states might be considered alike as they belong to a single European culture. But even within the same culture there is a great diversity. The European community includes now the Scandinavian people with their own northern mentality. It also has Southeast Europe with a very different outlook. The EU stronghold has always been Germany, which has always given priority to law and order and prefers better organized and more predictable relations. Bright colours are added to the picture by the highly emotional Mediterranean countries with their thousand years-long histories. The picture contains everything: conspicuous contradictions, as well as richness and diversity of cultures, so important for development.

But it comprises not just different countries and nations. There is disparity in the levels of historical, economic, and political development because the income of rich EU members is 35 times higher than that of the poorest ones. This gap is too large. And the diversity presents problems for the European Union: how to align different vectors of interests and bring them into agreement, how to harmonize economic relations without destroying the economies of individual countries and concurrently develop the entire economic space, and how to find so much money. However, such diversity may be considered an advantage, because within a large common market comprising millions of individual and collective consumers, regions at different levels of development, resources, and specialization can supplement one another. Skilful use of these advantages is instrumental for the delocalization of production, for rechannelling financial flows, and for encouraging labour migration without leaving the common economic space. And within that space, it is possible to seek for the best economic solutions.

The diversity is an obvious disadvantage, to put it diplomatically, in the external area. Each member state, or a group of states, has its own, sometimes diametrically opposed, interests, as in the case of Iraq's invasion. It is not always possible to find a common denominator. Thus Spain seeks to involve more Latin American countries in cooperation. For Finland, the northern dimension is closer.

Greece is engrossed in the Balkans. And the countries of this sub-region have their own agendas, while former imperialist countries make the affairs of their former colonies a priority.

The great powers that are members of the EU have global ambitions. They seek to establish an EU presence across the globe. They are directly involved in all the major international processes. Some of them meet in the United Nations Security Council (UNSC); others aspire to do so. No important international form of cooperation with limited composition (such as the G8 or G20) can do without them. The same is true of special structures for settling most serious international conflicts and problems, for example the initiative of the leading EU troika of Britain, France, and Germany on Iran and its specially designed format of negotiations. On the contrary, for most of the member states, and primarily for Central European and Baltic countries, the position of the EU as a regional power is a priority. They seek the active involvement of their direct and indirect neighbours in EU activities to bring them closer to the integration community.

There is a great variety of interest groups in the EU. While Old Europe is ready to criticize the United States and compete with it for world influence, the New Europe acts as a medium for US influence, which brings the latter tangible dividends: US support helps them to have more weight and independence in the EU affairs. The founding states would like to build up the EU's independent military capabilities and develop command and control structures. The newcomers tend to consider EU military power rather as a threat. With regards to energy, the major continental powers are struggling to retain a privileged position for their transnational corporations and to maintain their leading positions in the world economy. Those states that depend on external energy supplies are stubbornly imposing on others a transfer of competence to supranational level with the support of the European Commission. The EU members that modernized the structure of their economies and have staked all on the new economy and market deregulation insist on further globalization and liberalization of international trade. Those with populations largely engaged in the traditional and classical manufacturing sectors are not against balancing the freedom of trade by reasonable protectionist measures. Different countries are differently affected by the problems of legal and illegal migration, separatism, international terrorism, and organized crime. There is also a natural division between 'Euro-enthusiasts' and 'Euro-sceptics', advocates of a people's union and supporters of a union of states, and so on. The range of different interests and positions within the EU is enormous.

The EU is thus not able to achieve consensus on various foreign political and economic issues. Frequently, it is late with important decisions or even becomes paralyzed. Its position may be badly articulated or unclear. Instead of a single voice, there is a stunning and badly tuned chorus. Other international players tend to neglect the EU standpoint on certain issues of the world agenda.

But there is the other side of the coin. The variety of interests results in the EU being engaged in a wide range of issues and regions. It is ready to pursue an active foreign and economic policy in all directions. Working for and promoting their private priorities, individual EU countries can be supported by the consolidated power of the entire integrated community and can often resort to it (or even abuse it). When the EU does succeed in reaching a decision that is to everybody's liking and in elaborating a unified plan of action, it usually proceeds with implementation consistently, uncompromisingly, stopping short at nothing and giving priority only to its own benefit. The EU knows how to get what it wants, making a powerful and hard-to-resist fist to use in relations with outside countries. In such cases, the EU also manifests effective coordination and the skilful distribution of roles.

The lack of EU uniformity, as well as its diversity and the urgency of the challenges it faces, gives rise to another phenomenon that is usually hushed up in studies of the European project. European integration came about largely because Western Europe had to counter a common enemy. In a way, Josef Stalin was one of the godfathers of integration on the other end of the continent, although an evil one, unlike Robert Schuman and Jean Monnet. Even now, an external enemy remains ideal for EU solidarity. Brussels tries to use international processes and phenomena that are hostile to Europe, or individual countries, religions, and cultures to fill this role (although it would not admit to doing so). Concurrently, pursuing a tough and uncompromising policy in the international arena, Brussels seeks to make up for its internal looseness.

Holding member states hostage to the common and agreed-upon line on the international scene or to the private interests of one or several countries is just a secondary implement in the box of EU consolidation tools, which has become an entrenched aspect of the EU.

Solidarity Factors

The factors of solidarity among EU member states, in varying degrees, are the same geographical location, common historical background, cultural heritage and political values, close interests, and a shared hope that the community will neutralize contradictions and reinforce international competitiveness. Although these factors do not explain why Western European countries, now joined by most other European countries, have succeeded in their integration project. They could all have lived in peace, prosperity, and conciliation without testing new forms of organization for coexistence fraught with losing independence and sovereignty, as well as yielding power to each other. The organizational solutions tried and tested among the EU members have not taken root elsewhere. The integration project has become irreversible thanks to a special and unique legal order, a qualitatively new political culture of common decision making, and the implementation and joint governance of sovereignty.

Supremacy of Legal Provisions

The European Union is at once both an extravert and an introvert. It separates itself from the rest of the world, creating external borders along the perimeter of the entire community and a legal space regulated by its own internal mechanisms different from international ones.

Accordingly, the relations between member states, as well as with the subjects of the internal law of those member states, are increasingly regulated by EU law. When there is a conflict between national legislation and the EU law, the latter applies – exclusively. It is applied by all national, administrative, and judicial bodies. Individuals and legal entities use it directly to establish their legal relations.

Disputes that arise within EU competences cannot be resolved by bodies that follow common international law. The EU itself decides which international agreements apply within its territory. It also decides how member states implement the obligations contained in those international agreements.

At the same time, the EU seeks to propose a regulatory framework for its partners and the rest of the world. This became particularly pronounced in the financial and economic crisis that began in 2008, when the EU member states called for stronger law and regulatory mechanisms in the global economy and for putting the activities of all financial institutions in order. There were demands not only for strengthening the regulation of financial markets through control, transparency, responsibility, and strict compliance with the rules but also for elaborating new standards. Confident that this was the right time for such an initiative, Brussels wanted to put its projects of national, supranational, and international legislation on the negotiating table, because no one would be able to neglect them.

The EU has established a network of relationships supported through regulatory frameworks throughout the world. These relationships are expressed in agreements on customs unions and free trade zones, on association, stabilization, partnership and cooperation, on common and single spaces, and so on. The resulting cooperation and interaction are conditional, which means that certain conditions must be met for a third party to benefit from the relationship. This implies compliance with the rules of the game set by Brussels, including approved legal prescriptions. The only country that has not agreed to such conditionality with the EU is Australia. It refused to include in the agreement with the EU a standard clause affecting the European Union and its bilateral relations. Brussels did not have enough ways to exercise pressure on Canberra. Others assumed obligations to go, more or less, along the way of harmonizing their national legislations with the EU law.

It is worth clarifying why regulatory aspects are so important. It is the EU regulatory nature and regulatory features that make it so distinct. The EU is not just an economic or social and economic community, nor is it just an economic and monetary union. It functions through law and on the basis of legal instruments. All political, economic, and any other solutions are shaped as EU legal norms and executed as norms of law, rather than because of their feasibility or political setup.

They are endowed with a force of law, and the entire power of law enforcement of national states is available to defend them.

All the members, in all their diversity and despite such varied geography, economies, and politics, are integrated through – and thanks to – common law. The EU is thus zealous about its uniform application. No staggering as is typical of international law is allowed. The EU is well equipped with excellent structures, procedures, and mechanisms that have been tried and tested. Even more important is that supranational law and national law make up a single whole. Consequently, EU legal norms are guarded by the national subjects of law whose interests are served by integration better and more efficiently than by the national law. And the interests consist in the day-to-day use of the advantages of the common market and freedoms it is based on.

Thus the EU provides for the provisions and agreements of the supranational level to be actualized in the internal law of its member states. Without this, it cannot and will not exist. And the actualization in the member states' internal law is either uniform or similar and comparable. This is the meaning of EU legal harmonization. The common law is ramified and layered, modern and efficient, covering all areas of activities under the EU jurisdiction. Through it, the common market becomes effective and very fruitful, and beneficial for business, EU citizens and member countries. The accumulated experience of creating a common market by legal means can thus be extended to create common market analogues in various promising areas, from education to mutual recognition and the execution of court judgements – all that is covered by the concept of freedom, security, and justice.

Political Culture of Solidarity

To exist as a legal community is not sufficient to explain how the European Union succeeds in weakening its strong centrifugal forces, coping with heterogeneity, and resolving internal conflicts. Another component of its success is the specific political and legal culture nurtured by it.

It is not enough to have state-of-the art laws; They must work; It is not enough to create objective prerequisites for united action; United action should become routine practice; It is fine to lay down the basis for coordinating foreign economic activities and foreign policy and to create an organizational framework for consolidating efforts in this direction; But much more is needed to implement it. There should be readiness to make concessions and a political will to sacrifice individual ambitions and interests, consistently aiming at specific results. An appropriate political culture is required.

Such a culture is needed for the member states and all EU systems to proceed from a definite set of principles. The member states, as minimum, do not allow their private national interests to prevail over the common interests and subordinate theirs to the common interests, work for identifying these common interests, articulate them, consistently defend and promote them. In parallel, they seek to use the advantages of individual countries and groups for the common good.

An example of an efficient combination of high individual and collective political culture is the smoothness of the accession to the EU by Sweden, Finland, and Austria in 1995. Before this, several times running, the European Community had accepted economically less developed countries that had rid themselves of authoritarian yoke. The Nordic countries and Austria compared well with the most advanced members of the European Community, and their values did not differ at all. Moreover, they made a tangible contribution to the EU's economic potential, and in no way did they impair its homogeneity. On the contrary, they made integration even more sustainable.

Yet outsiders remain outsiders. It takes time to master the traditions of the core member states, to perceive common imperatives, and to comply with foreign legal practice. Therefore, although the newcomers had to meet very high standards, their arrival might have affected the discipline and quality of decision making, but it did not. The EU managed to avoid the temporary malfunctioning that might have been expected during a period of acclimatization when the common denominator of decision making is usually lowered.

The Nordic countries added value to the EU's internal policies and international activities. They gave the EU and the world an environmental agenda, enriched the European model of social and economic development with new elements, and introduced to the world the concept of sustainable development. Other EU members had their own preferences. At first, they considered the proposals by the Nordic countries a superfluous burden. But in the final analysis, the Nordic members got their way and all the other member states had to accept their approach. Environmental protection became a horizontal requirement for any type of EU activity and a major foreign policy priority. The common economic and foreign policy was agreed upon on the basis of the highest, not the lowest, standards.

The EU's political culture of mutual concessions and compromises in accordance with the highest standards, rather than a common denominator, had long been regarded as a 'specialty of the house' (and compared favourably to other classical international organizations that were, typically, making little headway). One of its ingredients is a formula by which the member states work together if they are interested in cooperation, and do not interfere with the others if they are not interested. The EU founding documents envisage mechanisms of integration at different pace, and they are actively used.

Nonetheless, the political culture that has emerged over decades has now seriously degraded. At the stage of negotiating accession, New Europe supported Old Europe unconditionally in all its initiatives. The latter became convinced that it would last forever. However, on acquiring EU membership, New Europe acquired its own voice. And the new members do not always agree with the practice of the European Union. For them, it is not an axiom that they should sacrifice something for the sake of others. They have their own vision of the ways and aims of European integration. After restraining themselves for so many years, they would not give up their individualistic plans and intentions easily.

Indeed, the negotiations between the EU and Turkey became more problematic after the EU accepted Cyprus. Relations between the 27 and Russia have not stabilized yet and the saga of the trying to negotiate a constitutional treaty and the subsequent Lisbon Treaty will be remembered by Old Europe for a long time. In the process, Poland demanded to retain the privileges that it had won a few years earlier under the Nice Treaty, presumptuously promising to block the approval of the treaty and to disrupt the emerging consensus.

By late 2009, a fundamentally new situation had arisen: the initiative of formulating ideological and foreign policy orientations shifted partially to the Baltic countries and Poland, as well as countries supporting them. They proposed their own interpretation of the solidarity principle and the way the emerging balance of interests within the EU should be counted. Still, strong individualism, blackmailing and obstructionism, minority rule, coercion to reject reasonable and rational steps under the pretext of a distorted slogan of solidarity temporarily disrupted the evolution of EU general political culture.

The strength of European integration has always been in its positive programme. A negative one can only contribute to losing soft power and weakening international competitiveness. The sooner Brussels refuses to move at the speed of the slowest camel in the caravan, the better for the EU and for those countries that are seeking to establish partnership relations with it.

Joint Management of Sovereignty

Another element of the heterogeneity of the EU is the partial transfer of sovereign powers by member states up to the supranational level. Logically, yielding sovereignty should imply that the states become in a way flawed. No longer fully legally capable on the international scale, they lose self-sufficiency and, to a certain extent, control over their internal and external policies.

In the case of the EU, this logic does not work. The transfer of some sovereign powers to the supranational level does not impoverish but enriches the member states. In return for part of their sovereignty, dozens of 'parts' shared with them by their integration partners. As a result, they engage in the joint management of numerous sovereignties, reinforcing each and every member state, opening up new prospects, and enabling them to use the cumulative potential of integration to achieve common and individual goals.

From this perspective, the major EU institutions act as managers administering the sovereign powers delegated to them. The future of the EU depends on their professionalism, leadership qualities, and ability to formulate tactical and strategic targets and replace or coordinate the efforts of member states. Brussels and other capitals have long focused on readjusting to meet the needs of the European Union of three dozens of states and adapt to a new competitive international environment. Before the Lisbon Treaty came into force in 2009, more fragmented palliative methods were used, which consisted of gradual, not always visible, incremental reforms using the recipes tested by the constitutional debate and the Lisbon Treaty and in building political and legal culture, as well as governance culture.

The transfer of sovereign powers by the member states to the supranational level, creation of supranational structures to manage them, mastery of the acquired powers, and development of appropriate practice among various governance levels entail complex, even intricate, vertical and horizontal symbiotic links. That is why the EU is perceived by all, internally and externally, as an extremely complex entity. However, it is the hierarchy, multiplicity, durability, and flexibility of the links and their mutual support and complementarity that make the integration community highly sustainable and dynamic and the European project irreversible.

There is a strong internal logic in the enormous diversity of the ligaments drawing the community into a tight knot. The EU is endowed with four types of competences. In other words, the system of relationships among the member states, between the member states and EU institutions, and among the EU institutions proper is made up of several models. In the areas of EU-exclusive competence, the member states no longer perform any regulatory functions, which are transferred completely to the supranational level. In those areas where the EU has a mixed competence, the member states and the EU act jointly. The member states retain regulatory functions, which they can use on their own as long as they have not reached agreement on a single legislation. When such legislation enters into force, the member states lose their regulatory functions and become a kind of an agent for enforcing common legislation. In the areas where the EU has only supporting competence, the role of the union is reduced to helping the member states in multilateral cooperation, assisting but not interfering in administering regulatory functions. Finally, if the EU is entrusted with parallel competence, it can replace the member states anywhere without preventing them from playing an independent role and acting individually. Legislative mechanisms are not used in this case. The role of the European Commission is weakened. Control by the European Court of Justice is not envisaged. The factor of political will becomes critical: when the EU has exclusive competence, the negative consequences of a conflict of interests are actually prevented from coming into play. Political culture of decision making and execution becomes much more important.

A parallel competence is used for establishing ties in foreign, security, and defence policy. The European Community had exclusive, mixed and supporting competence. Under the Lisbon Treaty those ties are inherited by the European Union. The cooperation of the police and judicial bodies in combating crime involves the use of instruments of both the interstate and supranational levels. The new treaty envisages their organization on a EU-wide basis.

With the Lisbon Treaty coming into force, the EU's horizontal three-pillar structure sinks into oblivion. Cooperation between the police and judicial bodies loses its uniqueness. It is regulated the same way as the common market. But most of the special features of foreign, security, and defence policy are retained even though the European Community is renamed the European Union, and becomes the legal successor to itself.

But what really matters is that the supranational nature of integration is reinforced. Supranational ties have become more diverse. Their share and importance in the overall balance of governance within the EU has grown. The system of institutions and their work has been restructured accordingly. Consequently, the factors that have tightened the EU's loose heterogenic space have become stronger. The EU should be able, to a greater extent, to come out as a single entity, including in the international arena.

Legal and Institutional Reform in the Governance of Foreign Affairs

A major weakness of the EU in the international arena is the disunity of its external economic policy and foreign policy. That disunity is often taken for granted as something that requires no proof. The EU political elite consider it an obvious shortcoming.

In fact, there is no, and cannot be any, barrier between what the EU does internationally in terms of both economic policy and foreign policy. Experts and politicians exaggerate the problem, intentionally or not. Researchers study the EU's external activities and the Common Foreign and Security Policy (CFSP) separately. These two areas are even referred to as different specializations. For politicians, state officials of various levels, and EU leadership, disunity has been a convenient excuse for inaction and failure at the international level. Compromise solutions were taken in the past because member states were not ready to give up more of their sovereignty. The European Union was denied international legal standing. It was created in a way that merely supplanted the European Community with new directions of foreign policy. But the European Community and the CFSP were combined only formally. No union or merger actually happened.

In reality, however, the European Community and the European Union have a single institutional structure. The Maastricht Treaty authorizes the EU Council and the European Commission to coordinate all activities irrespective of their sphere. The General Affairs Council and the Foreign Affairs Council both consider external economic and foreign policy issues in the same format, just changing hats. In practice it is absolutely impossible to separate them.

Here are some examples. One of the EU's calling cards in foreign affairs is environmental protection, which it promotes by purely political means, through political dialogues with other countries and in international organizations. But the basis of the EU environmental foreign policy is purely economic. The Kyoto Protocol is written to this end. With this in view, a new global market has been created for trading in carbon emissions quotas.

Another highly politicized example is the EU's external energy strategy, as well as the concept of energy security. In the name of energy security the EU takes economically ungrounded and very costly decisions to diversify the suppliers of hydrocarbons and energy sources and to build bypasses and alternative transcontinental pipelines. It is guided by primarily global considerations, as well as political and strategic concerns. But the energy plans it promotes are rendered consistent only because the EU is writing new rules of the game (the third gas package) and creating a common market for importing, producing, transporting, and distributing electric power and hydrocarbons.

The fight against organized crime is an example from a different sphere. It presents an acute problem of illegal drug trafficking and illegal immigration, as well as challenges in regulating migration flows. The problem can be solved, even partially, only through broad and efficient international cooperation. The EU is urged to engage in such cooperation by all countries with which it is developing trade and economic relationships and to which it provides technical assistance, although only on its own terms. Moreover, this cooperation is stated directly in the new generation of agreements concluded by the EU and other countries. Assistance and benefits from the access to the vast and attractive EU market are provided on condition of compliance with the requirements to limit emigration to the EU, to change legislation and law enforcement practice, and so on.

Yet there remain grounds for complaints that the EU foreign policy and external economic activities could be much better, that they lack coordination, that something must be changed, and that it is high time to introduce reforms. These complaints are related to the fact that the EU acts as both a supranational body in the economic sphere and as an intergovernmental one in the foreign policy. The gap between the two is difficult to overcome, but possible because of the EU's appropriate and robust procedures.

That gap results from the implementation of foreign policy and external economic policy using different methods, procedures, and management systems. In its external economic policy, the supranational law of integration is used as a legal basis for its actions. The EU proper comes out as an integration community. Accordingly, natural and legal persons, along with the member states, become the subjects of law that regulates external economic activities. The difference between external and internal commitments becomes blurred.

The situation is different with regard to the CFSP. Common principles, targets, strategies, and positions accepted by the EU are binding only for the member states. They do not have intra-state dimension, they are not law, and they are not binding for individuals. Priority is given to the vertical governance framework. The European Council and the Council of the European Union are dominant, and the European Commission plays a subordinate role. The European Parliament has an advisory vote. The Court of Justice is taken out of the game. EU interests are represented by the presiding state, which is assisted by the high representative for CFSP or in accordance with the Lisbon Treaty by the permanent president and much more powerful high representative. Decisions on all major issues, except for implementing what has already been agreed upon, are taken by consensus.

In external economic affairs, by contrast, decisions are usually taken by a qualified majority. The driving force is the European Commission. The European Parliament is rather strong, and decisions are reinforced at a fast rate. The Court of Justice may be involved in exercising control over the legality of any actions and agreements.

The difference is striking. Member states have given up a great, but limited, amount of their sovereign powers in external economic activities, primarily involving trade. In certain cases member states have lost completely their regulatory function. According to the concept of legal support, the EU has all the competence it needs to achieve its goals, particularly those related to the creation and functioning of the common market. In the areas of EU-exclusive and mixed competence, where common supranational legislation is effective, the EU prohibits member states from individually adopting competitive regulatory acts. In those cases when it has already happened, the EU is entitled not only to act and to act along with the member states but also to replace or side-line them.

Exclusive competence cannot exist in foreign policy. The member states have endowed the EU with almost limitless powers in foreign and security policy, but they have not lost their powers. They still play an autonomous role on the international scene and act in parallel with and alongside the EU. Therefore, the member states seem to retain all their powers while being concurrently vested in the EU institutions. The consolidation of efforts thus becomes an imperative for both the member states and EU institutions. The CFSP is implemented through a coordination method that excludes, in principle, the subordination of one state to another or supranational governance.

The differences in regulating and organizing external economic and foreign political activities create many problems for the EU and member states. The following simple example can demonstrate the challenge of seeking the best solution all the time. A country in Africa, having gone through a civil war, is full of weapons. To bring it back to peaceful life, the EU intends to buy out the weapons from individuals – a method that has already proved efficient elsewhere. The European Commission suggests doing it through a technical assistance programme, which means it would be funded by the EU's regular budget, it would be decided upon by a majority of votes, and its execution would be the responsibility of supranational institutions. A group of member states support carrying it out under the auspices of the CFSP, which means the decision would be have to be unanimous, the member states would have to provide the funding, and the Council of the EU and interested states retain full control the programme.

Thus, it is not a matter of what to do or how to do it, but a matter of the distribution of influence within the EU. What seem to be technicalities matter a lot in the EU. They predetermine the internal efficiency of the community, its ability to smooth over conflicts of interests, and its capacity for transforming the perpetual problem of conciliation of sovereignties from weakness into strength.

EU Positioning in the International Arena

There are always certain political forces behind foreign political and external economic decisions, tactical steps, and the choice of strategy. The EU mixes them. It pretends to be anonymous. It claims that its position reflects common interests. In fact, there are always players, primarily non-state ones, for which benefit most from Brussels's position and actions. It is sometimes easier and sometimes more difficult to identify them. But they are always there.

Meanwhile, many EU external economic and foreign political priorities are of statutory nature, set out in the founding treaties. Those priorities include protecting and promoting the interests of the EU as a single whole, spreading the EU's common values around the world, and achieving standard goals such as peaceful relations in compliance with the UN Charter and even prosperity for all, as well as a fair international order.

In its foreign activities the EU used to give priority to eliminating barriers to global trade and to free competition. In practice the EU had always pursued a pragmatic policy. It actively subsidized its own producers, particularly in agriculture. It tried to bind the developing countries to itself using non-economic methods. It did not hesitate to close its internal market when it deemed it to be feasible. It now supports a system of measures designed to impose strict national control over foreign investments in strategic sectors. At the initiative of France's Nicolas Sarkozy, freedom of competition was taken off the list of the EU objectives in the Lisbon Treaty. Thus the emphasis is placed primarily on free access to the markets of external countries while having a free hand to protect its own market from undesirable competitors.

In the 1990s, the EU proclaimed sustainable development as a major foreign economic slogan. Brussels did its best for it to be included in the world agenda and reflected in the declarations of international forums and organizations. Under the banner of sustainable development the EU succeeded in taking up leading positions at all international negotiations on economic issues. Its model of social and economic development was supplemented by the quality standards of economic growth, which implied less pressure on the environment. Sustainable development is considered by Brussels, tactically and strategically, to be a major competitive advantage. Recently the EU started interpreting environmental issues broadly. Brussels has engaged all available forces to organize a broad international front for combating climate change.

The EU is also positioning itself as a world leader of development aid. It allocates up to 20 percent of the total contribution by its member states to development aid programmes. However, its role is particularly important because it acts not on its own but as a coordinator. Its aid and technical assistance are conditional on policy changes, adoption of democratic values, changes in legislature, and so on. Brussels believes that external assistance is efficient only when the recipients are helping themselves. Yet it is difficult to judge how efficiently the money received is used. Nonetheless Brussels is very sensitive to the way China has recently been actively promoting its interests in developing countries through development aid.

On the political agenda, the non-proliferation of weapons of mass destruction and missile technologies and the settlement of local and regional conflicts are EU priorities. The EU has let the relations between India and Pakistan slip in the same way as the United States, although, unlike the US, Europeans were simply unable to prevent the nuclear ambitions of the Asian giants. Brussels is involved in the major ongoing negotiations, and working with Iran and closely watching North Korea. It has articulated proposals for improving the Non-Proliferation Treaty regime. However, the EU is not the number-one player in nuclear weapons, and the members of the nuclear club are not afraid to sidestep the EU in international diplomacy.

The EU is much better at settling local conflicts. It has conducted more than a dozen and a half civil and military operations on various continents. All of them were successful, although very limited contingents were engaged. The EU and its member states have gained unique experience and have worked out procedures, interaction schemes, logistics, and management by objectives. The EU is especially good at conducting post-conflict rehabilitation in affected countries, and not only because Brussels allocates impressive sums of money for this purpose. It has a clear idea of what should be done for the central and local authorities to start working in a way acceptable to the West. The EU seems to willing to transfer this experience over to the post-Soviet space. Not without the influence of the new members of the EU, Brussels is ever more insistent on its involvement in current post-conflict situations. It has already arrived in Georgia, most likely, to stay.

The EU is also involved in the Middle East. It is a member of the Middle East 'Quartet'. It has privileged relations with Israel, as well as with Arab countries. It launches foreign political initiatives and conducts secret negotiations. Nonetheless, having recognized the undisputable leadership of the United States, it plays a secondary role. Moreover, the EU bears a responsibility together with the US for what has happened in Iraq since 2003. Resolving the situation in Afghanistan is becoming a hard trial for the EU and for the North Atlantic Treaty Organization (NATO). The image of the EU as a leading international player and its international standing, to a great extent, depend on how it will cope with this task.

In terms of the geographic component of the EU's external economic and foreign policy priorities, the United States is the EU's most important partner. This is the top priority for the EU. The US is not just its strategic partner, but it is its only truly reliable ally. The allied relations are secured through the North Atlantic Treaty and the Transatlantic Charter as bilateral instruments, although neither the EU nor the US needs any contractual commitments for their special relations. Those are assured by massive mutual investments, economic mergers, enormous volumes of mutual trade, common interests, US military presence in Europe, and harmonious legal orders.

Nonetheless, when Germany held the rotating presidency of the EU in 2007, the EU proposed creating a common North Atlantic market. The institutions for serving mutual consultations were updated and sectoral dialogues were launched. After Barack Obama took office in the White House in 2009, the EU suggested a comprehensive treaty with the US and a ramified institutionalized mechanism for engagement and coordination.

It is hard to believe that such ideas will be realized. The United States considers it disadvantageous to develop relations with the EU as a single entity. It prefers the arrangement contained in NATO, with each EU country represented individually. The EU is not legally constituted as a group of states, and the US can work with each one on its own. This works well for the US taking into account their different weight.

EU-US relations are certainly far from ideal. Regular trade wars are not worth mentioning. By and large, the EU has not been content with the US financial policy over the last decades. Brussels dislikes Washington's unjustified use of force in international affairs. It resents America's unilateral approach to various problems and unwillingness to consult the EU. The EU would like the US to accede to the Kyoto Protocol, to ratify the Rome Statute of the International Criminal Court, and to abolish the death penalty. The EU would require a bilateral treaty so it could engage in relations on legal terms, with which it is much better familiarized, and impose restrictions and make bilateral economic ties with the US more efficient. But the US has also claims to make of the Europeans. Americans regard Europeans as afraid of the hard work of imposing order on the world and preferring to seek shelter behind America's back. Yet, whatever the psychological background, there is no alternative to a close EU-US union. This is, among other thing, the reason for the ecstatic reception that met Obama in Europe after the change in the US administration in 2008.

China ranks second in terms of external relations for the EU. The trade turnover between China and the EU grew up to €400 billion before the 2008 crisis, although it was developing in an irregular fashion. The EU deficit of its balance of payments in the trade with China is remained at the level of €150 billion. But the EU has no doubts that China presents extraordinary opportunities: it is a promising market with which the EU must establish long-term and stable cooperation.

However, China is not an easy partner. The EU does not know what kind of policy should be pursued towards it. There is no unity among the member states in this respect. Moreover, some are excluded from participating in the policy elaboration, because the political agenda is determined by those doing the 'heavy lifting'. Economic interests in expanding ties with China also vary. Moreover, China defies the European model of social and economic development. It forces member states to adapt faster to the changing conditions of global competition. However, they cope differently. One group of member states (led by the United Kingdom) proposes shutting down outdated production enterprises, to give preference to high technologies, and not to be afraid of Chinese exports. Those member states claim that it is necessary to run up the technological staircase higher and higher and accelerate technological development, so China cannot catch up or get ahead. In this context, there is no alternative to international trade liberalization. Others (for instance, Italy and Germany) are concerned about mass unemployment in the traditional economic sectors, and maintain that the economic structure will be rational and sustainable only if all sectors – not just high technologies – including sectors that are labour intensive, with relatively low or medium added value, are retained and supported. They do not want China to be the only world factory. The EU should remain a manufacturer and producer as well.

The European Commission has issued about a dozen statements related to the policy towards China. It has repeatedly suggested that the member states should introduce new specifications, should diversify and extend ties with China, and use more varied instruments in the relationship. China condescended to formulate its policy regarding the EU. Beijing did not hurry to respond to Brussels' proposal to draw up a comprehensive treaty for their rapidly developing relations. Thus, it was the EU that sought to establish close political ties with China and to institutionalize bilateral relations, in particular, after the United States had normalized relations with China and agreed upon regular political consultations.

The general pattern of interstate interaction now includes a hierarchy of contacts, political dialogue at all levels, and about 30 sectoral groups covering all major areas of economic and political cooperation, from industrial property protection to human rights. The EU and China have been working on a basic strategic partnership agreement for a number of years. It should replace their traditional agreement on cooperation and trade. But the nature of communication between the EU and China is changing dramatically. Brussels seeks tougher positions on economic issues, in particular on those related to intellectual property protection and market access, although without tangible results so far. It stubbornly works to include autonomy for Tibet and human rights issues in the agenda in order to justify its embargo on military equipment supplies introduced long ago and in completely different conditions.

The EU thus values its relations with the US and China. In official documents Brussels also counts among its strategic partners Japan, India, and Russia, but the scope of relations with them is much narrower.

Interaction with the countries in Asia, Africa, and the Caribbean also figures on the EU agenda. The EU seeks formal political and economical ties and to introduce its own model of social and economic development and state and law construction. It renews its agreements on association regularly, making them ever more comprehensive and intensive. These agreements are asymmetric, providing developing countries a preferential regime, access to the EU common market, status as technical assistance recipient, and possibilities to get involved in the EU policies, programmes, and projects.

These agreements are highly beneficial for the EU and for its member states. They secure the situation in which Brussels is helping the rest of the world by undertaking a 'hard' mission of integrating the developing countries in the world economy and teaching them democracy and the rule of law. Together with those countries it works on overcoming poverty, improving state administration, modernizing legislation and law enforcement, and combating corruption.

The approaches described here are the colonial legacy of Belgium, the UK, Spain, Italy, the Netherlands, Portugal and France, which has been transformed by the EU. It was especially important for these leading members of the EU not to lose their influence in their former colonies and to shift the responsibility for their development on to the EU. The EU has coped surprisingly well. The world is convinced that these former imperial powers are to blame for colonialism and that the EU has nothing to do with it. Because those countries do not act on their own but through the EU, the heavy burden of their colonializing past is removed, including claims for plundering resources and exterminating aboriginal communities. Thus the legitimacy of their presence and their influence is retained.

Political dialogues, economic interaction, and institutionalized cooperation with developing countries make the EU a truly global power. However, its expansion is carried out strictly on a regional and geographical basis and not according to zones of interest. It focuses first on managing the neighbouring territories and establishing efficient control over them, or (to use appropriate EU terminology) creating a neighbourhood belt with all the benefits and advantages of integration. Until recently, the Mediterranean region, the Middle East, and North Africa were given absolute priority by Brussels. After its most recent enlargement in 2007, growing importance has been given to East European countries, the Commonwealth of Independent States, the Trans-Caucasian states, and even to Central Asia.

It is evident why there are such trends in the evolution of the EU foreign policy and external economic activities. The EU core started considering new vectors of expansion after the EU borders had moved eastwards. New opportunities have emerged. The new Central European and South European member states are lobbying the EU ever more insistently and dogmatically. They want to use to advantage the economic and political might of the integrated community in their relations with their non-EU neighbours. In this respect, the solidarity brought produced by the EU's growth is taking on new and unexpected meanings.

Consequently, the EU's Eastern policy runs counter to the interests of Russia. Between 2003 and 2009, bilateral contradictions reached their peak. In August and September 2008, Paris and Brussels brokered an agreement on cease-fire terms between Russia and Georgia after the latter's army attacked South Ossetia and Russian peacekeepers did not resolve those contradictions in any way. The situation revealed what had long been unspoken: the mechanisms of managing partnership and cooperation created by both parties did not work and should be replaced or readjusted. 'Business as usual' has no prospects if one partner undermines the other by demonizing it while trying to persuade its political elite otherwise. Similarly, in the late 1980s Jacques Delors's concept of concentric circles, which placed the EU at the centre of world order with all other countries in surrounding circles, inflicted great harm on the EU-Russia relations. For more than two decades this approach predetermined the policy towards Russia formulated and pursued by the EU and its member states. Both sides will benefit if the paradigm is changed. And it cannot be otherwise as the potential of EU-Russia cooperation is virtually unlimited. The current negotiations on a modernized EU-Russia partnership should pave the way for its realization.

What the Future Holds

The European Union already exerts a great influence on the global agenda and development, as well as on the resolution of international problems in areas such as environmental issues, sustainable development, and climate change. However, there have been several damaging failures of EU foreign policy (such as in the Balkan war, in failing to prevent genocide in Africa, and in its own internal crisis related to Iraq). The EU political elite and member states are convinced that the EU international activities could and should be more offensive and efficient.

The EU carries much less political weight than economic weight in international affairs. The elite blame bad management of EU foreign affairs, disunity of structures, volatility, lack of continuity, and excessive decentralization. But the reasons do not lie in the EU's management of its foreign affairs. They arise out of a clash of member states' interests in an area as delicate as foreign policy. They are associated with the parallelism of the foreign policy activities of the EU and member states and with the inherent uncertainty in the transfer of sovereign powers to the supranational level. These contradictions will remain. But Brussels intends to do away with the shortcomings in shaping and executing foreign policy and external economic actions through improving the technology of management.

With the entering into force of the Lisbon Treaty, the European Union obtains permanent presidency instead of the previous six-month rotation. Some states manage the presidency better than others. Some have turned the EU into a political dwarf – and this has nothing to do with the size or might of the presiding state. France's 2008 presidency has been recognized as a role model: under President Nicolas Sarkozy, Paris and Brussels took the lead in settling the conflict in the Caucasus in August–September 2008, in countering the first wave of the global financial and economic crisis, and in implementing numerous important and far-reaching initiatives. Italy, while not much less influential in the world, was considered by most observers less successful and productive as EU president.

However, according to Brussels, the presidency is only one part of the problem. All EU countries have different visions of the foreign policy and external economic policy to be pursued by the European Union. They have different ambitions and different priorities. Thus under each presidency, certain problems are advanced and others are set aside or shifted to the back burner. Sometimes the EU does not know what to do with the initiatives supported before. The permanent president is entrusted with speaking out on behalf of the entire union and with providing continuity in foreign and foreign economic policy. This new arrangement will rid the EU of hasty and ill-considered initiatives and will bring more respectability to its foreign policy and external relations more respectable.

The Lisbon Treaty established the position of high representative for the EU's minister for foreign affairs. With the status of the highest EU official responsible for foreign policy, the high representative has great power and deals with both foreign policy and external economic policy, being concurrently a deputy chair of the European Commission and assuming the functions of the commissioner for foreign affairs. The authors of the constitutional treaty and the Lisbon Treaty believed that the concentration of powers in the position of high representative would bring continuity and integrity to the EU's foreign policy and external economic activities. Political goals will be reached by means of economic levers. In turn, the EU economic interests will be promoted through political methods.

Another advantage of this arrangement is that the office of the high representative bridges the two leading institutions of the European Union: the EU Council and the European Commission. The two can now work in a more coordinated and efficient way. Furthermore, in planning and executing foreign policy, the high representative can draw on the enormous expert potential available in the European Commission and used only in the EU external economic activities. The fact that all the European Commission delegations are subordinate to the high representative illustrates the qualitative leap that is theoretically possible in the EU's international activities.

With the Lisbon Treaty coming into force, new prospects have opened up for reinforcing EU's foreign policy and external economic activities using a power component. Although there is no discussion of creating an European armed force, the new arrangement makes it much easier to use military means, well trained and equipped, ready to serve in any region of the world. Moreover, the member states will be able to pursue structured cooperation within the EU framework. This means that those who can and wish to promote military integration will be able to do so without hindrance.

The Lisbon Treaty provides for many crucial changes in its very content. It is still premature to make any assessments and it remains difficult to predict how those changes will affect the EU's international position in the long run. At the same time, there is no doubt that in the foreign policy the EU will become a much more confident, tough, and ambitious entity. The time will soon come for reconsidering all international activities of the integrated European community and for rewriting them in the context of the ever growing potential of the European Union.

Chapter 7

The Representation of the European Union in the G8

Judith Huigens and Arne Niemann

Since 1977, only two years after the first G7 summit in Rambouillet, France, Europe has been officially represented at every summit, a fact often overlooked by the general public and scholars alike.[1] Despite its longstanding presence at the G7/G8 summit, the European Union has remained the odd one out, for a number of reasons. First of all, and most notably, the EU is the only regional institution among a select group of nation-states considered a fully fledged participant at the summit. The G8 formation, with France, the United Kingdom, Italy, Germany, the United States, Canada, Japan, and Russia, has always been an issue of debate (Merlini 1994; Silvestri 1994). Nonetheless, EU participation has, apart from some disagreement over the initial invitation in the 1970s, never been disputed since. Second, there is the issue of dual representation, stemming from the fact that, up until recently, the European Union could be represented by, at some occasions, as many as six representatives: the four European G8 members, the European Commission and the country holding the presidency of the Council of the European Union (Penttilä 2009, 38).

This chapter investigates the ambiguous nature of this unique representation and its effect on the contribution of the EU to the G8 debate. It claims that the dual structure of EU representation results directly from the characteristics of the EU itself as well as those of the G8. The EU's quest for supranationalism makes the presence of both the commission and member states inevitable, but this complicated situation is in fact not very complicated in the G8 context.

This analysis begins with a brief introduction to the concept of EU international representation. This will be followed by an overview of the development of the aforementioned representation construction (especially of multiple EU actors in the G8), including the (advantageous and problematic) implications culminating from this situation.[2] Finally, the chapter ends with two case studies that illustrate

---

1 See, however, see Susan Hainsworth (1990), Heidi Ullrich and Alan Donnelly (1998), and Fischer (2001). In the early years, the European Community was represented by the president of the European Commission, who was later joined by the rotating president of the European Council.

2 This chapter draws on interviews conducted with officials of the European Union member states and European Commission and also members of the G8 delegations.

some of the important challenges and opportunities of EU representation as well as some of the conditions that determine effective EU participation within the G8.

Conceptualizing the International Representation of the EU

In order to grasp the EU's unique position at the G8 summit, it is first necessary to understand the nature of these two very different international bodies. Their distinctive characteristics explain not only EU participation, but also the ambiguous nature of EU representation. Both the informality of the G8 and the supranational nature of the EU contribute to this delegation structure, which can be explained using principal-agent theory.

The G8 is often framed as a story of states. Born out of frustration with the inefficiency and slow decision making of existing international institutions such as the International Monetary Fund (IMF) or the World Bank, the initial meeting was intended to bring together a small party of powerful state leaders for a 'direct, unscripted, unbureaucratic exchange between a few heads of government' (Bayne 1995). The original composition has changed somewhat, by extending invitations to Canada in 1976 and Russia in 1997, and later including the so-called 'Outreach Five' or 'Group of Five', as well as by expanding the ministerial meetings (Kirton 1999, 51). Nonetheless, the G8 remains primarily a gathering of state governments. The G8 can not be considered an international governmental organization (IGO), however, as it does not fit all necessary characteristics: a formal treaty, voluntary membership, a permanent character, a distinctive constitutional structure, common interests, and a formal conference (Fischer 2001). G8 members have joined the group voluntarily to cooperate on common interests, and the summit has taken place every year since 1975, but it lacks those more formal characteristics (Kirton 2004, 453).

The dubious nature of the G8 as an international organization suggests it is rather a 'quasi-intergovernmental organization' or an 'informal group' (Fischer 2001). This kind of international organization can also be considered 'concert diplomacy', which is based on informal rules and serving mainly to coordinate policy (Schwegmann 2001). Concert diplomacy springs from growing interdependence and density of institutional relations between states, which cause a security community to develop. Concerts remain informal, with a core that is hard to pinpoint. They revolve around comprehensive deliberations and negotiations among powers that respect each others' rights. Due to its lack of mandate, fixed agenda, or bureaucratic infrastructure, the G8 can act very quickly and decisively when its members agree (Weiss 2006, 2).

If the G8 holds a position on one end of the institutionalization spectrum, the EU occupies a spot at the opposite end. The EU fits the aforementioned criteria for IGOs. Not only does it have a formal treaty and a distinctive constitutional structure, but the EU even goes beyond these characteristics by also possessing all the qualities of a supranational IGO. It is bound by decisions approved by a majority; independent organs within the organization have binding authority; the institution has the authority to pass legal acts applying directly to member states, which can influence individual citizens directly; and it has obligatory jurisdiction in case of conflict (Fischer 2001, 136).

That supranational nature deems EU's presence at the G8 summit necessary. Simultaneously, the conceptualization of the G8 as an informal group or concert helps explain how, in a setting that seems so adamantly state-centric, the EU as a regional body has managed to obtain a seat at the table. Without any clear rules excluding the EU, and based on principles of normative consistency and effectiveness, the G8 had no good reason to exclude the EU. The informality of the G8 facilitated EU participation. However, while the lack of rules and regulations offered the EU the opportunity to join in, the supranational nature of the EU itself made participation not only convenient but also necessary. After all, the most robust argument for EU participation is the fact that its member states have transferred a number of competences to the EU level, making it impossible for the individual states to make any agreements or promises on some issues. As the highest authority on subjects such as trade, the EU must be involved in global governance in order to ensure effectiveness. Not including the EU would thus negatively affect the legitimacy of the G8. EU participation thus contributes to the legitimacy and effectiveness of both the G8 and the EU (Hainsworth 1990; Lamy 1988; Ullrich and Donnelly 1998).

Not only did the characteristics of these very different international organizations result in EU participation, but they also shaped the distinct ambiguous structure of EU representation in this case. The EU's continuing inability to create a unitary international representation is once again facilitated by the informality of the G8.

With the foundation of the European Economic Union in 1957, a new and unique international player was born. Ever since, however, the EU has struggled with its international representation. After 50 years, the reality is still a pluralist and ambiguous hybrid entity, with strength in some contexts and marginality in others (Hill and Smith 2005). This patchy and uneven nature of representation is due to consistency issues, occurring in a number of contexts (Marsh and Mackenstein 2005, 71). One of the biggest issues stems from the diversity in competence in different areas, with the EU having full competence in common commercial policy, for example, and mixed, limited, or even non-existent competence in others.[3] Another challenge results from the fact that, even after the ratification of the Lisbon Treaty, international representation is divided among different EU institutions (Penttilä 2009, 35). Depending on the subject or the discussion partner, the EU might be represented by the president of the European Union, the high Representative for

---

3   The principle of conferral ensures that the EU is inclined to act within the limits of the powers conferred upon it by the treaties and the objectives assigned to them therein (Dehousse and Coussens 2002; Tóth 2002, 1). The doctrine of parallelism on the other hand ascertains that only when internal competence is gained, the EU automatically gains external competence too (McGoldrick 1997, 42).

Foreign Affairs and Security Policy, the president of the Council of the European Union, the president of the European Commission, or any combination of the four (Cameron 2004, 159; Rosamond 2005, 465). And apart from the diversity among institutions, there is also diversity within, since the council can be represented by 27 different member states and the commission consists of 27 commissioners, each with his or her own specific directorate-general. Moreover, decision-making procedures and policy developments may differ by issue area, as do legal bases and available policy instruments (Soares 2005). Finally, there is the difference in extent to which the member states are willing to lose sovereignty (Marsh and Mackenstein 2005, 71).

And if internal dynamics were not enough reason for ambiguity, there are also external factors: pressures and constraints from other participants in the international arena for the EU to define its international policies more clearly and international developments that demand a European answer, sometimes resulting in rash solutions (Hill and Smith 2005, 61). Despite the fact that the EU explicitly aims for the creation of a coherent international identity, the variety of views on this identity creates a serious obstacle to the development of such an identity (Ibid., 13). In a way, the European Commission exemplifies the ambiguous nature of the phenomenon that is the EU. It is much more than an international secretariat, but not quite a government; its international role is defined by both supranationalist and intergovernmentalist elements (Egeberg 2003, 131). The commission is one of the EU's main policy-making institutions, drafting most of the legislation. Internationally, the commission formulates and negotiates on certain aspects of the EU's external relations, but only if the power to do so has been explicitly conferred to it (Groenleer and Van Schaik 2007, 971). In this international context, the European Commission represents the interests of the EU's interests rather than those of the individual member states. This means that, formally, the commission constitutes an autonomous actor.

Most, if not all, of these inconsistencies also apply to the EU's participation in the G8. In an international forum with few rules, however, the EU can participate despite these challenges. Several inconsistencies can be considered problems of delegation and often are cases of incomplete, informal delegation of power from member states to EU institutions. Principal-agent theory, a reasoning that originally emerged in microeconomics, helps explain the delicate relationship between the principal and the agent that represents its interests (Dür and Elsig 2011, 328).

Generally, the member states – the principals – grant authority to the European Commission and the council presidency – the agents – to act on their behalf. The principal-agent approach, which is derived from rational choice theory, seeks not only to understand why delegation takes place but also to comprehend the policy consequences for any particular principal-agent relationship (Pollack 2006; Dür and Elsig 2011, 329). Given that EU representation in the G8 suffers from consistency challenges, principal-agent theory might clarify the position that the EU holds in this group. This approach is even more relevant because of the complexity of the relationship, with member states delegating power to EU representatives while also enabling several of them, namely France, Germany, Italy, and the UK, to monitor the agent(s) as so-called 'attending' principals in the G8. Moreover, the informality of the G8 encourages an informal principal-agent relationship, leaving even greater room for possible 'cheap talk' and political pressure on agents from member state principals (Pollack 2006, 196).

Multiple EU Actors in the G8

This section turns to the practicalities of the representation construction that result both from the informality of the G8 format, as well as the EU's struggle to attain international standing. This construction offers the several actors involved both challenges and opportunities. In the context of an informal principal-agent relationship, the European Commission has transcended the original intentions of its principals, while the influence of the European Council and the non-G8 member states has remained minimal (see Niemann and Huigens 2011).

The participation of France, Italy, Germany, and the UK in the economic summit in 1975 at Rambouillet was met with indignation by the other EU members and the European Community itself, which criticized the fact that some, but not all, individual states were present (Hainsworth 1990, 11). Prolific discussion within the European Community followed, over the issue of community representation versus that of certain member states acting individually (Ullrich and Donnelly 1998, 10). Smaller member states feared that decisions might be made without consulting them or reflecting their interests (Putnam and Bayne 1987, 149). Additionally, there were concerns that the summit might present the potential to rival (or even replace) 'the [European Community] as the principal entity to resolve and manage West European and transatlantic issues' (Hainsworth 1990, 14). Furthermore, as highlighted by Gaston Thorn, foreign minister of Luxembourg, those member countries that were not participating were concerned that they might become second-class members and lose the enhanced voice they had gained through community membership (Ullrich and Donnelly 1998, 18). Thorn also argued that the European powers present at the summits as national governments lacked the legitimacy to act as 'ambassadors' of the European Community (Bonvicini and Wessels 1984, 174).

Opposition to this position came not from the non-European summit participants, but from the European instigators of the summit – France, Germany, and the UK (Garavoglia 1984, 14). France, under Valéry Giscard d'Estaing, took a leading role in the process and held the firmest preferences for European Community exclusion from summitry, advocating the state-centric view that only representatives of sovereign states had sufficient legitimacy and authority to participate at a summit and contribute to it.

It was not until March 1977 that an agreement was reached, after mediation by the European Commission and the European Parliament. The commission would be represented in areas of its competence by two representatives, namely the president of the council and the president of the commission (Hainsworth 1990, 18; Ullrich and Donnelly 1998, 10). Meanwhile, the four existing G8 member states would participate alongside these European representatives. A so-called 'pooling of sovereignties' would occur on those issues of European Community competence, without a fixed or binding mandate (Hainsworth 1990, 13).[4] The profound disagreement led to a lowest common denominator solution – an 'informal contract' – with many contingencies left unspecified (Farrell and Héritier 2007; Hawkins et al. 2006; Tirole 1999). Both the G8 members and the smaller non-G8 members could thus pursue their interests through the use of control mechanisms and limitations to participation. The smaller member states attempted to stay in the loop as much as possible through insisting on involving the European Commission in regular consultations and substantial debriefings before and after G8 summits through the Committee of Permanent Representatives II (COREPER II), which consists of heads of missions. The Netherlands and Belgium, the strongest advocates of exclusive Commission representation, used these control mechanisms extensively (Hainsworth 1990).

Conversely, the European G8 members sought to restrict the position of their agents wherever possible by ensuring that the council presidency was always held by a G8 member at the time of the summit (Hainsworth 1990, 52). As a result, the Council was in effect not independently represented until 1982 (Hainsworth 1990, 11). Even then, the commission was only granted participation on issues of its competence. Moreover, the four European participants' continued presence at the summit allowed them to 'police patrol' or directly monitor the agent (McCubbins and Schwartz 1984). The greater availability of information to these present or attending principals coupled with their inevitable immediate and direct influence over the agent privileged them over the smaller member state principals. These privileged principals could further expand their influence through other means. For example, as hosts they could exercise a measure of control over the levels of courtesy, recognition, and leeway afforded to the commission through their management of procedures and agenda setting (Huigens and Niemann 2011).

Despite this precarious starting position of the EU delegation and the incomplete contract that was agreed upon, the European Commission was able to transcend the original intentions of its principals and become the main EU representative within the summit. Even though the commission was initially invited only to discuss trade and North–South issues, in 1978 its participation was extended to all economic issues. When the focus of the summit shifted to more political topics, the commission was also included in the discussions in 1981

---

4   According to the European Commission, a mandate is not necessary, since no formal decision making takes place at the G8 summit and agreements are mainly political. Since the G8 has no legal mandate, there are also no voting procedures at the EU level. The legal instruments that are available to the commission are limited to directives and opinions and recommendations, as derived from summit agreements (interview with Jooste Korte, a member of the European Union delegation to the G8).

regardless of competence.[5] The European Commission has in fact been described almost as a separate country in the way it operates. While the EU may not be a sovereign state like the other G8 members, it is generally treated like one at the summit. Its presence is not as a courtesy or for ceremonial purposes. Rather it is required for tackling the important global issues that are the priority of the G8. Other G8 members want the EU's involvement because of what it can contribute. Finally, the EU's performance and compliance, as measured by the G8 Research Group, has always been on par with that of other G8 members, suggesting that the EU has been successful as an autonomous delegate (Huigens and Niemann 2011).

The European Commission currently participates independently in all components that make up the summit structure. It sends its president, the head of cabinet (who serves as sherpa), and three sous-sherpas (for financial, political, and foreign affairs). In the course of the summit, the delegation remains separate from the other (EU) G8 members. It has its own administration, expertise teams, and media officers, conducts individual press conferences, and distributes its own press statements. As such, the European Commission is not connected to or dependent on any other G8 delegation in any of the summit activities or preparations. In view of distinct institutional resources, the commission acts as the ninth member at the table. The informal contract of 1977 ensured limited institutionalized means of control for the non-G8 EU member states. The informative meetings prior and after the summits have diminished in importance, with the commission now merely informing COREPER II on G8 aims. The only aspect where EU summit participation formally differs from that of the other G8 members is the fact that the EU cannot host a summit (Ullrich and Donnelly 1998, 11).

However, although the EU official participates in all summit proceedings, including preparatory meetings and informal elements, actual involvement differs by issue area. This variable commission strength is due to diverging levels of competence as well as to other factors, such as experience, national interests, or international context. The G8 context tends to neglect legal boundaries, due to its informal and unscripted nature. Competences matter in the sense that they define political boundaries, but the flexible nature of the EU system of legal competences, in combination with the ad hoc and informal nature of the summit, enables the EU delegation to develop a unique dynamic according to subject. The commission's influence has increased as its competences and experience have increased. A more elaborate illustration is offered in the next section.

Meanwhile, the position of the European Council representative is more problematic. It took six years for an independent EU representative to be present at the summit, in the shape of Belgian president Wilfried Martens in 1982. Nonetheless, the G8 aims to keep the group as small as possible by manipulating

---

5   Three factors contributed to the development of the European Commission position within the summit: the flexibility and informality of the G8; the evolving European integration process; growing capabilities, standing, and entrepreneurship of the European Commission. For more detail see Arne Niemann and Judith Huigens (2011, 428–9).

the date of the summit. Between 1977 and 2008, there were 23 mixed years in which the EU presidency was held by both a G8 country and a non-G8 country. Of these 23 cases, the G8 chair decided 21 times to hold the summit during a G8 member's six-month presidency of the council.[6] This is a way to avoid bringing in an 'unknown player' that would otherwise not be in the G8. If there is no other choice, the G8 will choose the country with the most experience (Belgium or the Netherlands, for example). When the council is represented by a non-G8 member, that country has a purely ceremonial role. It is not invited to any of the preparatory meetings and usually has very limited summit experience. It therefore tends to join forces with the commission delegation. However, when a G8 member holds the council presidency, that separation disappears: as one official says, 'France may hold EU presidency, but when it speaks, it speaks as France'. With regards to the European Council representative, there is no formal mandate or feedback system at all. The presidency of the council usually works according to its agenda as determined by that specific country.

The originally agreed 'parallel approach' left the question of who represented whom up in the air, and therefore never explicitly dealt with the issue of 'dual representation' (Penttilä 2003). With as many as six European representatives present at a summit table with only 10 official seats, it is remarkable that the issue seems hardly pertinent for summit members (Huigens and Niemann 2011). Generally, participants agree that the European Commission president represents first and foremost the commission, and not so much the present or not-present member states. The commission cannot represent the entire EU, which would mean its view is also the view of the UK, France, Germany, and Italy. The EU as such is therefore not represented; only the European Commission is. The individual member states, however, are not expected to represent common EU interests. Nevertheless, today there are few international issues on which the EU states have not already established a common position, which explains why, even in the abundance of formal means to enforce a cohesive EU position at the summit, often the same basic goals are still pursued.

Nonetheless, European bloc forming is not considered a problem by summit participants, as it is generally occurs only on certain issues, and not always along EU lines. Most G8 members agree that too much European unity could lead to the polarization within the G8 – the Europeans versus the rest – which would be counterproductive. If there was a united EU voice all the time, the Americans or the Japanese might simply decide only to deal with the European Commission, which would be unfortunate for the G8. In practice such complaints are rare, as was the case in 2008 when the united European position forced the pace on the issue of climate change and the Japanese delegation openly expressed reservations about 'the number of Europeans at the table'. But as such alignments tend to vary across

---

6   In that period, two summits (Tokyo 1993 and Evian 2003) were held in mixed years but during the presidency of a non-G8 country rather than during the presidency of the G8 member.

time and issue areas, European bloc formation has not emerged as a persistent area of contention. Thus the absence of consistent unity among EU members, partly facilitated by the flexibility of the G8 structure, preserves the construction as it is.

Despite its distinctive infrastructure, the European Commission, unlike individual EU G8 members, must always take into account the positions of the other EU G8 participants, and is therefore less likely to be pressing for the more radical approaches (Putnam and Bayne 1987). Furthermore, in practice the opinion of the commission will never completely contradict that of the other EU members. For instance, it would not back a new proposal of one member prior to other EU members doing so. Division among the ranks of the EU members is possible, and the commission does choose sides, but only after at least one other EU member has expressed support for that side. This means that the EU will not act unilaterally, but will act in most cases with the support of at least two European G8 members. In contrast, individual member states do not hesitate to act independently.

Hence, the informal contract of 1977 did not conclusively deal with the disagreements that arose among the different groups of principals. As such, the developed representation construction was not so much a conscious decision as it was more a gradual development, resulting directly from internal EU developments and facilitated by the flexible nature of the G8. The unique composition of EU representation within the G8 is thus the outcome of a supranational body represented within a flexible non-binding forum.

Case Studies:
The Challenges and Opportunities of EU Representation within the G8

To illustrate the challenges and opportunities presented by the specific structure of EU representation in the G8, two specific issues are more thoroughly discussed here: nuclear energy, and the Millennium Development Goals (MDGs) and overseas development assistance (ODA).[7] Both cases are characterized by diverging principal preferences and mixed competence, which means that both the EU and the member states have competence but the EU can impose binding rules upon member states and they may not implement measures that are not in accordance with EU objectives (Leal-Arcas 2001). As such, the issue of dual representation is particularly pronounced in these cases. In the case of nuclear energy, diverging principal preferences and dual representation have hampered the European Commission's representation, but in the case of ODA its presence alongside its divided principals has resulted in a proactive and independent commission.

The issue of nuclear energy has been disputed within the EU for decades, making it particularly difficult for the commission to make any international

---

7   The research conducted for this chapter predates the 2011 Fukushima nuclear accident.

statements on the subject. In 2000, the commission released a green paper tentatively declaring nuclear energy a risky and undesirable source of energy (European Commission 2000). At that time five out of the eight member states with operating nuclear power stations had started phasing out nuclear energy, including Italy and Germany, while the UK remained neutral on the issue and France and Finland remain positive (De Esteban 2002, 1). More recently, however, most of the opponents of nuclear energy have changed position, reversing their strategies and even planning new reactors to enhance energy security and reduce carbon dioxide emissions (Wood 2010, 317). Germany remains one of the few adversaries of nuclear energy, and announced its decision to take all its nuclear plants off line by 2021 and phase out nuclear power entirely by 2022 (Speigel Online 2011). In the meantime, the European Commission released more green papers on the issue of energy security, emphasizing the need for alternative energy sources but avoiding direct statements on the use of nuclear energy (European Commission 2006, 2007). Indeed, the issue of nuclear energy remains a member state issue, despite the fact that competence is formally shared between member states and the commission.

At the G8, the issue of nuclear energy has presented the European Commission with considerable challenges. With one G8 (powerful) principal – Germany – so adamantly opposing nuclear energy and others – France, the UK, and Italy – (strongly) supporting its inclusion in EU/G8 energy strategies, the principal preferences are so divergent that a united EU position becomes impossible. Although the individual EU member states can still actively participate despite disagreement, this becomes very difficult for the EU delegations. Moreover, some of the more powerful principals are 'attending principals', thus well equipped for monitoring and 'sanctioning' the agent. The European Commission has even kept a low profile given the presence of a member state 'heavyweight' constraining EU action, not expressing itself strongly, proactively, or independently on the issue. In line with G8 summit procedures, the commission and the council would never be excluded from any nuclear energy debates, given that the G8 is about effectiveness, participants aim to talk to those in charge. Since the European Commission is neither an expert nor a decision maker when it comes to nuclear energy, its position at these discussions is marginal. Double representation becomes a challenge in this case, because the attending principals tend to advocate their individual perspective as opposed to a united European position.

The second case study is characterized by a complex actor constellation. The UK, the Scandinavian countries, the Netherlands, Luxembourg, and the European Commission favour the progressive targets of the MDGs and have shared the most ambitious commitments. On the other hand, the member states that have joined the EU since 2004, together with earlier members Italy, Spain, Portugal, and Greece, have seemed less enthusiastic and more moderate in their goals. Germany, France, and a few other countries take an intermediate position. Although their goals and real commitments are somewhat more modest than the progressive group, their policy rhetoric is far-reaching (G8 Research Group 2007, 2008a). Against this backdrop, the commission adopted a strong, proactive, and independent role, which it carried over to the G8. At the UK-hosted Gleneagles Summit in 2005, European Commission president José Manuel Barroso was the only leader to mention the MDGs in his press conference (G8 Research Group 2006, 28). Before the German-hosted Heiligendamm Summit in 2007, Barroso criticized member states such as Germany for counting debt relief to meet aid targets (G8 Research Group 2007, 132). In addition, at the Japan-hosted Toyako Hokkaido Summit in 2008, it was the commission that encouraged non-European G8 countries to match EU targets (G8 Research Group 2008b, 130). Concerning the MDGs and ODA, even the more reluctant EU member states (including Italy) and those with intermediate preferences (including Germany and France) have emphasized the importance of this issue and articulated significant ambitions (Rampal 2005; G8 Research Group 2008a). Under such circumstances, it is more easily justifiable for the commission to speak out and take advantage of member states' rhetorical commitments (G8 Research Group 2007; Barroso 2008). Indeed, given such exaggeration, the European Commission could take the opportunity to lead the G8, regardless of the conservative preferences of member states. The commission could be seen use the platform afforded by the G8 to leverage its own internal EU agenda, using international pressure on the laggards in the EU to accelerate their efforts. In some cases, the commission could act more self-confidently and independently in the G8 because of its status as a major international aid donor. The commission could use not only the flexibility of the G8, but also the symbolism of the summit to pursue its own policy goals. Dual representation in this context was used to the advantage of the European Commission, which managed to exploit the member states' 'cheap talk'.

These two examples illustrate both the challenges and the opportunities that the dual representation structure of EU representation in the G8 holds. An experienced European Commission can sometimes use the G8 flexibility and media exposure to its own advantage, but when principals are strongly and unambiguously divided and commission experience is limited, so is their influence at the summit. As such, dual representation can be a nuisance or a blessing, depending on the circumstances.

Conclusions

Valéry Giscard d'Estaing once recommended not bringing up the issue of European representation at the G7/8. 'We don't want to draw attention to the fact that there are four EU members at the G8 table and that the EU is there as well,' he said. 'It might cause instability'. While a closer look at the issue of EU representation in the G8 may raise some eyebrows, in the history of the G8 it has rarely caused any problems.[8] Participants have accepted the necessity of representation by member states as well as the European Commission. The actor that drew the short end of the stick was the president of the Council of the EU when represented by a non-G8 member state. Excluded from many of the supplementary summit proceedings, the council plays a marginal role within the summit structure. Not only is dual representation necessary due to differing competence transferral, but it is also, at the same time, not considered problematic because of the loose G8 structure, in which leaders can be leaders and effectiveness is key. Overall, the informality of the G8 has tended to play to the EU's strengths. The EU has not clearly defined its international status yet, but the G8 might just be the perfect setting for it. The EU's participation is unhampered by the fact that it is not a nation-state. The informality of the G8 has meant that the question of what exactly the EU as such is doing at the summit can be safely ignored. The two institutions seem generally well suited: the EU can improve the effectiveness of the G8, and the G8 reinforces the international legitimacy of the EU and also provides a forum where the EU can develop its international standing.

References

Barroso, José Manuel (2008). 'Statement at the G8 Outreach Session with Leaders from Africa.' Speech/08/377, Hokkaido, Japan, 7 July. <europa.eu/rapid/ pressReleasesAction.do?reference=SPEECH/08/377&type=HTML>   (July 2011).

Bayne, Nicholas (1995). 'The G7 Summit and the Reform of Global Institutions.' *Government and Opposition* 30(4): 492–509. <www.g8.utoronto.ca/scholar/ bayne1995> (July 2011).

Bonvicini, Gianni, and Wolfgang Wessels (1984). 'The European Community and the Seven.' In *Economic Summits and Western Decision-Making*, edited by Cesare Merlini, pp. 167–93. London: Croom Helm.

Cameron, Fraser (2004). 'After Iraq: The EU and Global Governance.' *Global Governance* 10(2): 157–63.

De Esteban, Fernando (2002). 'The Future of Nuclear Energy in the European Union.' Background paper for a speech to senior representatives of nuclear utilities, 23 May, Brussels. <ec.europa.eu/energy/nuclear/doc/ brusselsfdemay2002.pdf> (July 2011).

Dehousse, Franklin, and Wouter Coussens (2002). 'Which Distribution of Competences for the EU?', 18 April, Egmont Institute for International

---

8   One instance of friction was in 1990, when US president George H.W. Bush expressed his annoyance about the tendency of the European countries to streamline their positions before the summit, making negotiations difficult for outsiders such as the United States or Canada (Silvestri 1994).

Relations, Brussels. <www.egmontinstitute.be/papers/DISTRIBUTION%20 OF%20COMPETENCES.pdf> (July 2011).

Dür, Andreas, and Manfred Elsig (2011). 'Principals, Agents, and the European Union's Foreign Economic Policies.' *Journal of European Public Policy* 18(3): 323–38.

Egeberg, Morten (2003). 'The European Commission.' In *European Union Politics*, edited by Michelle Cini, pp. 131–47. Oxford: Oxford University Press.

European Commission (2000). 'Green Paper on the Security of Energy Supply.' COM(2000) 769 final, Brussels. <europa.eu/legislation_summaries/energy/ external_dimension_enlargement/l27037_en.htm> (July 2011).

European Commission (2006). 'Green Paper: A European Strategy for Sustainable, Competitive and Secure Energy.' COM(2006) 105 final, Brussels. <europa. eu/legislation_summaries/energy/european_energy_policy/l27062_en.htm> (July 2011).

European Commission (2007). 'An Energy Policy for Europe.' COM(2007) 1 Final, Brussels. <europa.eu/legislation_summaries/energy/european_energy_ policy/l27067_en.htm> (July 2011).

Farrell, Henry, and Adrienne Héritier (2007). 'Introduction: Contested Competences in the European Union.' *West European Politics* 30(2): 227–43.

Fischer, Klemens (2001). 'The G7/8 in the European Union.' In *Guiding Global Order: G8 Governance in the Twenty-First Century*, edited by John J. Kirton, Joseph P. Daniels and Andreas Freytag, pp. 123–42. Aldershot: Ashgate.

G8 Research Group (2006). 'Issue Assessment Report: 2006 St. Petersburg Summit.' Toronto. <www.g8.utoronto.ca/evaluations/2006stpetersburg/2006-issue-assessment.pdf> (July 2011).

G8 Research Group (2007). 'G8 Country Analysis Part II: Assessment Reports.' Toronto. <www.g8.utoronto.ca/evaluations/2007heiligendamm/2007countri es-perf.pdf> (July 2011).

G8 Research Group (2008a). '2007 Heiligendamm G8 Summit Final Compliance Report.' Toronto. <www.g8.utoronto.ca/evaluations/2007compliance_final> (July 2011).

G8 Research Group (2008b). '2008 Hokkaido Toyako G8 Summit Country Assessment Report.' Toronto. <www.g8.utoronto.ca/evaluations/2008hokkaido/2008-countries-080709.pdf> (July 2011).

Garavoglia, Guido (1984). 'From Rambouillet to Williamsburg: A Historical Assessment.' In *Economic Summits and Western Decision-Making*, edited by Cesare Merlini, pp. 49–65. London: Croom Helm.

Groenleer, Marijn L.P., and Louise G. Van Schaik (2007). 'United Stand? The European Union's International Actorness in the Cases of the International Criminal Court and the Kyoto Protocol.' *Journal of Common Market Studies* 45(5): 969–98.

Hainsworth, Susan (1990). 'Coming of Age: The European Community and the Economic Summit.' Country Study No. 7, G7 Research Group. <www.g8.utoronto.ca/scholar/hainsworth1990/index.html> (July 2011).

Hawkins, Darren G., David A. Lake, Daniel L. Nielson, et al. (2006). 'Delegation under Anarchy: States, International Organization and Principal-Agent Theory.' In *Delegation and Agency in International Organization*, edited by Darren G. Hawkins, David A. Lake, Daniel L. Nielson, et al., pp. 3–38. Cambridge: Cambridge University Press.

Hill, Christopher, and Michael Smith (2005). *International Relations and the European Union*. Oxford: Oxford University Press.

Huigens, Judith, and Arne Niemann (2011). 'The G8 1/2: The EU's Contested and Ambiguous Actorness in the G8.' *Cambridge Review of International Affairs* 24(3): 1–29.

Kirton, John J. (1999). 'Explaining G8 Effectiveness.' In *The G8's Role in the New Millennium*, edited by Michael R. Hodges, John J. Kirton and Joseph P. Daniels, pp. 45–68. Aldershot: Ashgate.

Kirton, John J. (2004). 'Cooperation between the EU and the G8 in Conflict Prevention.' In *The European Union and Conflict Prevention: Policy and Legal Aspects*, edited by Vincent Kronenberger and Jan Wouters, pp. 451–66. The Hague: TMC Asser Press.

Lamy, Pascal (1988). 'The Economic Summit and the European Community.' Bissell Paper No. 5, Centre for International Studies, University of Toronto, Toronto. <www.g8.utoronto.ca/scholar/lamy1988> (July 2011).

Leal-Arcas, Rafael (2001). 'The European Community and Mixed Agreements.' *European Foreign Affairs Review* 6(4): 483–513.

Marsh, Steve, and Hans Mackenstein (2005). *The International Relations of the EU*. Harlow: Pearson Education.

McCubbins, Mathew D., and Thomas Schwartz (1984). 'Congressional Oversight Overlooked: Police Patrols versus Fire Alarms.' *American Journal of Political Science* 28(1): 165–79.

McGoldrick, Dominic (1997). *International Relations Law of the European Union*. London: Longman.

Merlini, Cesare (1994). 'The G7 and the Need for Reform.' *International Spectator* 29(2): 5–25.

Niemann, Arne, and Judith Huigens (2011). 'The European Union's Role in the G8: A Principal-Agent Perspective.' *Journal of European Public Policy* 18(3): 420–22.

Penttilä, Risto E.J. (2003). *The Role of the G8 in International Peace and Security*. Oxford: Oxford University Press.

Penttilä, Risto E.J. (2009). 'Multilateralism Light: The Rise of Informal International Governance.' Centre for European Reform, London. <www.cer.org.uk/pdf/penttila_essay_july09.pdf> (July 2011).

Pollack, Mark A. (2006). 'Delegation and Discretion in the European Union.' In *Delegation and Agency in International Organization*, edited by Darren G.

Hawkins, David A. Lake, Daniel L. Nielson, et al., pp. 165–96. Cambridge: Cambridge University Press.

Putnam, Robert, and Nicholas Bayne (1987). *Hanging Together: Co-operation and Conflict in the Seven-Power Summit.* 2nd ed. London: Sage Publications.

Rampal, José (2005). 'Belgium Urges Rich to Meet Aid Pledges.' Inter Press Service, 17 February.

Rosamond, Ben (2005). 'Conceptualizing the EU Model of Governance in World Politics.' *European Foreign Affairs Review* 10(4): 463–78.

Schwegmann, Christoph (2001). 'Modern Concert Diplomacy: The Contact Group and the G7/8 in Crisis Management.' In *Guiding Global Order: G8 Governance in the Twenty-First Century*, edited by John J. Kirton, Joseph P. Daniels and Andreas Freytag, pp. 93–121. Aldershot: Ashgate.

Silvestri, Stefano (1994). 'Between Globalism and Regionalism: The Role and Composition of the G7.' *International Spectator* 29(2): 141–59.

Soares, A. Goucha (2005). 'The Division of Competences in the European Constitution.' *European Public Law* 11(4): 603–21.

Speigel Online (2011). 'Germany to Phase Out Nuclear Power by 2022.' 30 May. <www.spiegel.de/international/germany/0,1518,765594,00.html> (July 2011).

Tirole, Jean (1999). 'Incomplete Contracts: Where Do We Stand?' *Econometrica* 67(4): 741–81.

Tóth, Ákos G. (2002). 'Vertical and Horizontal Distribution of Competences in the European Union.' *ERA Forum* 3(3): 134–38.

Ullrich, Heidi K., and Alan Donnelly (1998). 'The Group of Eight and the European Union: The Evolving Partnership.' No. 5, November. <www.g8.utoronto.ca/governance/gov5> (July 2011).

Weiss, Martin A. (2006). 'The Group of Eight: Evolution and Possible Reform.' Congressional Research Service, Library of Congress. <www.au.af.mil/au/awc/awcgate/crs/rs22403.pdf> (July 2011).

Wood, Steve (2010). 'Europe's Energy Politics.' *Journal of Contemporary European Studies* 18(3): 307–22.

Chapter 8

The European Union in the G20

Marina Larionova and Thomas Renard

If you build the present in the image of the past you will miss out entirely on challenges of the future.

– Winston Churchill, quoted by Gordon Brown, April 2009

The first meeting of the leaders of the G20, originally set up as a forum of finance ministers and central bank governors at the initiative of the G8 in 1999 after the Asian financial crisis, launched a new phase in the development of the international financial architecture and the global governance system. The European Union has participated fully since the beginning, unlike its gradual inclusion into the G7/G8. The reasons are clear, notably the EU's adoption of a single currency and its global economic and monetary success, both defining factors of its influence in the G20.

The EU is generally considered the 20th member of the G20. It is different from its counterparts in the sense that it is not a national entity. In addition, it includes both European members and non-members of the G20, creating a sophisticated system for European influence on G20 debates and outcomes. However, analysis of the EU's role within the G20 remains largely understudied (Debaere 2010, 141–54).

This chapter contributes to this scant literature, focusing on analysing the EU's input and impact on past summits. This analysis emphasizes institutional mechanisms that allow the EU to increase its influence within the G20 process through greater coordination (of European G20 members) and greater inclusion (of European non-G20 members). Indeed, the permanent presidency of the European Council has brought more coherence and continuity than could be achieved through the concerted efforts of the rotating presidencies.[1] Such continuity and durability are essential not only for forging consensus with the EU partners in the G20, but also, most importantly, for building internal consensus within the EU, necessary for effective common foreign policy. One of the hypotheses of this chapter is therefore that the Lisbon Treaty, which provided the European Union with a permanent president of the European Council and a high representative for foreign affairs and security policy, will strengthen the EU's role within the G20.

---

1 The capacity of the country holding the presidency is another vital factor. For example, the Czech Republic's presidency in 2009 was haunted by domestic crises and awkward statements by Prime Minister Mirek Topolánek.

The Emergence of the New G20

The first G20 summit, in Washington DC on 14–15 November 2008, was driven by the initiative of Nicolas Sarkozy, as France was at the helm of the EU at the time, and José Manuel Barroso, president of the European Commission (Barroso 2008). The historic event was immediately considered a success by many G20 leaders as well as by experts and international institutions. The 'Declaration of the Summit on Financial Markets and the World Economy' and the 'Action Plan to Implement Principles for Reform' should not be underestimated. Russian president Dmitri Medvedev (2008) said while the documents were not 'ideal' or did not provide 'immediate solutions to the crisis' or a 'new configuration of financial relations', they were 'comprehensive', 'met the expectations of practically every delegation', and reflected the proposals put forward by all the different countries.

Those documents represent the tip of the negotiations iceberg and give scarce material for assessing the stakeholders' contributions to the consensus and their influence on the commitments forged. However, analysis of the preparatory documents and facts shows that countries that shared positions (such as the EU or the BRIC countries of Brazil, Russia, India, and China) had an advantage. The EU, in fact, made extensive use of this advantage.

The EU stance was defined as 'Agreed Language' in the outcome of the Informal Meeting of Heads of State or Government on 7 November 2008 (EU 2008). The many levels of building blocks of the common position on collective and coordinated recovery measures had been laid systematically, although the Washington Summit was not formally announced until 22 October. On 7 October 2008 the Economic and Financial Affairs Council (Ecofin) issued its conclusions on the immediate response to financial turmoil, economic slowdown, and financial supervision (Ecofin 2008). This paved the way to the presidency's conclusions on 16 October reinforcing the EU commitment to 'work with its international partners on a genuine, all-encompassing reform of the international financial system based on the principles of transparency, sound banking, responsibility, integrity and world governance' (Council of the European Union 2008). The presidency emphasized that the initiatives on transparency, global standards of regulation, cross-border supervision, and crisis management would be carried out in consultation with the EU's main partners and the relevant international financial institutions. On 12 October the euro area leaders had announced concrete measures to ensure appropriate liquidity conditions for financial institutions to continue financing of the economy and enhancing cooperation among European countries (French Presidency of the European Union 2008a). Thus within a very tight timeline and in spite of divergent positions, the EU member states worked out common provisions, many of which were reflected in the final plan of action issued at the Washington Summit.

The G20's measures to strengthen transparency and accountability were in line with EU objectives and reflect the spirit of the October Ecofin conclusions and the letter of the 'Agreed Language'. The principle that 'no financial institution, no market segment and no jurisdiction must escape proportionate and adequate regulation or at least oversight' (Agreed Language 2008) clearly was registered in the Washington Declaration paragraphs (Declaration of the Summit on Financial Markets and the World Economy 2008) on enhancing the quality of regulation.

The risk management package adopted by the G20 was promoted ardently by and supported by the European Commission (French Presidency of the European Union 2008c). The US administration stuck to a more frugal approach (White House 2008). The Bush administration supported the principle of a weighted regulation that would not impair the economic growth. Ultimately, the US was able to maintain the tempered approach in the final Washington document (White House 2008).

Most participants at the Washington Summit advocated that the quality of international regulation begins at the national level. Most adopted unprecedented measures both to alleviate the crisis through supporting financial institutions and to implement institutional changes.

European participants could rely on EU efforts to establish a system of coordination. Ecofin set up a working group to assess possible policy responses that might 'mitigate undue potential pro-cyclical effects of the financial system' (Ecofin 2008). Ecofin also agreed 'to make EU-wide common reporting formats for a single set of data requirements and reporting dates, to ensure ... an efficient and convergent supervision and to reduce administrative burden for groups, operational by 2012'. At their 12 October meeting, the eurozone heads of state and government agreed to strengthen the procedures for exchanging information among their governments, the European Council, the European Commission, the European Central Bank (ECB) and the Eurogroup (French Presidency of the EU 2008b). The European Council set up the 'financial crisis cell', a new mechanism for information sharing and evaluation involving all these institutions as well (Council of the EU 2008).

Reinforced coordination based on common standards to overcome internal and transnational threats to financial stability and restore that stability was adopted by the G20 at Washington as a pillar of future cooperation. All the EU documents focused on concerted action and emphasized the need for multilevel coordination, including among national and regional authorities and international financial institutions (IFIs), the International Monetary Fund (IMF), the Financial Stability Forum, and other international forums defining the standards of financial operations. Furthermore, Sarkozy repeatedly stressed that all countries including developing ones be part of that coordination and that eliminating grey zones is key to success (French Presidency of the European Union 2008c).

One of the core disagreements between the EU and its G20 partners came on IFI reform (EU 2008). According to the EU, reforms were needed to strengthen and modernize the old institutions and ensure rapid progress in making those reforms. The necessary reforms included updating the instruments used by the IMF, increasing its resources, and creating facilities for exchanging information and co-ordination, while preserving the IMF's central role in the new architecture.

The Washington declaration went beyond financial policy and regulation, committing G20 members to refrain from raising new barriers to investment or to trade in goods and services, imposing new export restrictions, or implementing inconsistent measures to stimulate exports at the World Trade Organization (WTO) (G20 2008).

Leaders also pledged their intention to reach an agreement within a year on the modalities for a successful conclusion to the WTO's Doha Development Agenda, instructing their trade ministers to achieve this objective. Thus the G20's trade commitment aligned with the EU's priority of promoting free trade through the rapid conclusion of the Doha Round.

The EU also influenced the subsequent pace and rhythm of IFI reform and the G20 process. On 7 November, they agreed that 'a period of 100 days starting on 15 November should be used for drawing up measures to implement the principles that have just been restated' (European Union 2008). At the end of that period, they proposed a 'new summit' to discuss a report on the implementation of those measures, new decisions taken to implement the principles adopted on 15 November to improve the regulation of the financial system, and new proposals to enable meeting macroeconomic challenges.

It can thus be concluded that not only did the impulse for G20's Washington Summit come from Europe, but also that the EU was able to exert influence on the meeting's outcomes. G20 members came forward with a common position affecting the summit results. The presence of the Spanish and Dutch delegations, representing the EU alongside the European Commission in addition to Sarkozy's delegation representing France, illustrated European solidarity.[2]

The New Global Deal

The spontaneous character of the Washington G20 changed radically in the run-up to the second summit in April 2009. The causes of this shift are rooted in the further exacerbation of the economic and financial situation, the impulse from Washington, and the transition of the G20 presidency to the United Kingdom.

British prime minister Gordon Brown (2008f), undertaking measures to overcome the financial crisis in the UK, promoted the principle that national actions were inadequate. He managed to embed his imperatives on IFI reform, international cooperation for regulation and economic stimulus into the European and global approaches on the way to the Washington summit consensus.

Brown's anti-crisis package included transparency and accountability at all levels, better banking practices, integrity and international cooperation, international colleges of regulators, convergence on accounting standards, a

---

2   Sarkozy was nonetheless not prepared to yield his position as a leader defining the development of regional and global processes even after handing over the EU presidency to the Czech Republic on 1 January 2009.

review of executive compensation that encouraged excessive and irresponsible risk taking, the disclosure of toxic assets, and the reform of credit-rating agencies. Brown made good use of the summit potential for domestic policy governance to legitimize and enhance the effectiveness of national policies through the instrument of international collective decision making. More than any other leader, he was able to balance the objectives of countering the crisis and developing the global agenda for the future, although the EU was no less skilled at harnessing the G20 for its own domestic purposes (Brown 2008a, 2008b, 2008c, 2008d, 2008e; Brown and Ban 2008).

The process of preparing for the second G20 summit scheduled for 1–2 April 2009 was boiling with expectations, events, ambitions, experts' recommendations, political statements, members' position papers, reports from international organizations and working groups, and other preparatory documents. Rhetoric was flying high, as illustrated by Brown's speech at the Foreign Press Association, in which he described 'international economic hurricane sweeping the world and lashing our country' but stated the government was 'taking action to calm the storm, to bring order out of chaos' (Brown 2009e). He said that Britain was 'better placed to benefit as the storm passes' but success was only possible 'if we leave behind yesterday's solutions and reshape our international institutions for the challenges of today and tomorrow'. The upcoming event seemed historic in its essence: 'History is not destiny, it is the sum total of the choices of each generation … we now need the widest possible international agreement on how to proceed to the next stage as we focus on the London G20 Summit at the start of April. The priorities I believe are clear.'

Rhetoric aside, Brown's (2009e) steps to build an 'international financial system for the twenty-first century' included an early warning system to monitor international financial flows and systemic global imbalances. It also included expanding the membership of the Financial Stability Forum and redefining its role as well as cooperating with the IMF and the Bank for International Settlements (BIS) to strengthen institutional foundation for international governance.

In addition, to overcome regulatory deficits in a world of global capital flows and national regulators, Brown (2009e) proposed that the G20 enter 'a new era of global cooperation and coordination'. He suggested the G20 discuss creating a charter of principles to guide financial regulation and supervision and incorporating non-bank financial institutions and complex new markets and products' into the regulatory system.

Brown also sought agreement on transparent standards of corporate governance, including an international standard of best practice for financial institutions. He wanted to ensure that the IMF and other financial institutions play a bigger role in crisis prevention as well as crisis management. IFIs ought to be capable of lending to replace private sector flows and thus enable restructuring the domestic financial system in many countries. Brown's objectives for the London Summit also included continued development aid with the World Bank increasing lending to vital infrastructure, environmental and poverty reduction and providing an active cyclical boost to the global economy.

Indeed, the commitment to the Millennium Development Goals (MDGs) and development itself constituted a core priority of the UK presidency of the G20. Brown (2009g) consistently underscored that official development assistance (ODA) should remain on top of the international agenda and that the G20 ought to lay the foundation for a new global deal 'that continues to form the basis of our international policy for years to come'. He said it should underpin the subsequent G8 summit, the climate negotiations in Copenhagen, the 2010 MDG review, and 'herald a new era of rights and responsibilities that it is incumbent on each of us ... to develop and fulfill'. The theme of commitment to development in the face of the crisis ran through Brown's speech to African leaders and in a briefing to foreign media in the lead-up to the summit (Brown 2009c, 2009f).

Brown's work with the World Bank and his G20 partners to build support for a new fund to help the world's poorest was supported by the EU (Council of the EU 2009b). The G20 leaders committed to cooperation for development, including on the MDGs, food security, and support to social protection (G20 2009).

Rejecting protectionism and coordinating trade policy remained priorities at all stages leading up to the summit. All G20 members intended to comply with the declaration at Washington to avoid contravening WTO provisions and to reach a successful conclusion to Doha. The World Bank, the EU member states, the IMF, and the WTO proposed monitoring trade-restrictive measures regularly. At the initiative of secretary general Pascal Lamy, the WTO reported on its own self-initiated monitoring, although it refrained from making any assessments (WTO 2009). The EU and its members reiterated their commitment to the principle of fair and open trade at various meetings, including at an informal summit on 1 March 2009. They undertook various trade-related measures, while remaining within the WTO the Temporary Community Framework for State aid measures to support access to finance in the crisis (European Commission 2009a).

The agenda for the London Summit seemed to expand infinitely as consultations continued and more and more stakeholders were included in the preparation process, reflecting tensions over resources and possible future growth. The range of problems and the number of participants involved raised questions about the risks of failure and inefficiency. A month into the process, Brown (2009d) discussed the possible institutionalization of the G20, saying that the current format would need 'an executive that is effective, ... a continuing presence ... to be able to take on functions that are continuous and regular and not just passing depending on when a meeting is going to take place'. France resuscitated this idea when it assumed the presidency of the chair in 2011, but the idea received little enthusiasm.

There was also some discussion of the division of labour between the G8 and the G20 and the continuity of priorities and agendas. In a joint article, G8 chair and Italian prime minister Silvio Berlusconi and Gordon Brown (2009) agreed to coordinate and reinforce the two summit agendas, suggesting 'a Charter of Principles for financial regulation and supervision' come out of the London

Summit and using the G8's La Maddalena (later L'Aquila) Summit to adopt 'common principles and standards on propriety, integrity and transparency of international economic and financial activity'. They described their intention to use both summits to protect the poorest in the global recession and to make sure that actions taken to secure economic recovery are consistent with their shared aspirations for a low-carbon future and sustainable growth. Therefore, the summits will also focus on 'the challenges of development, climate change and energy, and how to relaunch global sustainable growth'.

Labour sharing, continuity, and cooperation were also supported by the G7 finance ministers and central bank governors. The statement they released at their February meeting called for joint action so their fiscal policy measures would adhere to principles that would increase their effectiveness, remain consistent with medium-term sustainability, and be temporary (G7 Finance Ministers and Central Bank Governors 2009).

In Search of 'Agreed Language'

Gordon Brown got the go ahead for his proposal by the leaders of the EU's six largest economies when they met in Berlin to prepare for the G20 summit on 22 February 2009. Reminiscent of G7 founder Valéry Giscard d'Estaing, Sarkozy (2009) said that Europe wanted a 'full review of the system' in London: 'We cannot afford a failure of the summit. We do not talk of cosmetic measures, but of structural measure that must be undertaken.' The leaders agreed on the goals of global financial market regulation, short-term crisis management, a return to sustainable economic growth, improved international coordination, and the strengthening of international institutions.

The European leaders called on both the G20 and the G8 to come up with a 'new charter for sustainable economic activity' at the London Summit, noting that the work on common principles and standards on 'propriety, integrity, and transparency of economic and financial activity' had already started within the G8 process (Germany 2009). EU members thus contributed to the continuity of the G20 and the G8 agendas and to the sustainability of the processes of reform and renewal of the global financial and economic architecture.

An informal summit held on 1 March was another stepping stone on the path to a EU common position. The European leaders endorsed the principles and actions agreed in October 2008 and the European plan for economic recovery approved in December 2008 (European Union 2009b). They welcomed, but did not act on, the recommendations of the High-Level Group on Financial Supervision in the EU (2009), which included a wide range of institutional changes such as establishing a European systemic risk council and European system of financial supervision. The recommendations proposed enlarging the Financial Stability Forum (FSF) to include all systemically important countries and the European Commission and endowing it with more resources, as well as reforming its accountability and governance systems by linking it more closely to the IMF. The high-level group also recommended that the IMF, in close cooperation with the FSF, the BIS, central banks and the systemic risk council, be put in charge of developing and operating a financial stability early warning system, accompanied by an international risk map and credit register.

However, the main decisions of the informal summit related to internal EU regulation and efforts to restore financial stability. At the global level the members underlined that the EU should lead the G20 process and ensure that its efforts were adequately reflected at the international level, while taking into account the particular situation of developing countries and remaining committed to rapidly concluding the Doha Development Agenda. Both the February and March meetings not only prepared the ground for the subsequent European Council, but also built resources to support Gordon Brown for his meeting with the US President Barack Obama immediately following the informal summit.

Brown was the first European leader to visit the new American president, taking the opportunity to discuss anti-crisis measures to stimulate the banks and economy and the reform of the international institutions. Speaking in Congress, Brown (2009h) called on all countries to share the responsibility and the workload of pulling out of the crisis: 'America and a few others cannot be expected to bear all the burden of the fiscal and interest rate stimulus ... So let us work together for the worldwide reduction of interest rates and a scale of stimulus that is equal to the depth of the recession around the world and to the dimensions of recovery, and most of all equal to the millions of jobs we must safeguard and create.'

Germany and many EU members viewed large-scale stimulus as threatening to regional and global macro financial stability. They agreed on the need for a new charter for sustainable economic activity and on the principle of selective, targeted and weighted measures and stimuli consistent with the long-term sustainability of public finances. However, Brown's position was closer to that of the US rather than the EU. Thus, on his return from America, he intensified the shuttle diplomacy within the EU, working both with the European leaders and the institutions. On the eve of the European Council meeting, Brown and German chancellor Angela Merkel emphasized that there are no contradictions between the EU and the US, indirectly indicating that there is a zone of concern (Brown and Merkel 2009). Merkel was characteristically diplomatic, calling the Washington Summit the 'first steps' but noting that 'substantive results' were now required. She said she was 'very optimistic' that the Europeans would agree with the United States as well as emerging economies such as China and India to see to it that new regulations and supervisory functions would prevent such a crisis from recurring (Brown and Merkel 2009). Brown's statement was even more resolute: 'The Americans are ready to support us in these changes that we are going to bring about'. However, although he repeatedly underlined the relevance of Merkel's proposed charter, it did not work its way into the final summit documents. The only surviving reference was a formula in the London Summit's Global Plan for Recovery and Reform that reflected the commitment to ensure long-term fiscal sustainability and price stability and to put in place credible exit strategies from the measures taken to support the financial sector and restore global demand. In fact, this weakening of resolve revealed a yield to Obama's push to large-scale stimulus shared by Brown.

Given the European Commission's competence in trade policies, at a meeting on 16 March Brown and Barroso (2009) emphasized the imperative of trade stimulus measures, particularly to support trade credit, increase in the financing of trade and stimulating demand. They also called for tighter surveillance of tariff and non-tariff barriers, with the WTO given a clear mandate to monitor protectionist measures undertaken by countries.

Finally, Brown, who had previously ignored EU institutions, spoke to the European Parliament about sharing the principles of close regulation for ensuring macroeconomic stability. His remarks were somewhat contradictory, however: Europe should 'take a central role in replacing what was once called the old Washington consensus with a new and principled economic consensus' although it was now the time to start a 'new era of heightened cooperation between Europe and America' (Brown 2009b).

International cooperation for sustainable macroeconomic policy was one of the priorities spelled out by Ecofin for the EU common position at the G20 summit (Ecofin 2009). The position was formalized and endorsed by the European Council meeting in March as 'Agreed Language' (Council of the EU 2009a). The main lines of action included the EU taking the lead in international actions to return to sustainable growth, strengthening capacities to manage the crisis and prevent recurrences, improving financial market regulation and transparency, and supporting developing countries. EU members approved a loan of €75 billion to the IMF to improve its lending capacity, and supported the quota and voice reform of April 2008, a review of selection process for top management, the expansion of the FSF to include all G20 members as well as Spain, and the institutional reinforcement of the FSF. They also reiterated the need to seek consensus and adopt a global charter for sustainable economic activity.[3]

Brown sought to coordinate approaches beyond the EU and the US as well. He held bilateral meetings with China's Hu Jintao, Australia's Kevin Rudd, Brazil's Luiz Ignácio Lula da Silva and Mexico's Felipe Calderón to forge agreements on the summit documents. Particularly with regard to Brazil and Mexico, due consideration was given to the necessity of coordinating the agendas of the G20 and G8 and also the Group of Five (G5) – Brazil, Mexico, China, India and South Africa, whose leaders had traditionally been invited to the G8 summits since 2005 (Brown and Lula da Silva 2009; Brown and Calderón 2009). Indeed, these consultations confirmed the eminence of the G8–G5 dialogue, in spite of the G20.

---

3 Although the idea of a charter was repeated throughout the EU documents and was included on the agenda of the G8 L'Aquila Summit, it did not find its way into the G20 documents until the Pittsburgh Summit in September 2009.

In the Language of Finance

The work of the G20 finance ministers and central bankers attracted less attention than the summits but was critical to brokering the leaders' decisions. The Washington Summit established four working groups to support the coordination of the national finance authorities.[4] The first formal presentation of the UK objectives for the April summit was presented in a letter from British exchequer Alistair Darling (2009) to his G20 colleagues on 7 January 2009. He focused on restoring financial markets.

At their meeting on 14 March, the G20 finance ministers and central bankers (2009) welcomed the decision to expand both the FSF and the Basel Committee on Banking Supervision (BCBS), which had been announced on the eve of the meeting (see Table 8.1). They committed to coordinated and comprehensive action to restore lending, boost demand and jobs, fight all forms of protectionism, and maintain open trade and investment. The framework for financial repair and recovery defined the main principles to guide the international cooperation among national authorities: programmes should be implemented quickly and comprehensively and should have a limited enrolment period, government support must come with strong conditions and should be closely monitored and be temporary, and support measures should be part of a sustainable medium-term fiscal strategy. The EU members' position that financial measures should be consistent with the long-term stability of public finances was fully reflected in the communiqué.

The BRIC finance ministers met just before the G20 finance ministerial to discuss fiscal and monetary policy responses, as well the forthcoming G20 summit agenda and the expected outcomes. They emphasized that anti-crisis measures should be implemented in a way that would not hamper efforts needed to ensure mid-term and long-term macroeconomic sustainability according to the particular conditions of each country. They also welcomed the expanded membership of the FSF and BCBS, and stressed that the International Accounting Standards Board and other standard-setting bodies also needed to become more representative and reinforce the presence of emerging market economies.

The BRIC ministers' position on IMF reform and changes in the international currency system deserves special mention, although there was nothing on the new reserve currency basket. India and Brazil opposed the proposal by Russia and China to replace the dollar with the IMF's special drawing right (SDR) as the reserve currency. The finance ministers of the Eurasian Economic Community also proposed a 'code' of principles and best practices for macroeconomic and financial discipline, a so-called 'new Maastricht consensus' that concurred

---

4   These were Working Group 1: Enhancing Sound Regulation and Strengthening Transparency, Working Group 2: Reinforcing International Cooperation and Promoting Integrity in Financial Markets, Working Group 3: Reform of the International Monetary Fund, and Working Group 4: The World Bank and Other Multilateral Development Banks.

Table 8.1   G20 Membership in the Financial Stability Forum and Basel Committee on Banking Supervision

G20	Financial Stability Forum	Basel Committee on Banking Supervision
Argentina	**Argentina**	
Australia	Australia	**Australia**
Brazil	**Brazil**	**Brazil**
Canada	Canada	Canada
China	**China**	**China**
France	France	France
Germany	Germany	Germany
India	**India**	**India**
Indonesia	**Indonesia**	
Italy	Italy	Italy
Japan	Japan	Japan
Korea	**Korea**	**Korea**
Mexico	**Mexico**	**Mexico**
Russia	**Russia**	**Russia**
Saudi Arabia	**Saudi Arabia**	
South Africa	**South Africa**	
Turkey	**Turkey**	
United Kingdom	United Kingdom	United Kingdom
United States	United States	United States
European Union	**European Union (European Commission)**	
	Hong Kong SAR	Belgium
	The Netherlands	Luxembourg
	Singapore	The Netherlands
	Switzerland	Spain
		Sweden
		Switzerland

Note: Bold indicates new member.

with the notion of a charter of sustainable economic activity floated by the EU (Finance Ministers of the Eurasian Economic Community, Economy Ministers of the Eurasian Economic Community, and Central Bank Governors of Eurasian Economic Community 2009).

The Eurasian Economic Community ministers agreed on the need to reduce dependency on a single reserve currency in order to ensure the sustainability of national economies and on the need for greater use of multiple currencies. The BRIC ministers called for the study of developments in the international monetary system, including the role of reserve currencies. However, there was no indication that the EU would be prepared to debate the issue, which is understandable given the euro status as the second reserve currency. Similarly, the UK was not willing to change the status of the pound in the global currency system.

Outcomes and Assessments

The London Summit

The London Summit statement contained 52 commitments, 20 of which were aimed at strengthening financial systems: enhancing regulation and supervision (11) and strengthening global financial institutions (9). The leaders pledged to provide more than $1.1 trillion in new funding to stimulate trade and economic growth, to contain unemployment, and to aid developing countries. The funding was broken down as follows:

- $750 billion to the IMF;
- $250 billion in SDR allocation;
- $100 billion of additional lending for multilateral development banks (MDBs);
- $250 billion of support for trade finance;
- $5 trillion for fiscal expansion, intended to save or create millions of jobs that would otherwise have been destroyed;
- $50 billion to support social protection, boost trade, and safeguard development in low-income countries;
- $6 billion additional concessional and flexible finance for the poorest countries over the next two to three years.

In fact, the amount was lower, as the $5 trillion for fiscal expansion represented an assessment of funding earmarked by national programmes to stimulate G20 economies. The increase for the IMF had already been generated by pledges by Japan ($100 billion), the EU (€75 billion), Brazil ($35 billion), Canada ($20 billion), China ($40 billion), the US ($100 billion), and Norway (up to $5 billion), making $400 billion of the $500 billion committed by the leaders' statement.

Another source of new money was the replenishment of the IMF's SDR system. However, the benefits of this instrument were distributed unequally according to the IMF quota system. Most benefits strengthened the reserves of developed countries, which possessed larger quotas: the US at 17 per cent, Germany and Japan at 6 per cent each, the UK and France at about 5 per cent each.

The commitment of $6 billion in additional concessional and flexible finance for the poorest countries over the next two to three years was to come from sales of IMF gold, together with surplus income. However, the IMF had to come up with concrete proposals at its spring meeting a few weeks later, on 25–26 April.

With regards to additional resources for MDBs and the availability of at least $250 billion over the next two years to support trade finance, the funds should be generated by the new Global Trade Liquidity Pool (GTLP) of the International Finance Corporation (IFC). The GLTP would provide up to $50 billion of trade liquidity support over the next three years with significant co-financing from the private sector. In order to reach this objective, the G20 countries aimed to provide up to $4 billion in voluntary contributions to the GTLP.

The priorities of resisting protectionism and promoting global trade and investment flows were reflected in seven commitments. The G20 leaders reinforced their Washington pledge to avoid protectionist measures by agreeing to rectify promptly any such measures. They extended this pledge to the end of 2010. Gordon Brown's proposal that countries should notify the WTO of any such measures was formalized. The WTO, together with other international bodies, was mandated to monitor G20 compliance and report publicly on a quarterly basis.

In the Declaration on Strengthening the Financial System, the leaders referred to the MDGs and ODA, including aid for trade, debt relief, and the commitments made at the 2005 G8 Gleneagles Summit, especially with regard to sub-Saharan Africa. The six commitments in the declaration included the promise to make resources available for social protection for the poorest countries, through voluntary bilateral contributions to the World Bank's Vulnerability Framework, including the Infrastructure Crisis Facility, and the Rapid Social Response Fund.

The FSF was transformed into the Financial Stability Board (FSB) with a membership expanded to include the rest of the G20 members, the European Commission, and Spain, in addition to the existing FSF members. Its mandate was broadened to promote financial stability as detailed in the annex to Global Plan entitled Declaration on Strengthening the Financial System.

The discussion of IFI reform, begun by the G20 in the autumn of 2008, was modestly reduced to fast tracking the quota reforms already agreed upon in April 2008. Tough negotiations were required to agree to the completion of the proposed quota review by January 2011. Increasing the quotas of the developing countries required reducing the quotas of the US, Japan, UK, and France, which did not want to yield. Agreement on the recommendations for the fast track reform, to be presented in the IMF/World Bank spring meetings of 2010, proved no easier, and stalled. The final wording in the Plan of Action – that the leaders agreed that 'the heads and senior leadership of the international financial institutions should be appointed through an open, transparent, and merit-based selection process' – was a far cry from the principle of fair nomination irrespective of nationality (G20 2009).

The resource allocation mechanisms through the IFIs were spelt out in the Declaration on Delivering Resources through the International Financial Institutions, which contained seven commitments. The leaders delegated 30 mandates to international institutions, most of which were IFIs. Finance ministers were requested to ensure the timely implementation of the decisions indicated in the Action Plan. The FSB and the IMF were asked to monitor progress, working with the Financial Action Task Force and the Global Forum on Transparency and Exchange of Information for Tax Purposes, and to report to the next meeting of the finance ministers and central bank governors, in November 2009 in Scotland.

The Action Plan and the declarations were naturally a compromise. The statement on the new global consensus in which G20 leaders 'will together manage the process of globalization to secure responsibility from all and fairness to all and … will build a more sustainable and more open and a fairer global society' once again carried a lot of rhetoric (Brown 2009a). However, the sum of compromises and decisions was an important achievement made possible through the efforts of the UK and Brown himself, who managed tensions both within his government and with its opposition. At a press conference after meeting with Mexico's President Felipe Calderón, Brown (2009) listed 'five tests' for the G20 summit:

- restoring growth to emerging market economies through increasing resources to international institutions;
- agreeing on measures to clean up the banking system and to tighten regulation of markets and financial institutions and make it more transparent;
- committing to take all measures necessary to resume growth;
- kick-starting global trade and resisting protectionism; and
- committing to a low-carbon and sustainable recovery.

Based on an assessment of outcomes, the London Summit performed well on four of Brown's five tests.

The EU made a substantial contribution through the efforts of its member states and institutions, although it may be an overstatement to claim that the EU played a driving role (European Commission 2009b). Nonetheless the outcomes resulted from coordinated efforts. For the EU as a community, the summit became an effective instrument of political management. Its collective contribution, reflected in the formal and informal documents adopted on 22 February, 1 March, and, finally, 19–20 March 2009, as well as the conclusions from the Ecofin meetings and the meetings of the General Affairs and External Relations (GAER) Council, was both substantial and noticeable. The European Commission and Spain became fully fledged members of the new FSB.

The London Summit did well on direction setting, defining five main directions of collective action to bring the world economy out of recession – influenced by decisions made by the EU.

With regard to developing global governance, the G20 moved from being an anti-crisis management mechanism to being a mechanism of systemic governance. Having defined concrete directions and actions, and issued 30 mandates for their implementation to international institutions as well as national financial authorities, the G20 exerted systemic influence on the global governance processes. The EU contributed not only in providing recommendations on the IMF and World Bank reform, but also through outlining the algorithm on the G20's future work and the modalities of its coordination with the G8, the FSB and the Organisation for Economic Co-operation and Development.

The leaders' capacity to exert their political influence for forging acceptable and consistent decisions also proved substantial. Many of the propositions came from the EU perspective. The EU position had a strong impact on the commitments to ensure mid- and long-term fiscal stability, develop and adopt early exit strategies, and limit longer-term costs to the economies.

The Pittsburgh Summit

Ahead of the Pittsburgh Summit on 24–25 September 2009, the EU followed a similar path as for the two previous summits, holding internal meetings to develop a unified position, a stronger stance and therefore have a significant influence on the agenda and the outcome of the summit. This was again a carefully planned process, under the Swedish rotating presidency, consisting of meetings of ministers and informal meetings of EU leaders.

Early during its presidency, which started on 1 July 2009, Sweden announced that it would hold an informal European Council meeting ahead of the Pittsburgh Summit in order to better prepare the EU position, following an established pattern (Taylor, Jennifer, and Brundsen 2010). The meeting was held in Brussels on 17 September and led to the adoption of 'agreed language' for the Pittsburgh Summit (European Union 2009a).

Of course, the preparatory work started much earlier, with a meeting of the 27 finance ministers soon after the end of the summer, to reach a common position ahead of the G20 finance meeting in London on 4–5 September 2009. The Swedish presidency organized a working lunch in Brussels on 2 September, chaired by Swedish finance minister Anders Borg. The topics on the agenda were already illustrative of the EU's priorities for Pittsburgh (Swedish Presidency of the European Union 2009c):

- the general economic situation, including a strategy to safeguard stability and viability of public finances;
- measures to avoid future financial crises, notably through strengthening the monitoring of markets;
- reform of IFIs, as well as resources allocated to them;
- reform of credit mechanisms within international and multilateral institutions; and
- the financial aspects of climate change.

In a statement after the lunch, Borg concluded that 'having established common positions in these crucial areas, the EU can now contribute decisively and constructively to the G20 meetings, which will hopefully advance the agenda on financial sector reform, improved remuneration schemes, and climate change negotiations' (Swedish Presidency 2009a).

However, the finance meeting also confirmed the persistent disagreements among EU members on several issues, including bank bonuses, a topic that drew strong opposition between the UK and France. These disagreements would last for much longer and show that EU coordination efforts cannot force a consensus on all topics, although any internal feuding on the public stage during summits – which would have further hurt the EU's credibility – was averted.

Beyond regular meetings and informal gatherings called by Sweden, however, some EU members play a greater role than others in setting EU priorities for the G20. For instance, an agreement reached by Eurogroup members can be subsequently approved by other member states at Ecofin meetings. More obviously, some states (for example, G20 members) carry more weight than others, not the least because they have the capacity to undermine the EU's position at the G20 summit if their position is not taken into account. Indeed, most of the language agreed ahead of Pittsburgh was inspired by a joint letter sent by Nicolas Sarkozy, Angela Merkel and – apparently jumping into the boat at the last minute – Gordon Brown to Sweden's Prime Minister Fredrik Reinfeldt on 3 September (Brown, Merkel, and Sarkozy 2009).

Nonetheless, this is not to say that non-G20 members do not get their voice heard. Through this EU preparatory process, all EU members have a chance to voice their suggestions and concerns, and can have an impact on the discussions at the G20 summit through maximizing their weight thanks to the EU. Moreover, EU states that are not members of the G20 and do not get invited can be kept informed of the work of the G20. Furthermore, this preparatory process leads to a 'mandate' for the EU to speak at the G20 – if not with one mouth, at least with one single message.

The informal discussions among EU leaders on 17 September indicated three core priorities for the EU in Pittsburgh. They discussed the need to coordinate exit strategies to avoid a global recession if stimulus packages are terminated too early and global inflation if they continue for too long: 'exit strategies need to be designed now and implemented in a coordinated manner as soon as recovery takes hold' (EU 2009a). Another major discussion was on the topic of bonuses, which confirmed the European will to regulate them. Reinfeldt, chair of the meeting, declared that 'the bonus bubble burst tonight' despite disagreement with the US and reluctance from London (EurActiv 2009). In fact, despite French attempts, remuneration caps per se do not appear in the agreed language, although the document calls for 'bonuses to be set at an appropriate level in relation to fixed remuneration and made dependent on the performances of the bank, the business unit and the individuals', wording similar to the letter by Merkel, Sarkozy and Brown (EU 2009a). Italy, for its part, managed to secure a reference to countering speculation on various commodities markets. Climate change negotiations were also discussed at the meeting, and deemed to be proceeding too slowly (EurActiv 2009).

The Europeans emerged smiling from the Pittsburgh Summit. Barroso (2009) said: 'I am particularly happy with the decisions taken today'. The Swedish delegation emphasized EU unity at the summit: 'We arrived with a clear mandate from the EU, well prepared and united.' It said that the summit marked some progress in solving global challenges, calling it was 'a step forward' although it did 'not resolve the problems and challenges we are facing' (Swedish Presidency 2009b). Sarkozy was maybe the happiest of all Europeans, as he had secured that France would hold the presidency of the G8 and the G20 in 2011.

The Europeans managed indeed to secure some of the core items on their agenda, including strengthening IFIs, developing coordinated exit strategies, and reforming financial regulation and supervision. It even managed to get the US to abide by the Basel framework, a much-awaited decision. However, Pittsburgh essentially marked progress on the road paved by previous summits rather than setting new ground in terms of innovation or priorities. In fact, the EU suffered a few failures, including its inability to avoid discussing the reform of the IMF executive board, where Europeans are over-represented, as well as failing to speed up negotiations on climate change, which would eventually lead to significant if not unpredictable disillusion in the Copenhagen climate change conference later that year.

The Toronto Summit

Two months after the Pittsburgh Summit, on 1 December, the Lisbon Treaty entered into force, providing the EU (on paper) with a more consolidated stance on the international stage (EU 2010). One of the core innovations of the new treaty was the new position of permanent president of the European Council, in place of the rotating presidency, to represent the EU at the highest level in international gatherings related to foreign and security policies. The EU member states designated for this important position a relatively unknown but agile and experienced Belgian politician named Herman Van Rompuy.

The implementation of the Lisbon Treaty had a fundamental impact on the preparation of the Toronto Summit scheduled for 26–27 June 2010, although the EU was still essentially in a post-Lisbon transitory phase in the first semester of 2010. To begin with, the EU had to sort out who would represent it in Toronto. It was agreed that a new duet of Barroso and Van Rompuy would be the face of the EU in international summits, with each taking the lead in his own field of competence. The process was not tension-free, but an agreement was eventually found between the two, with Van Rompuy taking the lead for the G8 and Barroso for the G20. At the preparatory level, this would translate into Van Rompuy's cabinet providing the sherpa for the G8 summits and Barroso's cabinet providing the sherpa for the G20 summits (Pop 2010). This was the first and key innovation of the Lisbon Treaty to ensure that the EU would 'speak with one voice' on the international stage. The result has been an improvement relative to the past chaotic situation, although there remains room for improvement as the EU is still over-represented by two people, in spite of the fact that they speak into the same microphone.

Another consequence of this new position relates to continuity in EU actions. Indeed, Belgium, holding the EU rotating presidency in the second half of 2010, announced early that it would not seek to be represented at the Seoul Summit in November, to set a precedent for future presidencies, particularly those of big member states. With a permanent president designated for two and a half years, instead of a six-month rotating presidency, the EU should be able to plan over a longer term and to foresee more continuity from one summit to another.

In addition, Van Rompuy decided to put financial stability and economic growth at the top of his agenda, mirroring the G20 agenda to a certain extent. In fact, he started as soon as February 2010 by convening an informal meeting of heads of state and government in Brussels to discuss coordination and monitoring mechanisms for European economy, in the midst of the Greek economic crisis (Spanish Presidency of the European Union 2010a).

Indeed, in those first months of 2010, the EU's focus was turned mostly inward because of the Greek crisis. But more worrying signals were coming from other European economies. However, in the minds of EU leaders, there was no separation between these domestic issues to be dealt with and the G20 agenda. In fact, what was done in Europe to solve internal problems was in line with the recommendations of previous G20 summits. Moreover, successful policies were also seen – retrospectively perhaps naively – as a potential model for other economies world-wide (see, for example, Council of the EU 2010b).

Internal stability was a preoccupation at EU discussions, with many debates over bailing out Greece, which was finally voted on in May 2010 at yet another extraordinary council meeting, in which the 'solidarity clause' newly introduced in article 122.2 of the Lisbon Treaty was invoked for the first time to justify exceptional rescue measures (Council of the EU 2010e). This decision followed a political deal reached at a meeting of the euro area leaders (see Spanish Presidency of the EU 2010b). Also, coordinating the EU's economic and financial policies was a core concern of Van Rompuy (2010b), who called several meetings of a task force on economic governance consisting notably of representatives from the 27 member states, the commission, and the ECB. The first meeting was held on 21 May 2010.

As the conclusions of the 17 June European Council meeting state: 'The action [the EU] is taking to boost competitiveness, consolidate public finances and reform its financial sector will enable it to put forward strong positions for similar international action at the forthcoming G20 Summit' (Council of the EU 2010a).

On 13 May, in a letter to Jerzy Buzek, president of the European Parliament, and Van Rompuy, Barroso (2010) presented five priorities for the EU at G20 Toronto Summit, therefore also taking the lead in the G20 process as per the informal agreement with his European Council counterpart. Those priorities were to:

- set out general guiding principles for exit from the crisis;
- make progress towards agreeing on country recommendations by groups of countries or regions in the context of the G20's Framework for Strong, Sustainable, and Balanced Growth;
- implement the existing commitments to reform financial markets;

- make substantial progress towards agreeing on an ambitious package on IMF reform in order to conclude by November; and
- build momentum for the MDG Review Summit in September.

As preparations for Toronto continued, France's Sarkozy and Germany's Merkel once again played a prominent role, notably pressing for a tax on financial transactions. They issued joint letters to Barroso and also to Canada's prime minister and G20 host Stephen Harper (Sarkozy and Merkel 2010; Merkel and Sarkozy 2010). In a meeting on 8 June, the 27 European finance ministers agreed to submit terms of reference to the European Council 'with a view to preparation, at its meeting on 17 June, of the G20 Summit in Toronto' (Council of the EU 2010c). The 17 June meeting followed most of those terms of reference, although there was no agreement on a single levy mechanism on financial transactions, settling instead on referring to 'levies' (plural) mainly due to Britain's reluctance (Council of the EU 2010a). On 22 June, the EU's position for Toronto was laid out in a letter co-signed by Barroso and Van Rompuy (2010b) addressed to all G20 leaders.

In the end, the Toronto Summit did not yield ground-breaking results, but rather continued to build on previous meetings. The EU managed to have several of its priorities addressed, although it did not manage to impose a consensus on a global bank levy. From a European perspective, however, the most important achievement was to have weathered – temporarily – the double storm of the Greek crisis and the bumpy post-Lisbon transitory period to present a unified yet solid position at the summit.

The Seoul Summit

The Seoul Summit on 11–12 November 2010 was the first fully under the new Lisbon rules. The EU's position was prepared under the Belgian rotating presidency, the first to operate under the new regime. The Seoul Summit was also the first post-financial crisis G20 meeting, resulting in a slight modification of the group's internal dynamics.

The EU preparations proceeded along the same lines as for Toronto, with Ecofin and euro area meetings. In line with the new treaty, the rotating presidency adopted a much lower profile, although it still represented the EU (together with the commissioner for economic and monetary affairs) at the finance meeting on 21 October in Gyeongju, Korea, as mandated by the terms agreed to during a council meeting (Council of the EU 2010d).

A comparison of those terms with the communiqué issued at Gyeongju would lead to the conclusion that the EU successfully influenced the outcome Council of the EU (G20 Finance Ministers and Central Bank Governors 2010). However, many items on the agenda were imposed on Europeans, such as the reform of financial institutions where Europe is largely over-represented. Nonetheless, a European agreement on IMF reform would likely have been impossible outside the framework of the EU (with all its bargaining power and internal trade-offs possible).

Ahead of Seoul, the 27 European leaders met again in late October to discuss their priorities for the G20, informed by the discussions of the finance ministers. They identified several priorities, such as global recovery, global imbalances, the Basel agreement, and exchange rate policies. They also identified financial governance and climate change as two other core issues to be discussed (Council of the EU 2010a). In a subsequent letter to the G20 members, Barroso and Van Rompuy (2010a) declared the EU priorities in a manner strikingly similar to the October Council conclusions. Although the EU leaders declared themselves satisfied with the Seoul Summit, it did not yield significant results (apart from IMF reform) and showed still important divergence within the EU on several key issues, as well as between Europe and other G20 members.

Nevertheless, both the president of the European Commission and the president of the European Council claimed that the summit outcomes reflected the priorities the EU set out ahead of Seoul. Indeed, the G20 leaders committed to reducing excessive imbalances and maintaining current account imbalances at sustainable levels, although they rejected the use of indicators to assess macroeconomic imbalances. On currency rates, they agreed to refrain from competitive devaluations and to be vigilant against excess volatility and disorderly movements. They recommitted to implementing structural reforms to boost and sustain global demand, foster job creation, contribute to global rebalancing, and increase growth potential. On financial regulation, they endorsed the BCBS proposal for a new framework on bank capital and liquidity, to be translated into national laws and regulations starting on 1 January 2013. These commitments reflected the priorities that the EU members had agreed to promote at the Seoul Summit (see Council of the EU 2010a).

It remains to be seen how well the G20 deliver on the commitments made. It is also unclear if the model set up by the Belgian presidency will be embraced by the EU future presidencies, although it was followed for the Cannes Summit in France in 2011. Therefore, the success of the EU should be put in perspective.

Conclusions

In the run-up to the Washington Summit the leadership and contribution of the EU presidency and the European Commission were indisputable and striking. In the preparations for the London Summit, the EU yielded leadership through its institutions (the European Commission president, Ecofin, the GAER Council, the High-Level Group on Financial Supervision in the EU) as well as the leaders of Germany, France, and, to some extent, Italy (mostly due to the latter's chair of the 2009 G8 summit) and the influence of formal and informal EU summits. These institutions were able to bridge the leadership gap and harness resources despite the impotence of the rotating presidency, there was a strong argument in favour of the permanent EU presidency that would arrive with the entry into force of the Lisbon Treaty in December 2009.

Since 1 December 2009, when he took office as president of the European Council, Herman Van Rompuy has worked to strengthen coordination of foreign economic policy at the EU and international levels. He is convinced that 'the field of foreign economic policy relations is the most promising vector for Europe to speak with one voice in the world', with the G20 as 'an appropriate forum' (Van Rompuy 2010a). Time will tell whether the EU has become more influential in the G20 due to its recent institutional representation. However, in the G20 the EU can upgrade its status as an international actor in accordance with the level of its competencies due to several factors.

First, the established pattern of coordinating and agreeing upon the language (or terms of reference) for G20 meetings provides a reliable and coherent operational framework.

Second, while the EU promotes certain values, interests, and priorities at the G20 table, most importantly it ensures the implementation of summit commitments not only by the EU members states but also the other G20 members. The EU thus 'serves as the transmission mechanism' enhancing compliance and building the level of trust and legitimacy (Emerson et al. 2011). The commitments made by individual G20 members at Seoul referred to European regulations, directives, and structural reforms objectives in line with the Europe 2020 Strategy. Turkey – a member of the G20 but not of the EU – also committed to measures to regulate and supervise its financial sector in line with EU law. This evidence indicates the EU's role in providing a model for international standards.

Third, the EU has proven to be an effective member of the G20 forum, performing consistently and significantly higher than average on compliance. According to the assessments conducted by the G20 Research Group and the International Organisations Research Institute, the EU average is 85 per cent, compared to 69 per cent for the G20 as a whole (see Table 8.2).

Table 8.2   G20 and European Union Compliance Performance

	European Union	**G20**
2008 Washington Summit	100%	84%
2009 London Summit	80%	62%
2009 Pittsburgh Summit	69%	62%
2010 Toronto Summit	79%	64%
2010 Seoul Summit	91%	75%
Average	84%	69%

Source: G20 Research Group and National Research University Higher School of Economics (2011).

Fourth, by endowing the EU with a single legal personality, the Lisbon Treaty has strengthened the institutional and legal provisions for upgrading the EU's status in the G20. Unlike in the G8, where agenda priorities focus more on policy areas falling within the EU's shared competencies such as a common foreign and security policy, economic and employment policies, energy and development, in the G20 coordinated action is required in policy areas exclusive to the EU (as in monetary, competition, and trade policies) and in shared policy areas where the EU is already implementing certain policy (such as enhancing economic governance). The EU should continue to build on these strengths to enhance its influence within the G20 and to 'promote the international system based on stronger multilateral cooperation and good governance' (European Union 2010).

References

Barroso, José Manuel (2008). 'Fighting on All Fronts: Tackling the Global Slowdown and Climate Change.' Globalisation Panel, SPEECH/08/63, Lisbon, 21 November. <europa.eu/rapid/pressReleasesAction.do?referen ce=SPEECH/08/636&format=HTML&aged=1&language=EN&guiLangu age=en> (July 2011).

Barroso, José Manuel (2009). 'Statement by EU Commission President Barroso.' Pittsburgh, 26 September. <www.eu-un.europa.eu/articles/fr/article_9032_ fr.htm> (July 2011).

Barroso, José Manuel (2010). 'President Barroso on EU Priorities for G20 Summit in Toronto.' MEMO/10/192, Brussels, 13 May. <europa.eu/rapid/ pressReleasesAction.do?reference=MEMO/10/192&format=HTML&age d=0&language=EN&guiLanguage=en> (July 2011).

Barroso, José Manuel, and Herman Van Rompuy (2010a). 'Joint Letter of Herman Van Rompuy and José Manuel Barroso to the G20.' Brussels, 5 November. <www.consilium.europa.eu/uedocs/cms_data/docs/pressdata/ en/ec/117547.pdf> (July 2011).

Barroso, José Manuel, and Herman Van Rompuy (2010b). 'Letter Co-signed by Herman Van Rompuy and José Manuel Barroso to the G20 Leaders.' Brussels, 22 June. <www.consilium.europa.eu/uedocs/cms_data/docs/ pressdata/en/ec/115454.pdf> (July 2011).

Berlusconi, Silvio, and Gordon Brown (2009). 'Joint Article by President of the Council Berlusconi and British Prime Minister Brown.' 19 February. <www. g8italia2009.it/G8/Home/News/G8-G8_Layout_locale-1199882116809_ InterventoBerlusconi.htm> (July 2011).

Brown, Gordon (2008a). 'PM Broadcast on Financial Stability Programme.' Transcript of a podcast, London, 9 October. <tna.europarchive. org/20081209202104/http://www.number10.gov.uk/Page17138> (July 2011).

Brown, Gordon (2008b). 'PM's Words on EU Council.' Brussels, 7 November. <tna.europarchive.org/20081209202104/http://www.number10.gov.uk/Page17385> (July 2011).

Brown, Gordon (2008c). 'Speech in Doha.' Doha, 2 November. <tna.europarchive.org/20081209202104/http://www.number10.gov.uk/Page17364> (July 2011).

Brown, Gordon (2008d). 'Speech on Global Economy.' Reuters building, London, 13 October. <tna.europarchive.org/20081209202104/http://www.number10.gov.uk/Page17161> (July 2011).

Brown, Gordon (2008e). 'Speech to Business Leaders.' London, 27 October. <tna.europarchive.org/20081209202104/http://www.number10.gov.uk/Page17303> (July 2011).

Brown, Gordon (2008f). 'Speech to the Lord Mayor's Banquet.' London, 10 November. <tna.europarchive.org/20081209202104/http://www.number10.gov.uk/Page17419> (July 2011).

Brown, Gordon (2009a). 'G20 Press Conference.' London, 3 April. <tna.europarchive.org/20081209202104/http://www.number10.gov.uk/Page18934> (July 2011).

Brown, Gordon (2009b). 'PM Speech to European Parliament.' 24 March. <tna.europarchive.org/20090119005723/http://www.number10.gov.uk/Page18718> (July 2011).

Brown, Gordon (2009c). 'Pre-G20 Briefing with Foreign Media.' London, 13 March. <tna.europarchive.org/20081209202104/http://www.number10.gov.uk/Page18739> (July 2011).

Brown, Gordon (2009d). 'Q&A Session on the Global Economy with the Brookings Institute.' Washington DC, 9 February. <tna.europarchive.org/20081209202104/http://www.number10.gov.uk/Page18266> (July 2011).

Brown, Gordon (2009e). 'Speech on Global Economy.' Foreign Press Association, London, 26 January. <tna.europarchive.org/20090119005723/http://www.number10.gov.uk/Page18153> (July 2011).

Brown, Gordon (2009f). 'Speech to African Leaders.' Lancaster House, London, 16 March. <tna.europarchive.org/20081209202104/http://www.number10.gov.uk/Page18639> (July 2011).

Brown, Gordon (2009g). 'Speech to DFID Conference on Eliminating World Poverty.' Conference on world poverty, Department for International Development, London, 9 March. <tna.europarchive.org/20081209202104/http://www.number10.gov.uk/Page18554> (July 2011).

Brown, Gordon (2009h). 'Speech to U.S. Congress.' Washington DC, 4 March. <tna.europarchive.org/20090119005723/http://www.number10.gov.uk/Page18506> (July 2011).

Brown, Gordon, and Ki-moon Ban (2008). 'Doorstep with Mr. Ban Ki Moon.' London, 13 November. <tna.europarchive.org/20081209202104/http://www.number10.gov.uk/Page17475> (July 2011).

Brown, Gordon, and José Manuel Barroso (2009). 'PM and President Barroso Press Conference.' London, 16 March. <tna.europarchive.org/20090119005723/http://www.number10.gov.uk/Page18644> (July 2011).

Brown, Gordon, and Felipe Calderon (2009). 'PM and President Calderón Press Conference.' London, 30 March. <tna.europarchive.org/20081209202104/http://www.number10.gov.uk/Page18870> (July 2011).

Brown, Gordon, and Felipe Calderón (2009). 'A Joint Declaration with Mexican President.' London, 30 March. <tna.europarchive.org/20090119005723/http://www.number10.gov.uk/Page18853> (July 2011).

Brown, Gordon, and Luiz Inácio Lula da Silva (2009). 'A Joint Statement with Brazilian President.' Brasilia, 26 March. <tna.europarchive.org/20090119005723/http://www.number10.gov.uk/Page18772> (July 2011).

Brown, Gordon, and Angela Merkel (2009). 'Press Conference with Chancellor Merkel.' London, 14 March. <tna.europarchive.org/20090119005723/http://www.number10.gov.uk/Page18617> (July 2011).

Brown, Gordon, Angela Merkel, and Nicolas Sarkozy (2009). 'UK, France, and Germany Release Joint Letter on G20.' 3 September. <tna.europarchive.org/20081209202104/http://www.number10.gov.uk/Page20496> (July 2011).

Council of Economic and Financial Affairs (2008). 'Press Release, 2894th Council Meeting.' 13784/08 (Presse 279) SN4750/1/08 REV 1, 7 October, Luxembourg. <www.consilium.europa.eu/ueDocs/cms_Data/docs/pressData/en/ecofin/103250.pdf> (July 2011).

Council of Economic and Financial Affairs (2009). 'Press Release, 2931st Council Meeting.' 7048/09 (Presse 54), 10 March, Brussels. <www.consilium.europa.eu/uedocs/NewsWord/en/ecofin/106576.doc> (July 2011).

Council of the European Union (2008). 'Presidency Conclusions.' 14368/08, 16 October, Brussels. <www.consilium.europa.eu/ueDocs/cms_Data/docs/pressData/en/ec/103441.pdf> (July 2011).

Council of the European Union (2009a). 'Presidency Conclusions.' 7880/1/09 Rev 1, 19/20 March, Brussels. <www.consilium.europa.eu/uedocs/cms_data/docs/pressdata/en/ec/106809.pdf> (July 2011).

Council of the European Union (2009b). 'Press Release: 2943th Council Meeting.' 10009/09 (Presse 137), 18 May, Brussels. <www.consilium.europa.eu/uedocs/cms_data/docs/pressdata/en/gena/107921.pdf> (July 2011).

Council of the European Union (2010a). 'Conclusions.' EUCO 13/10, 17 June, Brussels. <www.consilium.europa.eu/uedocs/cms_data/docs/pressdata/en/ec/115346.pdf> (July 2011).

Council of the European Union (2010b). 'Preparation of 17 June European Council: Guidelines for the Conclusions.' Brussels, 31 May. <www.europolitics.info/pdf/gratuit_en/274094-en.pdf> (July 2011).

Council of the European Union (2010c). 'Press Release: 3020th Council Meeting.' 10689/10 Presse 162, 8 June, Brussels. <www.consilium.europa.eu/uedocs/cms_data/docs/pressdata/en/ecofin/115006.pdf> (July 2011).

Council of the European Union (2010d). 'Press Release: 3038th Council Meeting.' Presse 278/10, 19 October, Brussels. <www.consilium.europa.eu/uedocs/cms_data/docs/pressdata/en/ecofin/117209.pdf> (July 2011).

Council of the European Union (2010e). 'Press Release: Extraordinary Council Meeting.' 9596/10 Presse (108), 9–10 May, Brussels. <www.consilium.europa.eu/uedocs/cms_data/docs/pressdata/en/ecofin/114324.pdf> (July 2011).

Darling, Alistair (2009). 'UK Objectives for the G20 in 2009.' Letter to G20 finance ministers and central bank governors, 7 January. <www.icmagroup.org/ICMAGroup/files/08/088e7cd8-692b-4885-901a-044bc92030fc.pdf> (July 2011).

Debaere, Peter (2010). 'The Output and Input Dimension of the European Representation in the G20.' *Studia Diplomatica* 63(2): 141–54.

Emerson, Michael, Rosa Balfour, Tim Corthaut, et al., eds (2011). *Upgrading the EU's Role as Global Actor: Institutions, Law and the Restructuring of European Diplomacy*. Brussels: Centre for European Policy Studies. <www.ceps.eu/ceps/download/4134> (July 2011).

EurActiv (2009). 'EU Achieves Unity Ahead of Pittsburgh.' 18 September. <www.euractiv.com/priorities/eu-achieves-unity-ahead-pittsburgh/article-185574> (July 2011).

European Commission (2009a). 'Communication from the Commission: Temporary Community Framework for State Aid Measures to Support Access to Finance in the Current Financial and Economic Crisis.' *Official Journal of the European Union* 16: 1–9. <eur-lex.europa.eu/LexUriserv/LexUriserv.do?uri=OJ:C:2009:016:0001:0009:EN:PDF> (July 2011).

European Commission (2009b). 'EU Drives G20 Crisis Action.' 2 April. <ec.europa.eu/news/economy/090402_1_en.htm> (July 2011).

European Union (2008). 'Agreed Language.' Informal Meeting of Heads of State or Government, 7 November, Brussels. <www.consilium.europa.eu/ueDocs/cms_Data/docs/pressData/en/misc/103873.pdf> (July 2011).

European Union (2009a). 'Agreed Language for the Pittsburgh G20 Summit.' 17 September, Brussels. <www.consilium.europa.eu/uedocs/cms_data/docs/pressdata/en/ec/110166.pdf> (July 2011).

European Union (2009b). 'Informal Meeting of Heads of State or Government: Joint Press Lines.' 1 March, Brussels. <www.consilium.europa.eu/uedocs/cms_data/docs/pressdata/en/misc/106390.pdf> (July 2011).

European Union (2010). 'Consolidated Versions of the Treaty on European Union and the Treaty on the Functioning of the European Union.' 2010/C 83/01. Also referred to as the Lisbon Treaty. *Official Journal of the European Union* 53. <eur-lex.europa.eu/JOHtml.do?uri=OJ:C:2010:083:SOM:EN:HTML> (July 2011).

Finance Ministers of the Eurasian Economic Community, Economy Ministers of the Eurasian Economic Community, and Central Bank Governors of Eurasian Economic Community (2009). 'Joint Statement of Ministers of Finance, Ministers of Economy and Governors of Central (National)

Banks of Eurasian Economic Community Member States on Reforming International Financial Architecture.' 13 March. <www1.minfin.ru/en/news/index.php?afrom4=13.03.2009&ato4=17.03.2009&type4=&id4=7174> (July 2011).

French Presidency of the European Union (2008a). 'Declaration on a Concerted European Action Plan of the Euro Area Countries.' Summit of the Euro Area Countries, 12 October. <www.eu2008.fr/PFUE/lang/en/accueil/PFUE-10_2008/PFUE-12.10.2008/sommet_pays_zone_euro_declaration_plan_action_concertee.html> (July 2011).

French Presidency of the European Union (2008b). 'Eurogroup Declaration on the Concerted European Action Plan of the Euro Area Countries.' Summit of the Euro Area Countries, 12 October. <www.eu2008.fr/PFUE/lang/en/accueil/PFUE-10_2008/PFUE-12.10.2008/sommet_pays_zone_euro_declaration_plan_action_concertee.html> (July 2011).

French Presidency of the European Union (2008c). 'Propos introductifs du président du Conseil européen.' European Council session on the financial crisis, 15 October, Brussels. <www.ue2008.fr/webdav/site/PFUE/shared/import/1015_conseil_europeen/Conseil_europeen_Propos_introductifs_President_crise_financiere_FR.pdf> (July 2011).

G7 Finance Ministers and Central Bank Governors (2009). 'Statement of the G7 Finance Ministers and Central Bank Governors Meeting.' Rome, 14 February 2009. <www.g8.utoronto.ca/finance/fm090214.htm> (July 2011).

G20 (2008). 'Declaration of the Summit on Financial Markets and the World Economy.' Washington DC, 15 October. <www.g20.utoronto.ca/2008/2008declaration1115.html> (July 2011).

G20 (2009). 'Global Plan for Recovery and Reform.' London, 2 April. <www.g20.utoronto.ca/2009/2009communique0402.html> (July 2011).

G20 Finance Ministers and Central Bank Governors (2009). 'Communiqué.' Horsham, United Kingdom, 14 March. <www.g20.utoronto.ca/2009/2009communique0314.html> (July 2011).

G20 Finance Ministers and Central Bank Governors (2010). 'Communiqué of the Meeting of Finance Ministers and Central Bank Governors.' Gyeongju, Korea, 23 October. <www.g20.utoronto.ca/2010/g20finance101023.html> (July 2011).

G20 Research Group, and Internationl Organisations Research Institute (2011). '2010 Seoul G20 Summit Final Compliance Report.' 6 November. <www.g20.utoronto.ca/compliance/2010seoul-final> (November 2011).

Germany (2009). 'Chair's Summary of the Berlin G20 Preparatory Summit.' Press Release 86, 22 February. <www.bundesregierung.de/nn_6538/Content/EN/Pressemitteilungen/BPA/2009/2009-02-22-chair-summary.html> (July 2011).

High-Level Group on Financial Supervision (2009). 'The High-Level Group on Financial Supervision in the EU.' Chaired by Jacques de Larosière,

25 February, Brussels. <ec.europa.eu/internal_market/finances/docs/de_
larosiere_report_en.pdf> (July 2011).

Medvedev, Dmitri (2008). 'Press Conference on the Results of the APEC
Summit.' Lima, Peru, 24 November. <www.kremlin.ru/eng/speeches
/2008/11/24/1409_type82915_209638.shtml> (July 2011).

Merkel, Angela, and Nicolas Sarkozy (2010). 'Letter by Merkel and Sarkozy to
Canadian Prime Minister Harper.' 21 June. <www.bundesregierung.de/
nn_774/Content/DE/Pressemitteilungen/BPA/2010/06/Anlagen/2010-06-
21-bk-sarkozy-brief-engl,property=publicationFile.pdf> (July 2011).

Pop, Valentina (2010). 'Van Rompuy and Barroso to Both Represent EU at G20.'
EU Observer, 19 March. <euobserver.com/9/29713> (July 2011).

Sarkozy, Nicolas (2009). 'Conférence de presse conjointe – Réunion de préparation
du Sommet du G20.' Berlin, 22 February. <www.elysee.fr/president/les-
actualites/conferences-de-presse/2009/conference-de-presse-conjointe-
reunion-de.6033.html> (July 2011).

Sarkozy, Nicolas, and Angela Merkel (2010). 'Draft Letter to the President of
the European Union.' 8 June. <www.bundesregierung.de/Content/DE/__
Anlagen/2010/2010-06-08-brief-sarkozy-eng,property=publicationFile.
pdf> (July 2011).

Spanish Presidency of the European Union (2010a). 'Consensus on the Need
to Establish a Coordination and Control System for the Economy.'
Brussels, 11 February. <www.eu2010.es/export/sites/presidencia/en/
documentosynoticias/noticias/feb11_consejorompuy.html> (July 2011).

Spanish Presidency of the European Union (2010b). 'Statement of the Heads of
State or Government of the Euro Area.' Brussels, 7 May. <www.eu2010.
es/export/sites/presidencia/comun/descargas/unioneuropea/may08_
eurogrupo.pdf> (July 2011).

Swedish Presidency of the European Union (2009a). 'Establishing Common EU
Positions Ahead of the G20 Meeting in London.' Brussels, 2 September.
<www.se2009.eu/en/meetings_news/2009/9/2/establishing_common_eu_
positions_ahead_of_the_g20_meeting_in_london.html> (July 2011).

Swedish Presidency of the European Union (2009b). 'The G20 Meeting is a Step
on the Way.' Pittsburgh, 26 September. <www.se2009.eu/en/meetings_
news/2009/9/26/the_g20_meeting_is_a_step_on_the_way.html> (July
2011).

Swedish Presidency of the European Union (2009c). 'Informal ECOFIN's
Ministers Lunch.' Brussels, 2 September. <www.se2009.eu/en/meetings_
news/2009/9/2/informal_ecofin_ministers_lunch.html> (July 2011).

Taylor, Simon, Rankin Jennifer, and Jim Brundsen (2010). 'Swedes Prepare
for Extra EU Summit in September.' *European Voice*, 30 July. <www.
europeanvoice.com/article/imported/swedes-prepare-for-extra-eu-summit-
in-september/65627.aspx> (July 2011).

Van Rompuy, Herman (2010a). 'The Challenges for Europe in a Changing World.'
Address by the President of the European Council to the College d'Europe,

Bruges, 25 February. <www.consilium.europa.eu/uedocs/cms_data/docs/pressdata/en/ec/113067.pdf> (July 2011).

Van Rompuy, Herman (2010b). 'Remarks by Herman Van Rompuy, President of the European Council, Following the First Meeting of the Task Force on Economic Governance.' PCE 102/10, Brussels, 21 May. <www.consilium.europa.eu/uedocs/cms_data/docs/pressdata/en/ec/114606.pdf> (July 2011).

White House (2008). 'President Bush Discusses Financial Markets and World Economy.' Federal Hall National Memorial, 13 November. <georgewbush-whitehouse.archives.gov/news/releases/2008/11/20081113-4.html> (July 2011).

World Trade Organization (2009). 'Report to the TPRB from the Director-General on the Financial and Economic Crisis and Trade-Related Developments.' 26 March. <www.wto.org/english/news_e/news09_e/trdev_dg_report_14apr09_e.doc> (July 2011).

PART IV
Critical Case Studies

Chapter 9

The G8, the European Union, and Climate Change and Energy

John J. Kirton and Victoria Panova[1]

The issue of energy was a major cause of the creation of the G7 summit in 1975. With the challenge of climate change added as early as 1979, the subject has remained on the summit agenda, with increased attention and action since 2005. The major democratic powers needed to coordinate efforts to confront the challenges of ensuring security of energy supply, introducing energy-saving and energy-efficient technologies, and governing energy to help meet their economic, environmental, and security goals. The G7 and G8 summit has enabled them to do this effectively.

G7/G8 energy governance evolved over five phases (see Appendices 9.1 and 9.2). First, in response to the two energy shocks of 1973 and 1979, energy security took a prominent place on the G7 agenda and evoked effective action from 1975 to 1981. Second, during the period of much lower prices and a sustained excess of supply over demand from 1982 to 1986, energy arose in the context of the G7's emerging environmental concerns. Third, the years from 1987 to 1999 saw a post-Cold War shift to a dominant security concern, with new conflicts in the Middle East, the 1986 Chernobyl accident and its subsequent environmental and health costs, and the growing risks of proliferation of nuclear materials and technologies. Fourth, after 2000, energy security recaptured the attention of the G8, with climate change assuming prominence as well. Fifth, since 2008, the global financial and economic crisis along with soaring oil prices in 2008 and 2011 made the now closely connected energy-climate issue a G8 concern.

This chapter focuses on G8 energy and climate change governance since 1987, when the European Union emerged as an autonomous and important international actor within the G8 in the energy and climate field. It argues that the G8 has been a strong success in governing global energy and climate change. Indeed, it connected the two issues with increasing effectiveness, reaching ever higher peaks in the 1970s, 1990s and since 2008. This performance has been driven by severe shocks in terms of military, security, energy supply and price, ecology, and nuclear safety that exposed the vulnerability of the United States, the most powerful member of the G8. With no multilateral organizations able to provide an effective,

1   The authors are grateful to Jenilee Guebert, Laura Sunderland, Zaria Shaw, Tatiana Khanberg, and Sarah Jane Vassallo for their research assistance.

integrated global response, the G8 has been left to combine its own formidable capabilities, to address the expanding dimensions of the energy-climate challenge, and to support skilled leaders who offer ambitious solutions. The EU has played an important part in expanding the G8's capabilities and promoting ecologically sustainable solutions to offset the preferences of a United States increasingly unable or unwilling to assume the global lead.

The Post-Cold War Security Shift, 1987–1999

During the second half of the 1980s, the G7 viewed energy security primarily through the prism of traditional environmental concerns. Yet with conflict in the Middle East erupting again in 1987, and with the end of the Cold War and Soviet Union, security considerations acquired an increasingly dominant place.

At Venice in 1987, the Iranian ayatollah Khomeini's threat to block the strategically important Strait of Hormuz, G7 members demonstrated a unified front in support of America's unilateral warnings, advising the warring parties that such actions were inadmissible.

At Paris in 1989, another energy shock propelled the G7 into action. On 25 March 1989 the *Exxon Valdez* tanker ran aground, spilling 300,000 barrels of crude oil into Prince William Sound. Oil prices spiked due to news of the spill and potential shortages caused by refinery fires. While such dramatic accidents account for only 6 percent of total oil pollution, they generate great attention, related to spills that occur during off-loading and stowing oil and throwing the wash-over, ballast, and bilge water into the ocean. At Paris the G7 thus noted the importance of cooperation with the International Maritime Organization to improve measures to prevent oil spills. On climate change, the G7 leaders deepened their consensus on the environmental implications of greenhouse gas emissions and the need to strengthen energy-saving measures to reduce them.

Energy came to the forefront again after Iraq invaded Kuwait on 2 August 1990. Crude and product prices soared, exchange markets reacted wildly, and jet fuel prices broke records due to increased defence demand. In late August, the Organization of Petroleum Exporting Countries (OPEC) failed to organize a formal meeting to respond to the crisis, although informal meetings resulted in record price falls. Conflicting reports of promises to increase OPEC output to compensate for the embargo of Iraqi and Kuwaiti oil further compounded market uncertainties. Oil supplies and prices remained vulnerable to political crises, even crises contained by effective market mechanisms, expansion of supply by exporting countries and coordination of the use of oil reserves with the International Energy Agency (IEA).

Several factors played against Saddam Hussein, including the strategic position of Kuwait, primarily due to its oil fields. His illegitimate act of aggression provoked an immediate response from a coalition led by the United States with the consent of the United Nations. Moreover, in a weakened USSR, Mikhail

Gorbachev wanted to support his western colleagues, for political and ideological reasons and to encourage western aid to the Soviet Union.

The crisis improved the relationship between hydrocarbon producers and consumers by promoting information exchange, transparency, and the effective functioning of market forces. Nevertheless, the Gulf War led to economic difficulties in several countries. The G7 leaders praised the Gulf Crisis Financial Co-ordination Group for successfully mobilizing $16 billion in direct aid to those affected by the crisis (G7 1991). They also supported the creation of the Gulf Development Fund. Less was done to deal with Iraq's burning of Kuwaiti oil wells and Iraq's deliberate spills into the sea, causing serious environmental damage.

The European Community first assumed a major role at the 1991 London Summit. G7 leaders supported the European initiative to create the European Energy Charter, first proposed by Ruud Lubbers, prime minister of the Netherlands, at a European Council session in Dublin on 25 June 1990. Full participation in the charter and its governing European Energy Conference was important to promote free trade in energy resources, strengthen security of supply, ensure environmental protection, and further economic reforms in Central and Eastern Europe and the Soviet Union, by establishing a regime of open, non-discriminatory commercial investment in energy. The European Energy Charter was adopted in December 1991. It was followed by the legally binding Energy Charter Treaty, which was signed in 1994 and entered into force in 1998.[2]

The conference soon proved unsuccessful, however, as several key participants, including Australia, Belarus, Iceland, Norway, and Russia did not ratify the Energy Charter. The US and Canada signed onto the conference but not the charter – the only G8 members to hold observer status. Subsequently, Russian prime minister Vladimir Putin, who did not think the charter reflected the interests of all parties, stressed the need for a comprehensive, regulated common energy regime for the Eurasian or even Eurasia-transatlantic territory.[3] Since such a major undertaking is difficult, smaller steps took place, including the unification of the EU and Russian electricity systems.

With the demise of the Soviet Union, the focus of the G7 shifted to nuclear security. The documents issued at Venice 1987, Paris 1989, and Houston 1990 devoted considerable sections to strengthening international cooperation to secure the use of nuclear energy, including, at Houston, the issue of non-proliferation. There the G7 proclaimed that each country bore individual responsibility for the security of its nuclear power plants. At Munich in 1992 the G7 created a multilateral mechanism to provide elaborate measures of operational and technical security, as well as to strengthen regulative regimes. Power plants that did not meet existing

---

2   At present, 51 countries have signed the Energy Charter Treaty. Of the G8 countries, the United States and Canada never signed the treaty and hold an observer status in the conference.

3   In particular, Russia would never accept provisions of the Transit Protocol to ensure freedom of transit that are inconsistent with its sovereign interests.

standards would be closed or, if possible, modernized, under the supervision of the IEA and the World Bank.

Further innovation came at the special, inter-sessional Moscow Summit on Nuclear Security, co-chaired by Russian president Boris Yeltsin and French president Jacques Chirac in April 1996, prior to the G7+Russia Summit in Lyon. The Moscow Summit went beyond the narrow issue of nuclear security to consider regional issues as well.[4] The eight leaders recognized the security of civilian nuclear reactors as an unquestionable priority and the need for a 'culture of efficient nuclear security'. They adopted a Nuclear Security Convention with a call upon all states to sign promptly so it could come into force by the end of 1996. The Moscow Summit also convened a meeting of experts in Paris in October 1996.

Nuclear energy inherently involves the issues of non-proliferation and weapons of mass destruction. Since 1996, these were both high priorities for various forums, although less so for the G8. Most cooperation occurred bilaterally, such as the American-Russian high-level task force on nuclear security set up by Russian president Putin and US President George W. Bush in February in Bratislava in 2005 to reduce stockpiles and guarantee safe storage of nuclear materials. As early as 1992 the Japanese government had adopted a programme for assessing mechanical facilities of nuclear power stations, which provided staff training.

The biggest step taken by the G8 was the creation of the Global Partnership against the Spread of Weapons and Materials of Mass Destruction at the Kananaskis Summit in 2002. Its priorities were the elimination of chemical weapons, decommissioning of atomic submarines, handling fissile materials, and managing former military scientists. A senior officials group met monthly to implement the partnership.

G7/G8 interest in more traditional energy issues also re-emerged. G8 energy ministers first met in Moscow in March/April 1998 to discuss the development of world energy in the 21st century, recognizing that the G8 accounted for 39 percent of world energy production, 48 percent of primary fuel resources consumption and a considerable share of international trade in energy resources. What assured the effectiveness of the ministerial was a consultation among international business and academic circles on world energy issues. Participants produced ideas that eventually fed into the Joint Oil Data Initiative (later the Joint Organisations Data Initiative, or JODI) created in 2001 to develop oil market transparency and increase competitiveness. Other issues discussed included nuclear security, energy transportation, and environmental protection.[5] Ministers agreed to continue dealing with such problems bilaterally or through existing international mechanisms.

---

4   Several reasons explain holding the special summit in Russia: it was the tenth anniversary of Chernobyl, and the G7 leaders wanted to show support for the extremely unpopular Yeltsin in the run-up to Russia's presidential election.

5   In 1998 a 50-year moratorium on mining and oil exploration in the Antarctic came into force. A protocol for the protection of the Antarctic had been adopted by 26 countries in 1991, but could not be implemented until Japan's ratification in 1998. Antarctica contains

A few months later, the G8 Birmingham Summit approved the ministerial's recommendations.

G8 leaders also noted the success of cooperation on pilot project to construct an international thermonuclear experimental reactor (ITER). Japan agreed that ITER would be built in Cadarache, France, after receiving a guarantee that the first full-scale reactor would be built in Japan.

Forging the Energy-Climate Connection, 2000–2007

The dramatic changes in world oil prices determined the next phase of G8 energy governance. Prices were affected by financial markets and inflation, which were in turn influenced by fundamental global economic trends and increased prices of raw materials. The hydrocarbons commodity futures markets set the level of prices for the real sector of the economy, while these prices were formed by financial agents. The volume of physical oil trading on the world trading flows was modest (according to estimates, about 1 percent of the world's oil trade) but, owing to the flexibility, high liquidity, and transparency of this comparatively small segment, it began to set the prices for the long-term contract, spot, and forward market segments.

G8 leaders proved unable to recognize these broader connections, especially with the new world of 21st-century finance. Yet they moved ahead in other ways. The 2000 Okinawa Summit brought together officials, private sector, and non-governmental organizations (NGOs) in the Renewable Energy Task Force, led by former Shell president Mark Moody-Stewart. The G8 also supported the 1992 International Convention on Civil Liability for Oil Pollution Damage and the International Oil Pollution Compensation Funds.

Russia was still not included as a full-scale G8 member at Okinawa, with the G7 still meeting separately.[6] While in some aspects this division was justified, as one of the biggest producers of hydrocarbon fuel, Russia should have participated in the discussions on energy, especially as the G7 (2000) noted the 'need for greater stability of oil markets to help ensure sustained growth and prosperity in both oil producing countries and oil consuming countries'.

At the 2001 Genoa Summit, the first for US president George W. Bush, differences arose over environmental issues, especially because the US had decided not to ratify the Kyoto protocol. There was no progress on energy. The Renewable Energy Task Force presented its report, recommending changing the

---

70 percent of the world's fresh water, and the moratorium attempts to preserve the world's least polluted continent.

　6　The years between 2002 and 2006 was a honeymoon period for the G8, with Russia included as a full member of the club. The relationship between Russia and the West reached its lowest point during the Ossetian-Georgian conflict in August 2008, when the G7 foreign ministers issued a statement about Russia's use of military force in Georgia.

structure of subsidizing energy projects in developing countries to reduce support for traditional suppliers. This strategy was intended to increase the share of renewable energy sources from 2 percent to 7 percent by 2003.

The issue of oil prices emerged during the G7 discussions. The conclusion was that 'high and volatile oil prices' constituted a concern for the world economy, especially for 'the most vulnerable developing countries' (G7 2001). Therefore the objectives were 'increased and diversified energy supplies, improved energy efficiency, expanded infrastructure and stable oil markets'. The G7 also welcomed the closure of the Chernobyl nuclear power plant on 15 December 2000.

The G8 energy ministers met again in May 2002 in Detroit, in a gathering co-chaired by the US and Canada. The meeting again raised the issue of improving information exchange, sending it for consideration to the eighth International Energy Forum in Osaka. Other points of concern included nuclear security, cooperation with the developing countries, and the use of new technologies. The decision to create an additional regular forum was never implemented.

At the 2003 Evian Summit, the G8, with Russia now a full member, shifted its focus to transport security. Despite a desire to establish a global regulatory regime for double hulls for oil tankers, Japanese resistance prevented a G8 consensus. Nevertheless, this provision advanced, with such standards introduced by the EU. The G8 also created the Nuclear Safety and Security Group to promote the safe, secure use of civilian nuclear technology.

As usual, with the US as host at the 2004 Sea Island Summit there was a stronger focus on security and thus also energy. The G8 leaders were concerned with how terrorist threats could hinder economic growth or recovery, influence energy prices, and add to uncertainty. Differences over the 2003 American invasion of Iraq constrained progress, as not all the G8 leaders agreed that Saddam Hussein presented a real threat.

At Gleneagles in 2005, the first working day of the summit was devoted to climate change, clean energy and sustainable development along with political issues. These issues caused considerable debate, especially between the US and the Europeans. Climate change had been a source of division between the G8 and civil society stakeholders since 1997. There was also speculation that the climate change document would pit the US against the rest of the G7, or that there would be no agreement, especially after leaked drafts were published in *The Guardian* on the eve of the summit.[7] Indeed, agreement on the climate change was reached only at the very last moment. The declaration on Climate Change, Clean Energy and Sustainable Development and its 10-page Plan of Action allowed each G8 country to interpret the problem the way it wanted. An additional document was released on the situation in the global economy and international oil market. Although it was

---

7   No G8 member would ever allow for disagreement to prevail and thus discredit the united front in the international arena. When there are profound divergences within the club, the issue is either dropped completely or, as happens more often, a generally worded document is issued that contains little substance.

intended to be voluminous and far reaching, it failed to offer comprehensive and innovative ideas. Much of the discussion was devoted to investing in alternative energy resources, mostly through research on auto engines. At the session with the Outreach Five members, or Group of Five (G5), the leaders agreed that the modern economy required flexibility, although it remained dependent on oil and gas (with greater emphasis on gas).

In 2006, the Russian presidency chose energy security as one of three priorities for the St Petersburg Summit. As the second largest exporter in the world, Russia was active in formulating a new paradigm for energy security. During its presidency several initiatives were adopted by the G8, including increasing transparency, predictability, and stability of global energy markets; improving the investment climate in the energy sector; enhancing energy efficiency and energy saving; diversifying the energy mix; ensuring the physical security of critical energy infrastructure; reducing energy poverty; and addressing climate change and sustainable development.

From the start Russia sought agreement on a common, comprehensive definition of energy security. There was limited success here. The declaration on energy security stated that G8 leaders were committed to 'enhanced dialogue on relevant stakeholders' perspectives on growing interdependence, security of supply and demand issues' (G8 2006). They realized the importance of diversifying both energy demand and supply. This was a major breakthrough, since many partners favoured a narrow approach, considering only the demand side.

The provision of 'transparent, equitable, stable and effective legal and regulatory frameworks, including the obligation to uphold contracts, to generate sufficient, sustainable international investments upstream and downstream' presented a positive example of cooperation (G8 2006). The St Petersburg Plan of Action went further, stating that 'better risks sharing between all stakeholders in energy supply chain [would] ensure reliable and sustainable energy flows' (G8 2006). It acknowledged the importance of 'economically sound diversification between different types of contracts, including market-based long-term and spot contracts'.

Another important statement concerned investments in the full energy chain, focusing on several priorities:

- generating electricity, including building new, more efficient power plants, upgrading plants to use renewables more, constructing transmission lines and interregional energy infrastructure, and facilitating the trans-border exchange of electrical power;
- introducing advanced energy-efficient and energy-saving technologies to revisit national goals for reducing energy intensity of economic development; and
- complementing existing regional systems of pipeline gas delivery to form a global market for liquified natural gas to lower investment risks.

The peaceful use of nuclear energy was also a priority, as a source of environmentally clean energy (in terms of greenhouse gas emissions) and as an alternative to hydrocarbon sources. However, due to resistance from Germany and Italy, only a vague statement emerged.

A similar situation arose with the Kyoto Protocol. In 2005 the US had acknowledged that human activity caused global warming. In 2006 European countries emphasized the need for emerging economies such as China and India to join international efforts to mitigate climate change. That the emerging economies did not agree to control their greenhouse gas emissions was the main reason the United States did not adhere to the Kyoto Protocol.

At the 2007 Heiligendamm Summit, much of the G8 Declaration on Growth and Responsibility in the World Economy was devoted to energy efficiency and climate change. The G8 leaders agreed to maintain the momentum, reaffirming their 'commitment to enhance dialogue on relevant share holders' perspectives on growing interdependence, security of supply and demand issues, facilitate diversification of different types of contracts, including market-based long-term and spot contracts, promote investment in upstream and downstream assets internationally, support the principles of the Energy Charter and the efforts of the participating countries to improve international energy co-operation' (G8 2007).

The 2007 summit created the Heiligendamm Dialogue Process (HDP), which institutionalized the now traditional outreach sessions with Brazil, China, India, Mexico, and South Africa. The HDP included the issues of energy efficiency and combating climate change.

From the start the German presidency suggested focusing on national programmes to introduce innovative technologies and set international standards of energy efficiency in different sectors of the economy, primarily regarding construction with minimum or zero energy consumption from external sources, 'clean coal' technologies, and increased efficiency of coal power stations.

The Energy-Economy Crises, 2008–Present

The fifth phase of G8 energy governance began with the global financial and economic crisis of 2008. On 3 July 2008, the OPEC basket peaked at $140.73 per barrel of oil, with the average price in 2008 at $94.45 per barrel. By early 2009, the price plunged to just over $40 per barrel, then held within a range of about $50.

Different causes explain the surge, including rates of oil depletion, fast-growing emerging economies, and political instability in oil-producing countries. Some temporary factors included economic growth rates, government decisions about greenhouse gas emissions and other environmental standards, biofuel production, and development of unconventional renewable sources of energy. Hydrocarbon prices had previously been low, which left the oil sector without sufficient investment and eventually led to its unpreparedness for increased demand from the most vibrant economies. In all, the cyclical nature of the economy seems the key cause.

At the 2008 Toyako Hokkaido Summit the G8 leaders faced challenges all too reminiscent of those that inspired the G8's birth in 1975. World prices for oil, again driven in part by conflict in the Middle East, surpassed those of the oil crises of 1973 and 1979, placing a new premium on energy conservation, efficiency, alternative energy sources, renewable energy, and climate control. Thus the Toyako Summit introduced a more engaged and broad approach to dealing with energy.

The Japanese focused on climate change rather than energy security in its own right. They divided the agenda and communiqué to treat energy and climate in separate sections, in contrast to the unified treatment at Heiligendamm and St Petersburg. Energy security was dealt with in the world economy section with strong language, but with no reference to oil prices. Some countries wanted it to be added, but others did not.

The summit in general was a substantial success. It earned a grade of B+, or 78 percent (Kirton 2008). It produced a striking success on its centrepiece subject of climate change, substantial advances on development and Africa, health, food security, accountability, and Zimbabwe, and solid management of many other issues.

However, it was a serious failure on the world economy and energy, worthy of only a C– (62 per cent) (Kirton 2008). The statement on the world economy suggested that all was well with the global economy and any negatives were merely future risks. It read: 'We remain positive about the long-term resilience of our economies and future global economic growth. Emerging market economies are still growing strongly though our growth has moderated. However, the world economy is now facing uncertainty and downside risks' (G8 2008c). On energy, little was said and even less was done. While noting the 'sharp rise in oil prices', it called for supply side measures that were well beyond G8 control (G8 2008a). On the demand side, there was no call for energy conservation or many of the other effective measures the G8 had invented and endorsed.

The leaders did not discuss oil prices at any length. They noted the need for producers and consumers to work together, and referred to the importance of the emergency meeting in Jeddah. The African leaders invited to participate said their economies were suffering because of increased oil prices, and that oil producers such as Nigeria and Algeria needed to help their fellow Africans. They recognized the responsibility of oil-producing countries, including themselves, to consider the impact of high prices. They expected G8 leaders to show stronger leadership in conducting a dialogue with OPEC.

On the contentious issue of biofuels, the US pushed for language on sustainability in the section on energy security rather than food security. Despite disagreements, solutions were found, although the bulk of the discussion was reflected in both the Environment and Climate Change declaration and the G8 Leaders Statement on Global Food Security.

On nuclear energy several countries, including the US, sought a stronger endorsement than the previous year. The Germans continued to resist. But there were some grounds for hope for further advances in the eyes of the US, if not of the Japanese host.

In keeping with Japan's traditionally strategic approach, Japan had begun preparing for its summit years in advance (Dobson 2004). In preparations beginning as early as March 2007 at the initiative of Prime Minister Shinzo Abe, Japan wanted the G8 to confront the challenge of climate change directly at Toyako. That focus was maintained by Yasuo Fukuda when he took office in September. The intention was to create a framework that would ensure the participation of the United States and China.

Japan's ambitious plan included four multi-year commitments to be met in 2008 from earlier G8 communiqués and five remit mandates from 2007.

However, at Toyako climate change achieved the least consensus, above all on medium and long-term goals. While the US saw it as a priority, it preferred the Major Economies Meeting (MEM) process and wanted the G8 to endorse the MEM's process of long- and medium-term targets from its members. The US also sought a strong G8 statement on clean technology.

In the lead-up to the G8 summit in July, Europe and Japan had been careful not to prejudge the MEM before its meeting in Korea on 21–22 June, immediately after which the G8 sherpas would meet on 23 June. While the issue was contentious, there was much mutual respect, with both sides suggesting targets. There was a good conversation on how the G8 might move forward.

In the end, Toyako produced an A-level performance on climate change. The summit affirmed a new set of norms for a new architecture to control emissions, which would be far more effective than the fundamentally flawed and failed Kyoto regime. The G8 with the MEM agreed for the first time that all major carbon polluters must control their carbon, that all G8 members – now including the United States and Russia – would do so after 2012, and that the G8's long-term goal was to reduce emissions by at least 50 percent by 2050.[8] The G8 declared that mid-term targets and national plans were needed and that the bottom-up sectoral approach pioneered by Japan was useful. The G8 members boldly bound themselves saying: 'we acknowledge our leadership role and each of us will implement ambitious economy-wide mid-term goals in order to achieve absolute emissions reductions' (G8 2008b). Several specific medium- and short-term actions reinforced these decisions. In the mid term, the summit identified energy efficiency, clean energy, national goals, renewable energy, and clean coal as subjects for action, through carbon capture and sequestration (CCS) by 2010. In the short term, it specified the aviation, maritime, and sustainable biofuel sectors, a nuclear energy infrastructure initiative, and 20 CCS demonstration plants by 2010.

---

8 An alternative view was that 'Bush agreed to a vaguely worded, essentially meaningless "aspirational" goal to reduce carbon emissions'.

To encourage other major carbon polluters to agree to this plan, the G8 offered abundant finance, technology transfer, trade liberalization, and action on sinks, and measures to reduce, reuse, and recycle (3R). On finance the G8 promised scaled-up support for disaster risk reduction, $10 billion in research and development with $6 billion for Climate Investment Funds, more for the Global Environmental Facility, and a reminder that it was providing more than $100 billion by 2010 to the Clean Energy Investment Framework. It offered free trade in carbon-reducing products, services, and remanufactured goods. It supported Reducing Emissions from Deforestation and Degrading (REDD), illegal logging, forest fire protection, and biodiversity co-benefits.

With the additional incentive of the Toyako Hokkaido Summit, the EU in December 2008 responded with a climate and energy policy that set 20-20-20 targets: by 2020 EU members would cut greenhouse gases by a minimum of 20 percent of 1990 levels (going up to 30 percent if followed by other developed countries), increase their use of renewables from the current 8.5 percent to approximately 20 percent, and cut energy consumption by 20 percent as levels forecasted for 2020. The EU's Emissions Trading System (ETS) grants emission allowances to power plants and energy-intensive industries (and the aviation industry starting with 2012) with the goal of reducing emissions to 21 percent below 2005 levels by 2020. Renewables were also introduced with binding national targets, with Sweden coming up with 49 percent by 2020.

The major developing countries responded, in partnership under the MEM, with just enough commitments to put the new G8-pioneered architecture firmly in place. They said they would 'continue to improve our policies and our performance' (MEM 2008). They pledged to control their own carbon emissions and pursue 'nationally appropriate mitigation actions to achieving a deviation from business as usual emissions'. They supported a 'shared vision for long-term cooperative action' with a 'global goal for emissions reductions'. They affirmed that 'deep cuts in global emissions' would be necessary and urged 'serious consideration' of 'ambitious' scenarios proposed by the Intergovernmental Panel on Climate Change. They thus made a politically binding commitment to control their own greenhouse gas emissions, just as the G8 had asked.

To give life to these commitments, the developing economies through the MEM declaration promised several actions that were highly compatible with the G8's plan in the short and medium terms. For the short term up to 2012, they endorsed the sectoral approach and, through it, promised to 'improve significantly energy efficiency.' For the medium term they emphasized how sinks could help stabilize greenhouse gases in the atmosphere and identified deforestation, forest degradation, forest fires, forest governance, and land use change as factors.

Most broadly the MEM endorsed an approach that was compatible with that of the G8. There was a convergence on the basic principles in both. There were only three major differences: the MEM's emphasis on the UN process; differences on financing, technology transfer, and capacity building; and the MEM's refusal to include reductions of at least 50 percent by 2050 as the long-term goal for themselves.

Amidst this major movement the MEM missed some opportunities to control climate change. First, only small steps were taken to endorse nuclear energy as a critical zero-emission source. Second, no effort was made to end the use of carbon-saturated coal, beyond the endorsement of the experimental, unproven technology of CCS. Third, no specific measures were taken to stimulate renewables such as wind, solar, geothermal, and hydro, although second-generation biofuels got a verbal boost. Fourth, energy conservation and the need to reduce energy consumption received only a passing nod. Fifth, there was no direct affirmation of the 1997 commitment to reduce greenhouse gases by 2010, nor any movement on that commitment.

Criticism came from some that G8 leaders were making their 50-2050 commitment using different years as the base, rather than using the Europeans' Kyoto favourite of 1990. This criticism had little merit. There was no scientific rationale for selecting 1990. The increase in emissions between 1990 and 2008 was much smaller than the business-as-usual increase in the 42 years from 2008 to 2050. In Japan's case, the promise of 'at least 50 per cent' meant a reduction of between 60 percent and 80 percent, with the additional cut more than compensating for the period between 1990 and 2008. A change to a 1990 base thus would mean that Germany, for example, would do less. And there was never any chance that the US or G5 would accept 1990 as the new base for themselves.

Toyako's relatively successful performance, especially on climate change, flowed from several forces. The first was the shock from oil prices reaching historic highs, from cyclones and floods showing the costs of uncontrolled climate change, and from bank collapses hurting G8 citizens already suffering from soaring food and gas prices, falling home and stock prices, contracting credit and confidence, and slowing wages and jobs. A second force was the internally equalizing and globally predominant capability among G8 members, thanks to an economically slowing US with its dropping dollar, a rising Japan and Russia, and an expanding EU and strengthening euro. A third force was the common commitment of the G8 countries and all their 16 invited participating countries – apart from China – to the G8's core values of open democracy, individual liberty, and social advance, as applied to energy security, African development, Zimbabwe, Afghanistan, Myanmar, the Middle East, North Korea, and Iran.

However, several substantial obstacles stood in the way of a big breakthrough codified in quantitative targets and timetables on climate change. There were no severe shocks to security, energy supply, national financial systems, or health to show the G8 leaders and their citizens the immediate vulnerability of their countries to global threats from outside and to propel them into the high performance of past summits such as Japan's first in 1979. Moreover, the UN system had already made promising efforts to respond to clean technology investment, the global food crisis and nuclear proliferation in Iran, if not to human security in Zimbabwe, Myanmar, and Sudan. The UN also offered an alluring Kyoto protocol precedent as an alternative process and a 2009 deadline at Copenhagen to tempt some G8 and G5 powers to delay acting on climate change at Toyako in the self-interested hope of getting themselves a better deal later on. The leaders of many of the most powerful G8 members, including host Japan, did not firmly control their parties or legislatures at home, were deeply unpopular with their voters, and would not be in office long enough to deliver the promises they made. There was a particularly strong temptation to delay doing any big deal on climate change, health, development, and trade until 2009, when a new American president and Congress would fulfil the hope that they would deliver on the G8 and G5 partners' most audacious demands. However, even with the arrival of the new administration and the Copenhagen conference demonstrating dubious results, climate change continued to be an unresolved issue.

There were no real breakthroughs the following year at the G8's L'Aquila Summit, although 2009 was considered to be particularly important due to the Copenhagen conference on climate change a few months later. The G8 followed the practice of the previous year, when the issue of climate change was taken up within the broader Major Economies Forum (MEF), as it was now known under the new Obama administration. The countries agreed to 'undertake transparent nationally appropriate mitigation actions, subject to applicable measurement, reporting, and verification, and prepare low-carbon growth plans' (MEF 2009). They pledged to work towards the goal of keeping the rate of growth of the global average temperature below the preindustrial level of two degrees Celsius. They also agreed to introduce such cuts before 2050, but they never agreed on specific targets.

Of particular note was the decision to establish a 'Global Partnership to drive transformational low-carbon, climate-friendly technologies' (MEF 2009). The MEF also agreed to public sector investments in research, development and the demonstration of these technologies by 2015, 'while recognizing the importance of private investment, public-private partnerships and international cooperation, including regional innovation centers', including international funding arrangements such as the Green Fund proposed by Mexico. Nonetheless, the Copenhagen meeting was a disappointment for most observers, with no legally binding document on post-Kyoto targets.[9]

At the G8 summits in Canada in 2010 and France in 2011, the levels of attention and action on both energy and climate declined. This was in part due to the focus of those summits – on maternal, newborn, and child health at Muskoka in 2010 and on the changes in North Africa and the Middle East including the war in Libya

---

9   There were, however, a few positive results, such as $100 billion by 2020 pledged for developing countries to cut emissions and adapt to climate change, with $30 billion for investments and the fight against deforestation by 2012. The level for carbon dioxide emissions cuts to be implemented by 2020 was identified. Also each country was required to provide information at the national level on the implementation of its plans, with possible international level consultations.

at Deauville in 2011. Moreover, the 2009 Copenhagen conference had failed, the MEF had disappeared from the G8 summit process, and the G20 summit had become institutionalized with an agenda that included climate change – although issue of nuclear safety was raised at Deauville, after the March 2011 Fukushima disaster in Japan. Thus the G8 agreed with the EU initiative to conduct stress tests on nuclear power plants as part of an international safety standards review. The EU started stress testing in June 2011 for all 143 nuclear power plants on EU territory.

The Causes of G8 Energy-Climate Performance

In all, the G8 has proven to be an effective, expanding governor of energy, climate, and their connection in several ways. Ideationally, the G8's seminal 1979 consensus on stabilizing carbon concentrations through energy conservation, efficiency, alternatives, nuclear power, investment, and technological innovation was restored and reinforced in 2005–06 by a new consensus on the centrality, urgency, and comprehensive nature of the connection between energy and climate itself. In initiatives and their implementation, the Bush-Blair breakthroughs of 1990 and 2005 have been central in producing this new consensus and converting it into ambitious commitments and high compliance to put it into effect. Institutionally, the G8 combined energy and climate actors in new G8-centred bodies, most vigorously in 1979–80, and again from 2003 to 2005. Inclusively, the G8 at the summit and ministerial levels increasingly involved the other consequential energy and carbon-producing and carbon-consuming countries, in a balanced G8-guided way.

The G8's generally strong performance in the interconnected energy-climate domain is driven by the key causes highlighted by the concert equality model of G8 governance and by a few beyond.

The first is shock-activated vulnerability in the energy domain, as reflected in and measured by high world oil prices. The energy shocks of the 1970s and 2004–06 showed G8 powers, led by the most capable oil-short members of the US, Japan, and Germany, that they must move away from carbon-creating oil use, towards cleaner fuels. Energy shocks also equalized capability within the G8, among those three great powers and the small but energy-rich powers of Britain and especially Canada and Russia, thus providing a basis for balanced deals to be made. Here it is important that energy-rich Canada and Russia were Kyoto members, even though the US was not. Shock-activated vulnerability from terrorism generated high G8 performance on energy but not on the energy-climate connection itself. That connection was forged at the 2005 Gleneagles Summit, when the United States adjusted its position in the days before the July 7 terrorist attack in London, but not at the 2002 Kananaskis Summit – the first after the September 11 terrorist attacks in the United States.

The second cause is the failure or even absence of other multilateral institutions and organizations governing global energy. The International Atomic Energy

Agency, World Bank (which deals with energy poverty), and the IEA, much like the Organisation for Economic Co-operation and Development (OECD), functioned largely as G7 secretariats or platforms (with Russia still excluded) rather than as global governance forums on their own. Nor did the multilateral system contain any established body to deal with the fast emerging issues on renewable, alternative and efficient energy sources. No new or extended institutions or action of any consequence came even when oil prices doubled to historic highs within a year.

The multilateral architecture on climate change also remained fragile and fragmented. The United Nations Commission on Sustainable Development, the United Nations Environment Programme, the World Meteorological Organization, the secretariat of the United Nations Framework Convention on Climate Change (UNFCCC), and the secretariat of the Convention on Biological Diversity (CBD) showed few signs of growing coherence or capability. The UNFCCC continued to focus on emissions sources, with little coordination with the CBD, with its expertise in sinks. The UNFCCC's Bali conference in December 2007 added nothing essential to the HDP's long- or medium-term targets to help define a fast-approaching post-Kyoto regime. Its belated recognition of the role of avoided deforestation did not propel it to include sinks, which the G7 had recognized as equally important at the summit hosted by George H. Bush in Houston, Texas, in 1990.[10] Nor did the UN's two follow-up meetings in 2008 advance the likelihood of agreement at the climate change conferences in Poland at the end of 2008 or Copenhagen at the end of 2009. They and the energetic, G8-centric new plurilateral institutions – the American-pioneered MEM/MEF of 16 countries, the Asia Pacific Partnership of seven countries (with the subsequent addition of Canada), the ministerial Gleneagles Dialogue and the HDP's energy efficiency group – needed the G8 summit if their work was to culminate in the intended way.

A third cause is iteration, both in the summit agenda and in the institutionalization that gives greater continuity and depth (Bayne 1999). By 1979 when it first mentioned carbon dioxide, the G7/G8 had a history and an official-level mechanism for dealing with energy in a de facto carbon-constraining way. Similarly, George W. Bush's energy-climate institutionalization in 2004 provided a basis on which Tony Blair could build in 2005. The latter in turn provided the intellectual foundation on which the G8 acted, in its commitments at Gleneagles in 2005 and St Petersburg in 2006. Yet the record from 1980 to 1981 and afterwards shows that iteration and institutionalization alone are not enough to make a difference when energy prices and economic growth plunge as they did in 1981 and the years immediately following.

A fourth cause is the agency of individuals, especially from an experienced, skilled and committed G8 leader who serves as the summit's host. Among the two-

---

10   As measured by deforestation, among the greatest contributors to greenhouse gas emissions were Brazil and Indonesia, rather than China and Japan. There was thus a strong logic in having the G5 and the additional three Asian countries at the summit to deal with climate change.

time summit hosts, Tony Blair did nothing on energy or climate at Birmingham in 1998, amidst the competing call of the Asian-turned-global financial crisis and world oil prices dropping to $11 per barrel. But he did at Gleneagles 2005, just as Britain was turning into a vulnerable net importer of oil and gas, and just as science was showing that global warning and rising sea levels could be destructive for small island states around the world. In sharp contrast, Jean Chrétien, the Canadian prime minister who had previously served as energy minister – but never environment minister – of his hydrocarbon-rich country hosted the G8 in both 1995 and 2002, when world oil prices were low and financial and terrorist shocks were high. He was thus not forced to learn to connect energy and climate and put his summit to work in this way. It remains a question for further research how much George W. Bush at Sea Island 2004 learned from his father George H. Bush as host of Houston in 1990. What is nonetheless clear is that leaders can craft their commitments at a summit in ways that enhance the chances they will be complied with, and that their premises forged and promises made will thus be turned into promises kept (Kirton 2006).

Conclusion

G7/G8 governance, supported by other international institutions such as the IEA, contributed greatly to countering the energy shocks generated by military, political, and structural threats. The policy of the leading industrial countries led to overall stabilization. Countries effectively implemented high energy-saving policies and technologies that allowed for the rapid economic development (or recovery). Changing the world energy balance helped achieve economic growth and foster environmentally sustainable development (with the gradual move to clean and alternative energy sources). Actions taken to diversify energy supply and demand and to create and increase oil reserves substantially reduced the risk of repeated energy shocks.

The basic priorities of future G8 strategy focus on adopting measures to stabilize the world energy market, create new infrastructure capacities, render assistance to the poorest countries (energy producers as well as consumers), set rapid reaction systems to respond to international energy security threats, neutralize the negative environmental implications of energy development and identify new energy technologies, including alternative energy sources.

The G8 now primarily seeks the stabilization of the world energy market, with priority given to price volatility. The threat of a supply shock is less dangerous than it was in the 1970s. Yet the interdependence of all global actors and all components of the global architecture, combined with finance and economic problems leads to instability in the energy domain. Thus the G8 and the EU are the appropriate bodies to address the combined challenge.

Major systemically important countries have the primary responsibility to increase the predictability of the world energy market, promote transparency, take preventive measures on infrastructure development, and coordinate exporting and importing countries' interests, taking into account their current and prospective place in the world economy.

Apart from the military protection of unstable oil-exporting regions, there are more aspects of international energy security: protection against short-term shocks such as the G8's support, in line with other international organizations (such as the IEA or the EU), of increasing strategic oil reserves and of the possibility to redirect funds from exploration to efficiency.

The problem with the first aspect lies in the reality that developing countries usually do not possess such reserves. Among the fastest growing economies are the emerging countries, which could suffer in the case of a short-term shock (hence the possibility for assistance from the G8 and OECD). With the second aspect, there are possibilities for G8 action in considering ways to improve legislation for international investments into the energy sector, since many oil-rich regions suffer from bad governance, which hinders foreign investment flows. That is why it is essential to maintain at a minimum a dialogue for solving the most urgent energy security issues in close cooperation with one another.

References

Bayne, Nicholas (1999). 'Continuity and Leadership in an Age of Globalisation.' In *The G8's Role in the New Millennium*, edited by Michael R. Hodges, John J. Kirton and Joseph P. Daniels, pp. 21–44. Aldershot: Ashgate.

Dobson, Hugo (2004). *Japan and the G7/8, 1975–2002*. London: RoutledgeCurzon.

G7 (1991). 'Economic Declaration: Building a World Partnership.' London, 17 July. <www.g8.utoronto.ca/summit/1991london/communique> (July 2011).

G7 (2000). 'G7 Statement.' Okinawa, 21 July. <www.g8.utoronto.ca/summit/2000okinawa/statement.htm> (July 2011).

G7 (2001). 'G7 Statement.' Genoa, 20 July. <www.g8.utoronto.ca/g7/summit/2001genoa/g7statement.html> (July 2011).

G8 (2006). 'Global Energy Security.' St Petersburg, 16 July. <www.g8.utoronto.ca/summit/2006stpetersburg/energy.html> (July 2011).

G8 (2007). 'Growth and Responsibility in the World Economy.' Heiligendamm, 7 June. <www.g8.utoronto.ca/summit/2007heiligendamm/g8-2007-economy.html> (July 2011).

G8 (2008a). 'Chair's Summary.' Hokkaido, 8 July. <www.g8.utoronto.ca/summit/2008hokkaido/2008-summary.html> (July 2011).

G8 (2008b). 'Environment and Climate Change.' Hokkaido, 8 July. <www.g8.utoronto.ca/summit/2008hokkaido/2008-climate.html> (July 2011).

G8 (2008c). 'World Economy.' Hokkaido, 8 July. <www.g8.utoronto.ca/summit/2008hokkaido/2008-economy.html> (July 2011).

Kirton, John J. (2006). 'Explaining Compliance with G8 Finance Commitments: Agency, Institutionalization, and Structure.' *Open Economies Review* 17(4): 459–75.

Kirton, John J. (2008). 'A Summit of Substantial Success: The Performance of the 2008 G8.' 17 August, G8 Research Group, Toronto. <www.g8.utoronto.ca/scholar/kirton-performance-080817.pdf> (July 2011).

Major Economies Forum (2009). 'Declaration of the Leaders: The Major Economies Forum on Energy and Climate.' L'Aquila, Japan, 9 July. <www.g8.utoronto.ca/summit/2009laquila/2009-mef.html> (July 2011).

Major Economies Meeting (2008). 'Declaration of Leaders Meeting of Major Economies on Energy Security and Climate Change.' Hokkaido, Japan, 9 July. <www.g8.utoronto.ca/summit/2008hokkaido/2008-mem.html> (July 2011).

Appendix 9.1   G8 Conclusions on Energy, 1975–2011

Year	# of words	% of total words	# of paragraphs	% of total paragraphs	# of documents	% of total documents	# of dedicated documents
1975	193	17	4	26.6	1	100	0
1976	30	1.8	1	4	1	100	0
1977	614	23	13	33.3	1	50	0
1978	643	21.4	14	28.5	1	100	0
1979	1309	62.2	26	76.4	1	50	0
1980	1742	43.5	24	40	1	20	0
1981	466	14.7	11	21.1	1	33.3	0
1982	163	9	2	10	1	50	0
1983	186	8.6	4	10.8	2	100	0
1984	156	4.7	2	4.0	1	20	0
1985	0	0	0	0	0	0	0
1986	521	14.5	7	21.8	2	50	1
1987	59	1.1	2	2.7	2	28.5	0
1988	0	0	0	0	0	0	0
1989	295	4.1	6	5	1	9	0
1990	334	4.3	4	3.2	1	25	0
1991	702	8.6	12	21.4	1	20	0
1992	496	6.5	9	5.3	1	25	0
1993	186	5.4	2	4.7	1	33.3	0
1994	325	7.8	8	11.7	1	50	0
1995	242	3.3	3	2.2	1	33.3	0
1996	411	2.6	4	1.7	2	50	0
1997	365	2.8	5	3.5	1	20	0
1998	356	5.8	5	7.8	1	25	0
1999	641	6.3	6	6.9	1	33.3	0
2000	444	3.2	7	4.8	2	40	0
2001	272	4.3	3	4.1	1	14.2	0
2002	43	0.35	1	0.68	1	12.5	0
2003	209	1.2	4	2.3	1	7.6	0
2004	68	0.17	1	0.29	1	4.7	0
2005	567	2.5	9	4.2	2	10	1
2006	5984	19.4	74	30.2	3	17.6	1
2007	1563	6.0	12	4.3	4	33.3	0
2008	2104	12.4	22	12.6	1	9	0
2009	6333	38.2	57	17.3	8	61.5	1
2010	787	11	4	7.5	1	50	0
2011	1701	11.2	20	10.8	2	66.6	0
Average	824.59	10.49	10.49	12.21	1.46	35.73	0.11

Notes to Appendix 9.1: Data are drawn from all official English-language documents released by the G8 leaders as a group. Charts are excluded.

'# of words' is the number of energy-related subjects for the year specified, excluding document titles and references. Words are calculated by paragraph because the paragraph is the unit of analysis.

'% of total words' refers to the total number of words in all documents for the year specified.

'# of paragraphs' is the number of paragraphs containing references to energy for the year specified. Each point is recorded as a separate paragraph.

'% of total paragraphs' refers to the total number of paragraphs in all documents for the year specified.

'# of documents' is the number of documents that contain energy-related subjects and excludes dedicated documents.

'% of total documents' refers to the total number of documents for the year specified.

'# of dedicated documents' is the number of documents for the year that contain an energy-related subject in the title.

Appendix 9.2   G8 Conclusions on Climate Change, 1975–2011

Year	# of words	% of total words	# of paragraphs	% of total paragraphs	# of documents	% of total documents	# of dedicated documents
1975	0	0	0	0	0	0	0
1976	0	0	0	0	0	0	0
1977	0	0	0	0	0	0	0
1978	0	0	0	0	0	0	0
1979	28	1.3	1	2.6	1	50	0
1980	0	0	0	0	0	0	0
1981	0	0	0	0	0	0	0
1982	0	0	0	0	0	0	0
1983	0	0	0	0	0	0	0
1984	0	0	0	0	0	0	0
1985	88	2.9	1	1.9	1	50	0
1986	0	0	0	0	0	0	0
1987	85	1.5	1	1.1	1	14.3	0
1988	140	2.7	1	1.2	1	33.3	0
1989	422	6	7	5	1	9.1	0
1990	491	5.9	5	3.6	1	33.3	0
1991	236	2.4	5	2.8	1	20	0
1992	137	1.8	4	2.5	1	25	0
1993	154	3.1	1	1.2	1	33.3	0
1994	107	2.6	2	2.1	1	50	0
1995	87	0.7	3	1.1	1	25	0
1996	167	0.8	3	1.4	1	14.3	0
1997	305	1.6	5	1.7	1	16.7	0
1998	323	5.3	4	4.1	1	25	0
1999	198	1.3	1	0.3	1	25	0
2000	213	1.6	2	0.5	1	20	0
2001	324	5.2	4	4.4	1	10	0
2002	53	0.2	1	0.7	1	14.3	0
2003	62	0.3	3	2.3	1	5.9	0
2004	98	0.3	2	0.5	1	5	0
2005	2667	9.3	68	9.9	3	8.1	2
2006	1533	3.1	26	2.6	3	12	0
2007	4154	12.0	47	9.0	5	41.7	0
2008	2568	17.5	21	14.2	3	60	0
2009	5559	33.3	52	15.8	7	53.8	0
2010	1282	12	7	7.1	1	33.3	0
2011	1086	7.2	12	6.5	1	33.3	0
Average	609.92	3.84	7.81	2.87	1.16	19.51	0.05

Notes to Appendix 9.2: Data are drawn from all official English-language documents released by the G8 leaders as a group. Charts are excluded.

'# of words' is the number of climate change-related subjects for the year specified, excluding document titles and references. Words are calculated by paragraph because the paragraph is the unit of analysis.

'% of total words' refers to the total number of words in all documents for the year specified.

'# of paragraphs' is the number of paragraphs containing references to climate change for the year specified. Each point is recorded as a separate paragraph.

'% of total paragraphs' refers to the total number of paragraphs in all documents for the year specified.

'# of documents' is the number of documents that contain climate change subjects and excludes dedicated documents.

'% of total documents' refers to the total number of documents for the year specified.

'# of dedicated documents' is the number of documents for the year that contain a climate change-related subject in the title.

Chapter 10

G8 and G20 Financial Crisis Governance: The European Union Contribution

John J. Kirton

Over the years, the G7/G8 has had extensive and even existential experience with financial crises (see Appendix 10-1). The group's creation at Rambouillet, France, in November 1975 was driven by financial crises created in the United States, in the form of the Nixon administration's unilateral destruction of the Bretton Woods system of fixed exchange rates on 15 August 1971 and the imminent bankruptcy of New York City.[1] Then came a succession of real and potential crises, notably the need for support from the International Monetary Fund (IMF) by Britain in the mid-1970s and by Italy in 1976, the developing countries' debt crisis of the early 1980s, the American stock market plunge of October 1987, the subsequent attack on the European monetary system, the Mexican peso crisis starting on 20 December 1994, the Asian-turned-global financial crisis of 1997–99, the 9/11 terrorist attacks on America, the dot-com bust of the early 2000s, and, since 2008, the American-turned-global financial crisis. Since 1975, such crises have been both created by others to afflict a vulnerable America and created in America to affect the rest of the world. Some have been conscious, calculated, controlled, and targeted, as on 15 August 1971 and 11 September 2001. Yet some have been unconscious, uncalculated, uncontrolled, and untargeted events characterized by contagion, complexity, and uncertainty that no one can fully comprehend, as in the global crisis from 2008 until now.

The key tests of the European Union and contribution to G8 and G20 global financial governance, in an era of intense globalization, the financial crises that erupted in 1997 and 2008. The international financial crisis that began in Thailand on 2 July 1997 and soon spread to the global economy outside Asia, was one of the defining international events of the second half of the 20th century. In the judgement of US President Bill Clinton and others, it was the world's worst financial crisis in 50 years. It destroyed the Asian export-led growth miracle of the post-World War II period that had long been presumed to be permanent. It assaulted the liberal economic ideology of growth through open trade and financial markets – the globalization consensus – that lay behind that miracle. It blunted the hope of

---

1   The G7, which consists of Canada, France, Germany, Italy, Japan, the United Kingdom, the United States and the European Union, began meeting annually in 1975. Since 1998, Russia has been included at the leaders' level, forming the G8.

many other emerging market economies in Latin America and elsewhere, which had joined Asia in the 1990s, that this was the proper path. It threatened to reverse a decade of hard-won progress towards the historic G7-guided accomplishment of the post-Cold War era – the peaceful transformation of Russia into a democratic, market-oriented country, fully integrated as a ranking member of the international economy and its governing institutions. Above all, with its unprecedented speed, spread, severity, and systemic impact, the 1997–99 financial crisis suggested that in the newly globalized world economy, national governments and their classic intergovernmental organizations, led by the IMF, were no longer in control.

Almost a decade later, another financial crisis erupted, this time beginning in America and going first to transatlantic Europe before going global. The sub-prime mortgage-generated credit crunch that erupted on 'Main Street', side streets and then Wall Street in the summer of 2007 grew rapidly to become a devastating global challenge by 2008. It brought the death of American investment bank Bear Stearns, and then the run on and rescue of Britain's Northern Rock Bank, the first in that country in more than 100 years. By January 2008 it featured a rogue trader who cost Société Générale, France's second largest bank, $7.3 billion, in a move reminiscent of Nick Leeson's bankruptcy of Britain's Barings Bank in 1995. But, above all, this crisis featured a general lack of transparency and trust in global credit markets – a crisis of confidence that rapidly spread through a globalized world.

A close examination of the G7/8's response to the 1997–98 and 2007–08 global financial crises sustains the case for effective, concert-based G8 governance, with the EU playing an increasing but still largely regional role. G7/G8 effectiveness came not in proactive or prescient preventative measures, inspired by the precursor Mexico crisis in 1994–95, the subsequent Barings Bank collapse, or the achievements of the G7's Halifax Summit in 1995, or even through incremental iteration (Bayne 1999). Rather, it came reactively, through flexible innovation on a just-in-time cadence of common aversion and disaster avoidance. At the height of the global phase of the crisis G7 governments, through their established institutions and new mechanisms at the official, ministerial and ultimately leaders' level, acted collectively to contain the burgeoning disaster, by stopping a rapid contagion and restoring confidence to markets gripped by proliferating panic. In short, the G7 successfully managed markets that had gone mad, hegemons that were themselves infected, multilateral organizations immobilized by legalized charters and procedures, and less powerful regional governments gripped by fear. The G7 did so with its globally predominant, equally shared financial capability, in response to the new globalized vulnerability of even the most powerful national economy, as successive shocks froze America's markets and domestic politics and overwhelmed its available resources. In such a situation, the shared sense of systemic responsibility, the common desire to defend and extend democracy, and the flexibility of a small, informal institution allowed the G7 to act effectively in America's stead.

These accomplishments were the results not of a hegemonic America using the G7 as a convenient legitimizing or burden-sharing tool, or of an America acting with support from a strong Japan or Germany or even its Anglo-American associate and former hegemon Britain. Rather, it was the result of concerted collaboration in which all members – even the weakest – played influential leadership roles, on the intellectual, policy, and structural levels. The ability of all members of the small group to act quickly to deploy the overwhelming resources required to calm markets, their use of the crisis to further internationally the democratic and social market principles they shared, and the ultimate role of elected ministers and leaders in generating innovative responses were all key to the G7's success.

In this G7/G8 governance, and subsequently in its expanded form especially at the G20 summit level since November 2008, the EU was a relatively minor player, as diplomacy and alignments among G8 members were dominated by fluid trans-regional coalitions rather than self-contained regional blocs. The EU's contribution, while growing, remained much more limited than its economic diplomacy in other fields, such as trade (Woolcock 2011). In the Mexican crisis and the Asian-turned-global crisis, the EU – led by unelected presidents of the European Commission or the chair of the European Council, which changed every six months – behaved predominantly as a regional governor wedded to hard law organizations and their procedures. The EU saw Mexico as America's or, at best, North America's problem. The EU and its European members considered the 1997 crisis to be Asia's problem, and subsequently one where a response had to respect the slow-moving legal formalities and procedures of the IMF, dominated by the EU's major members. Only with the American-turned-transatlantic and global crisis of 2008 and the advent of G8-led G20 summit-level governance has the EU increased its involvement and impact as a regional institution and begun, as a global actor, to play a more active role in providing global public goods. Even so, in the field of finance the essential character of the EU as a regional intergovernmental organization remains intense.

The Asian-Turned-Global Financial Crisis, 1997–99

The world and the G7 had a taste of how financial crises of the old and new varieties could erupt in an era of globalization in 1994–95 when Mexico suffered an old-style crisis of balance of payments and when speculative excesses by a rogue trader led to the collapse of Barings Bank (Kirton 1995; Daniels 1999; Wood 2005, 63–64).

The first crisis was ignited by the collapse of the newly floating Mexican peso, which began on 20 December 1994. The US responded unilaterally with financial assistance to support its new neighbour in the North American Free Trade Agreement (NAFTA). IMF procedures and politics prevented it from acting sufficiently swiftly. The IMF's high-ranking, over-represented European members, preoccupied with the plight of neighbouring Russia rather than with far-off Mexico – their new partner in the Organisation for Economic Co-operation and Development (OECD) – were reluctant to contribute to what they considered a distant, regional all-American concern. Among the G7 members, only NAFTA's Canada joined the US in providing timely and robust support. Mexico's new partners in the OECD and the Asia Pacific Economic Cooperation (APEC) forum stood idly by. The EU was not involved as an actor, but as a regional institution that helped keep its G8 members looking inward to focus on regional preoccupations, above all on a democratizing and reforming Russia, rather than assuming their responsibilities to provide global public goods half a world away.

Within weeks of the G7's Denver Summit in June 1997, another crisis erupted, although its dimensions were not recognized for some time. When distant, diminutive, if democratic, Thailand precipitated the crisis by devaluing its currency on 2 July 1997, there was little sense of a systemic threat. European G7 members saw the issue as a regional Asian responsibility. The US was equally prepared to leave the problem to the Asians. By August 1997, when a $17 billion support package for Thailand had been assembled, neighbouring Japan – the regional hegemon with extensive economic interests in the country – was the only G7 member to contribute national funds. By September 1997, when G7 finance ministers met in Hong Kong at the time of the semi-annual IMF meeting, they did agree to a 45 percent increase in core resources for the IMF, to strengthen its involvement in financial sector reform, improve national governance by reducing corruption, and expand the allocation of special drawing rights (SDRs). However, they still believed that further financial liberalization was wise. Despite Canada's objection, they agreed to amend the IMF Articles of Agreement within the year to make the IMF formally responsible for sweeping capital account liberalization.

In the autumn, the crisis and G7 involvement spread to still distant, but large and dictatorial, Indonesia, the world's fourth most populous country. When a support package for a beleaguered Indonesia was assembled, Japan was now joined by the US as a contributor to a hastily assembled new 'second line of defence' of national funds, to be deployed if those of the IMF and other international financial institutions (IFIs) proved insufficient. In November, the G7 formalized this arrangement and moved to ensure that all members had the legislative authority to contribute to it.

By December, this Asian financial 'flu' had spread to the more proximate, large, democratic and new OECD partner of South Korea. This time all G7 members acted together from the start. In early December, they agreed on a support package for Korea of $35 billion from the IFIs, to be reinforced, if necessary, by a second line of defence. To this second line, Japan pledged $10 billion, the US pledged US$5 billion, each European G7 member pledged $1.25 billion, and Canada pledged $1 billion. Shortly, after the Korean won plummeted in the face of a speculative market attack, G7 members agreed to activate the second line in return for an agreement from their private banks, pushed by the US and others, to roll over and reschedule their Korean loans. This private sector burden-sharing agreement was particularly valuable in light of the difficulty the US government was having in securing congressional authorization for its share of the IMF quota increase. Robert Rubin, US treasury secretary, had hoped that the mere existence of a large package with a second line would reassure markets, but now agreed with his G7 partners that it should be used. The 24 December announcement that national funds would indeed flow proved sufficient to stem the market's assault on the won. No national funds actually had to be expended in exchange markets, as the clarity and credibility of the G7's commitment was sufficient to deter market players from further attacks (Kirton 2002). G7 governments acting together had beaten panicking markets in this new globalized game of financial deterrence.

This G7 action immediately lessened the pressure not just on Korea but on the surrounding Asian economies as well. However, Suharto's dictatorial Indonesia resisted IMF prescriptions and suffered further attacks. As its situation deteriorated, the US intervened, reinforced by Germany and supported by the other G7 members. On 15 January 1998, the IMF and Indonesia negotiated a letter of intent according to which Indonesia accepted revised economic targets and more far-reaching structural reforms. The full G7 had now joined in to save Indonesia, and in the process to reform it in the economic and political domain.

By April 1998, it became clear that Indonesia and now Korea would be unable to meet their pledges, made in the summer of 1997, to the support package for a still struggling Thailand. Canada, the only country from outside Asia to contribute, assumed Indonesia's share of $500 million. The American administration – the obvious trans-Pacific donor – was deterred neither by fear of globalized markets nor by a domestic political 'lesson of the past' (Putnam and Bayne 1987; Bergsten and Henning 1996). Rather, it was concerned about congressional criticism of a 'bail-out' and any use of its Treasury's Exchange Stabilization Fund (as in the Mexican rescue package of 1994–95). It refused to contribute. By giving when the US could not, Canada became part of the 'first line of defence'. Its disbursements, which started to flow in June, ultimately totalled $300 million.

The Asian phase of the crisis was thus contained, just in time, through concerted G7 action. In a clear display of their power over markets, G7 governments often prevailed, at times without actually expending national funds. Instead, they induced the IFIs, banks, and other private sector actors to provide the required liquidity. Moreover, in mobilizing these additional funds, a congressionally constrained United States followed the policy leadership of its G7 colleagues, often having to rely on the structural leadership that these partners, from second-ranked Asian Japan through sixth-ranked European Britain to seventh-ranked North American Canada, made available in the form of new national funds. In such a situation, intellectual leadership also flowed freely and effectively from the G7's lesser members. Britain and Canada, on opposite sides, drove the debate over capital account liberalization, and Canada, with relatively few Asian investors of its own to protect, pushed with some success for significant private sector participation. The EU as an actor had no role.

With the acute phase of the Asian crisis over, G7 leaders and finance ministers turned their attention from crisis response to system reform at the Birmingham

Summit in May 1998. British prime minister Tony Blair as host focused on finance as one of the summit's three central themes (Kirton and Kokotsis 1997/98; Hodges, Kirton, and Daniels 1999; Bayne 2000). He also gave G7 leaders a full half-day immediately prior to the opening of the G8 to address finance and economic issues, rather than forcing them, as at Denver, to find a few minutes between G8 sessions to deal with the subjects that had historically been at the G7's core. Here, with the president of the European Commission present, they stressed the need for improved transparency, early warning and private sector burden sharing. Canada secured an endorsement for the concept behind its major initiative of establishing a mechanism for peer review of national banking and financial system supervisory authorities. Because France preferred to invest the supervisory function in the IMF under its Article 4 consultations, and Britain wanted to use a joint IMF-World Bank mechanism, the decision on how to implement the concept was left to the fall meetings of the G7 finance ministers, the IMF, and the World Bank.

The second phase of the crisis came in the summer and autumn of 1998, when the financial crisis went global and arrived next door to the EU. Following further disquieting events in Asia, on 17 August, Russia unilaterally devalued its currency and rescheduled its debt, only three weeks after receiving yet another large IMF support package that produced the funds from the General Arrangements to Borrow (GAB) for the first time in two decades. Although no one within the G7 had been enthusiastic about the prospects for the July package, the speed of Russia's collapse and the shock of its default and devaluation brought home the message that no country, even a member of the G8, was too big to fail. It was soon apparent that the IMF, which still lacked the agreed-upon increase in quota share as a result of American political stalemate, might not have sufficient funds to cope with crises of this scale. However, with the crisis arising in the greater European region, the G7 looked to Germany to take the lead. This time Germany applied its longstanding policy of 'help for self-help' to conclude that Russia was unwilling or unable to help itself. It thus decided to let Russia go down. Its G7 colleagues followed suit.

The contagion, driven by plummeting commodity prices, soon spread to the emerging economies of the Americas, as interest rate spreads ballooned in all emerging markets. Brazil, which had a large fiscal deficit financed at floating interest rates, was hit particularly hard. As its interest rates soared, capital started to flee the country at the rate of up to $1 billion a day. In early September, Colombia devalued its currency. Moody's downgraded Brazil's foreign currency bonds. Stock markets in the US, Canada, Mexico, and the rest of the Americas continued the sharp fall begun in mid summer.

By late August, the US itself came under attack. As even healthy companies in the US found it difficult to borrow money at reasonable rates, fears of an international credit crunch arose. The crisis peaked in mid-September with the de facto collapse of Long-Term Capital Management (LTCM), an American hedge fund, and its rescue by major American financial institutions under the guidance of the Federal Reserve. Although the rescue was reassuring, the fear that similar hedge funds might be on the verge of collapse compounded the move towards freezing credit markets in the United States. Congress continued to refuse to authorize the US share of the IMF quota increase. Consequently, the world was deprived of its traditional reliable lender of last resort. Indeed, the hitherto vibrant American economy itself appeared on the verge of being engulfed by the cascading crisis.

Throughout, Canada – along with the United States, Britain, France, and others – led in the IMF and other forums by producing and pressing for detailed proposals on an expanding agenda for crisis response and systemic reform. In September, Clinton outlined a package that emphasized the desirability of interest rate cuts, a new IMF precautionary lending facility, and support for Brazil. Canadian finance minister Paul Martin, dissatisfied with the central thrust of the American plan and judging that markets needed a stronger signal that governments were in control, prepared his own package. This he unveiled at the Commonwealth Finance Ministers Meeting in Ottawa, just a few days before the 3 October meeting in Washington of G7 finance ministers and central bank governors.

That G7 finance meeting, held during what Clinton called the worst financial crisis in 50 years, concluded by signalling an easing of monetary policy to provide needed liquidity. Canada, the US, and Britain promised to maintain conditions for sustainable growth. Continental European members did not. The EU's four G8 members were once again divided, with the continental countries opposed by Britain across the channel.

The G7 finance ministers issued a communiqué that also supported IMF programmes and a proactive role for the G7, through the IMF, the new Group of 22 (G22), on architectural reform and a consensus on the core principles to guide it. Canada, along with Britain and the US, pushed successfully for an emphasis on transparency. On banking and financial system supervision, although the American and British approaches largely prevailed Canada made some progress in principle. An emphasis on private sector involvement as a way of avoiding moral hazard reflected one of Martin's concerns, although a German conviction dominated and no particular mechanism for private sector bail-in was endorsed. Canada's greatest gain was in the crisis-bred diminished enthusiasm for rapid capital account liberalization. The process for amending the IMF Articles of Agreement, initially slated for completion at the meeting, was extended another one to two years. The G8's North American members were divided over this, too.

Despite this momentum, the G7 failed to provide the badly needed immediate, coordinated macroeconomic response required to stem a still burgeoning crisis in Brazil and in credit and equity markets in the US and the rest of the developed world. In early October, the IMF cut its earlier estimate of world growth to a modest 2 percent. Some relief came when Congress passed the American IMF quota share increase on 14 October, and Japan's Diet passed its banking bill shortly thereafter. But the situation remained unstable.

With markets clearly not absorbing the G7 message from the finance ministerial, the British led a campaign to send a stronger collective signal, and to do so at the leaders' level. Blair, still in the chair of the G7 for 1998, called for a special G7 summit. He received enthusiastic support only from the French, who demanded that such a special summit involve a broader group of countries. Gordon Brown, the British Chancellor of the Exchequer, returned from Washington convinced of the need for a new G7 statement that reflected a deeper degree of consensus than had previously been revealed. Canada, the US, and Japan, were initially sceptical. But when US Congress finally approved the increased IMF quota share, Japan passed its banking legislation, Brazil approached the IMF for assistance, and the G7 agreed – through conference calls – on Clinton's proposed precautionary facility (through contingent credit lines conceived and secured by the US), Canada concluded that a statement that cast these new developments in a positive light would be useful.

Britain, as G7 host, drafted the statements along two tracks. The first was among G7 sherpas, with Blair communicating through his sherpa John Holmes to his fellow sherpas, who were, in turn, in touch with their leaders. The leaders were also in direct contact with one another by fax and phone. This process included calls from Clinton to Canada's Jean Chrétien, Tony Blair, and, on several occasions, Germany's new chancellor and incoming summit host Gerhard Schröder, whose government strongly opposed Clinton's call for a new IMF precautionary facility. The second track was among the G7 finance ministers, with Brown working through the finance deputies. At the last minute, the two statements composed on separate tracks were rendered compatible. Despite the rush, with conference calls until the last minute, the substance was genuinely a G7 product, and reflected most of Canada's and Britain's core concerns.

The two statements were released on 30 October, with the first from the G7 leaders and the second from their finance ministers and central bankers. Martin's call for restrictions on short-term capital outflows, in the form of the emergency standstill clause, now received some support from other G7 countries. However, the US where private sector investors would be most harmed by such a proposal, remained adamantly opposed. The statements included carefully crafted language that amounted to a tacit acceptance of the concept of capital controls. The leaders' statement spoke of the need to minimize the 'risk of disruption' for 'an orderly and progressive approach to capital account liberalization' and for 'measures to ensure the orderly and cooperative resolution of future crises, in particular mechanisms to involve the private sector' (G7 1998). G7 officials were directed to work out the mechanisms to give this principle effect over the next year. The finance statement also endorsed enhanced supervision through 'a process of peer review' (G7 Finance Ministers and Central Bank Governors 1998). The IMF – France's preferred forum – also agreed to devote more attention to the quality and capability of such supervision in its annual Article 4 review of members' economies.

The final element was the G7's support package for Brazil, still being negotiated as the 30 October statements were released. The package, unveiled on 13 November, contained several novel components. Brazil had voluntarily adopted a restraint package prior to the extension of G7 assistance. In addition to IMF and other IFI funds, it would use bilateral national contributions from all G7 members and other countries as part of a first line of defence. Of the $41.5 billion total, the IMF provided $18 billion, the International Bank for Reconstruction and Development (IBRD) $4.5 billion, the Inter-American Development Bank $4.5 billion, and bilateral contributions, funnelled through the Bank for International Settlements (BIS), totaled $14.5 billion. For the first time, newly available funds from the New Arrangements to Borrow (NAB) were used to support a non-NAB member. These funds were authorized by phone calls to the G7 finance ministers, whose countries provided more than 90 percent of the total. The $41.1 billion package exceeded the $25 billion initially envisaged or the market-rumoured $30 billion. Of the total, $37 billion would be made available during the first year. The size and early availability of the package, and the willingness of all G7 members to put their national funds on the front line, was sufficient to demonstrate resolve and deter markets from continued attack. Canada's contribution to the bilateral first line of the Brazilian package, determined at a late stage in the process, was a relatively modest $500 million, or a deliberate one-tenth the US contribution. All European G8 members contributed, but not through or with the EU.

A subsequent G7 debate arose about the speed of repaying the NAB. The US, wanting to show a still sceptical Congress that the IMF could function as a profit centre, preferred to rely as long as possible on the NAB, so as to reap its very high interest rates and delay a use of the IMF's regular quota increase. France agreed. Canada, along with Britain, Germany, and Japan, wanted to pay off the NAB and revert to the lower cost regular IMF quota as soon as possible. Cross-regional coalitions, rather than a unified European regional bloc, again prevailed.

The US delay in making its IMF quota share increase available in time for Brazil to use it stemmed in part from a provision of the congressional legislation. It allowed funds to flow only 15 days after the treasury secretary and chair of the Federal Reserve received assurances from the major shareholders of the IMF that they were pressing for several conditions as part of IMF programmes. To enable Robert Rubin, the treasury secretary, to act, the G7 agreed that their executive directors at the IMF would collectively ask the managing director to meet such conditions. This unprecedented collective G7 action, which publicly directed the IMF's managing director to act, proved effective. It indicated that the G7 collectively, and not the US unilaterally, was the source of effective leadership for the IMF.

A third stage came during the first half of 1999 as the G7 moved from responding to the crisis in Brazil in early 1999 to constructing a strengthened system at the Cologne Summit in June. Canada was able to work in close partnership with Germany and its 'red-green' coalition government to advance its longstanding positions.

The G7 finance meetings in Berlin on 20 February, in Washington on 26 April, and in Frankfurt on 11–12 June, and the G7 Summit in Cologne on 18–20 June, led to the creation of the Financial Stability Forum (FSF). This German-designed institution contained a mechanism for peer supervision of national financial systems that gave life to an early Canadian proposal – if in a different institutional forum. Moreover, the FSF's architecture reflected Britain's recommended financial regulation and supervision even more than Canada's. The FSF's first chair was Andrew Crockett, a British national who headed the BIS. Yet, in the lead-up to Cologne, significant differences remained on the core architectural issues: private sector involvement, moral hazard and the emergency standstill mechanism, crisis prevention and resolution, international institutions and the role of the IMF, membership in the FSF, debt relief for the poorest, and the overall approach to globalization.

On reform of the international institutions, Canada faced strong demands from France and from the IMF's Michel Camdessus, who wanted primacy for the IMF. Canada had reservations about transforming the IMF's Interim Committee into what it considered a *directoire*. On the FSF, the earlier agreement of the G7 finance ministers had left to the leaders the issues of the breadth of participation and inclusion of emerging economies. Canada, in notable contrast to the US, was among those pressing for broader participation.

On debt relief for the poorest, during the spring, the newly elected German government – despite the reluctance of its central bank – reversed Germany's longstanding position and agreed that a debt initiative, including the sale of IMF gold, would be the centrepiece of the Cologne Summit. As spring proceeded, a G7 agreement on the sale of 5 million ounces of IMF gold led rapidly to a demand for the sale of 10 million ounces, to raise the substantial funds required to make the initiative credible. As Cologne drew near, Canada, Britain, and, now, Germany encountered strong resistance from France and Japan on a second component of the initiative. France and Japan had continued their programmes of official development assistance (ODA) through large loans rather than grants and would thus be faced with large costs to their national budgets if a proposed G7 programme required writing off loans. Within the G7, trans-regional coalitions were evident yet again.

The American-Turned-Global Crisis, 2007–09

A decade later, a new crisis saw the EU now as an actor, particularly in the context of the new G20 summit (Kirton 2012). The coming of the American-turned-global financial crisis of 2007–09 had its origins in the dot-com bubble and bust of 2000–01, the terrorist attacks of September 11, the resulting growth slowdown and interest rate reductions, the ensuing stimulus, the bubble in the American subprime mortgage and housing market, and the rise of securitization in America's financial system. Despite the mounting signs of distress, however, at the summit level the G8 was very slow to respond (Kirton 2011).

The 2007 G8 Heiligendamm Summit

For the G8's Heiligendamm Summit in 2007, the German host began with a wish to return the summit to its presumed economic origins, by focusing on global imbalances, financial stability and hedge funds, private investment, counterfeiting, and piracy and intellectual property rights (Freytag et al. 2011). The priorities on the German agenda included dealing with global imbalances through strategies to manage the current account deficit in the US, generate growth in Europe and Japan, and contain foreign exchange reserves in Asia. Also among the priorities was improving financial stability and transparency, including with regard to hedge funds.

But resistance from other G8 members and other priorities soon crowded out these central financial and economic objectives. In the end, the G8 leaders did little in response to Germany's desire for greater regulation of hedge funds, preferring to let the industry solve any problems through voluntary codes on its own. Germany acquiesced, preferring to use its scarce political capital as host for other priority concerns such as development, health, and climate change. Soon after the summit, G7 central banks started injecting ever larger liquidity into contracting inter-bank credit markets, first unilaterally and then in a coordinated fashion. By late January 2008, the US Federal Reserve had unilaterally slashed its interest rate by 125 basis points within two weeks, amid signs that the American and G7 economies were rapidly slowing down.

The 2008 G8 Toyako Hokkaido Summit

Nonetheless, for the Toyako Hokkaido Summit in July 2008 the Japanese host did not even try to put finance and economics back on the agenda in any serious way. On the summit's priority of the world economy and energy, G8 performance was poor, worthy of no more than a grade of C– (62 percent) (Kirton 2008). The concluding statement opened with a suggestion that all was well with the global economy and that any negatives were merely future risks. It poorly reflected the reality of the voters struggling to pay or secure their mortgages or trying to get or keep their jobs, and watching the world's major stock markets shrink by about 20 percent since October 2007 (apart from Canada, where the economy contracted in the first quarter of 2008). Consistent with the view that growth was not a problem, the statement issued tough inflation-fighting words.

The communiqué's one-paragraph treatment of macroeconomics was followed by a paragraph on finance. It merely endorsed what the FSF and G7 finance ministers and central bankers had decided to do before. The next paragraph on imbalances called on 'emerging economies with large and growing current account surpluses' to have 'their effective exchange rates move so that necessary adjustment will occur' (G8 2008). But it offered no signal that the dropping US dollar would stabilize or rise. The next morning, the headlines in the world's major newspapers announced a new round of financial distress, sparked by fears about the creditworthiness of America's Federal Home Loan Mortgage Corporation and Federal National Mortgage Association, better known respectively as Freddie Mac and Fannie Mae.

G20 Governance

September 2008 brought the collapse of Lehman Brothers and the full-scale globally contagious financial crisis. A week after the G20 finance ministers and central bank governors held their tenth annual meeting in Sao Paulo, Brazil, the institution leapt to the leaders' level, as the crisis was so serious that it needed the authority of leaders to solve it (English, Thakur and Cooper 2005; Kirton and Koch 2008, 2009; Martin 2008; Summers 2008; Savona, Kirton and Oldani 2011). On 14–15 November 2008, the G20 leaders gathered in Washington DC for the 'Leaders Summit on Financial Stability and the World Economy'. In calling for and hosting the summit, US President George W. Bush admitted that America could not cope with it on its own, and that more than the multilateral IMF or exclusive G7 or G8 clubs was needed.

Emerging power leaders agreed to assist America, its established G8 partners, and the world solve a crisis that had been born in the USA, on its many main streets, side streets, and Wall Street, where mortgages that had been recklessly issued and sold as transatlantic securities were now going bust. The G20 summit delved deeply and intrusively into the internal world of countries' regulatory systems, professional communities, and even firms. The summit launched a leaders-level G20 institution as a new centre of global economic governance, where finance was now globalized and driven by the private sector, and where power had passed to the emerging economies of Asia and the Americas from the established Atlantic-centred powers of old.

The 2008 G20 Washington Summit

French president Nicolas Sarkozy had been the first to call publicly for a summit to respond to the crisis (Alexandroff and Kirton 2010).[2] Soon after he met Bush in Washington, Bush announced that he would host a special summit before the end of November, and that he would invite the G20 leaders (including the EU's) and the IMF managing director, the World Bank president, the FSF chair, and the United Nations secretary general.

Sarkozy and Bush differed over what this summit should do (Brookings Institution 2008; Eichengreen and Baldwin 2008; Rotman School of Management 2008). Sarkozy and his continental European allies wanted ambitious, immediate action, including a comprehensive new international financial architecture and

---

2   The following sections draw on Alexandroff and Kirton (2010), whose relevant passages are in turn taken directly from Kirton (2009).

heavy, internationally imposed government regulation. The US and Canada viewed the Washington meeting as the start of a process of stronger intergovernmental cooperation.

Spain, Venezuela, Poland, and the Netherlands soon asked to be invited. Sarkozy announced that he would give up France's assumed 'second seat' as the rotating president of the European Council so that Spain could attend. He also suggested including the finance minister of the Czech Republic, which would replace France as EU president in 2009. The Dutch leader was also added to the French delegation. Demands from poor African countries were refused. The EU thus exerted influence as a regional international institution through the instrument of France, expanding the eurocentric bias of the new G20 summit.

As part of the preparatory process, on 12 October Sarkozy called the eurozone's first summit and invited British prime minister Gordon Brown (Bayne 2011). Brown and German chancellor Angela Merkel also met. An EU-Russia summit was scheduled. The Asia-Europe Meeting (ASEM) in Beijing addressed the Washington Summit's agenda. At the EU summit on 7 November, European members agreed on the state of the financial crisis and initiatives for the G20 summit. The EU was thus a central participant in the G20's preparatory stage.

All participants expected the Washington Summit to be followed by another, to be held outside the United States. Yet the Europeans wanted it to take place within 100 days, immediately after the new US president Barack Obama took office. The US wished it to set principles to be developed and applied by working groups for future summits to consider.

The G8 sherpas and G20 finance deputies agreed on the draft communiqué one week before the Washington Summit. But only on the day before the summit did an agreement arrive on a college of supervisors for the world's biggest international banks. FSF chair Mario Draghi and IMF managing director Dominique Strauss-Kahn finally agreed on the role and relationship of their respective institutions, for G20 leaders to endorse (Engelen 2008). The lightly institutionalized FSF would set new standards that the organizationally powerful IMF would monitor and enforce. On 14 November, beginning in the early afternoon, the sherpas and deputies finalized the communiqué and action plan, a task that kept them working through much of the night (Price 2009).

The leaders' dinner that evening began with short statements from Strauss-Kahn, the World Bank's Robert Zoellick, the UN's Ban Ki-moon, and Draghi. The next day's plenary working sessions lasted into the early afternoon.

In the end, the summit was a strong success. It acted decisively in areas controlled by government, notably trade, where the EU had full policy competence on behalf of Europe, and on fiscal stimulus and international institutional reform. On private sector–driven finance the leaders declared principles and a defined process for experts from the public and private sectors to devise solutions. They matched those specified by G7 finance ministers and central bankers at their meeting in Washington the month before.

The G20 leaders skilfully managed their domestic politics at the summit. Their presence showed their electorate that they were personally seized with the crisis. Just being there brought great prestige, in particular, especially in hard-hit Spain and the Netherlands, which were both left out of the G8.

The summit enabled the leaders to adjust their positions above all on fiscal stimulus. Brown abandoned his longstanding two 'golden rules' of fiscal sustainability by producing a major stimulus package, citing the meetings of the G7 finance ministers and the G20 leaders to justify his move. His summit performance boosted his plummeting standing in public opinion polls at home, although it was not long-lived. Canada's Stephen Harper, having been re-elected on 14 October with a promise to keep Canada in fiscal surplus, used the G20 summit to justify his post-election move to stimulate despite the deficit that would result. The summit also boosted public approval for Bush, as host, and for Merkel. India's Manmohan Singh declared his initial scepticism had been overcome by the summit's accomplishments.

The leaders' deliberations went well. Despite having only half the time of a G8 summit but more than double the number of participants, there was considerable personal engagement among the leaders. Several intervened energetically to condemn trade protectionism, a shared sentiment that was recorded in the communiqué in strong terms. The communiqué with its action plan contained 3635 words, many more than the first G7 summit's in 1975, if fewer than more recent G8 ones. The G20 declaration emphasized finance above all, followed in turn by the economy, trade, development, and IFI reform. It also noted 'energy security and climate change, food security, the rule of law, and the fight against terrorism, poverty and disease', covering several EU competences and concerns (G20 2008).

The G20 summit also engaged in principled and normative direction setting, highlighting the benefits of open markets and putting calls for strong government regulation secondary. The leaders made 95 decisional commitments, above all on macroeconomics and finance, followed by trade – far more than the first G20 finance ministerial in 1999 or the most recent one in Sao Paolo.

The leaders acted to ensure that these commitments were delivered. They promised to implement many short-term decisions by 31 March 2009 and to hold another summit by the end of April. Their commitments contained 139 catalysts proven to enhance compliance with G8 commitments (Kirton, Roudev, and Sunderland 2007; Kirton 2006). The commitment to have another summit by 30 April 2009 was fully met. By the time of the subsequent summit on 1–2 April – which fulfilled the Washington commitment to hold another summit by the end of April – the average level of compliance was +0.60 (on a scale from –1.00 to +1.00), with the three assessed trade commitments, focused on the anti-protectionist pledge, averaging +0.59 compliance, on financial regulation averaging +0.47, and on macroeconomic policy averaging +0.75. The EU's average compliance was a perfect +1.00.

More broadly, the anti-protection pledge was quickly violated by Russia, India, the US, and France over the Common Agriculture Policy. The commitment to reach a modalities agreement by 31 December 2008 to advance the Doha Round of multilateral trade liberalization was not met. Despite its perfect compliance performance, on some issues EU competence in trade appeared to impede the compliance performance of the Washington Summit.

The Washington Summit also performed well in developing global governance. Its call for a second summit announced the birth of a new summit-level institution. It induced the G20 finance ministers and central bankers to meet far more frequently and created four official-level working groups – and soon joined by a fifth. It also called for G20 trade ministers to come together.

The summit went beyond the G20 members. It issued instructions to the G7-created FSF to add new members and to strengthen itself. It similarly instructed the Bretton Woods bodies to reform. It guided several governmental and non-governmental professional supervisory bodies, notably the International Organization of Securities Commissions (IOSCO) and the International Accounting Standards Board (IASB). It created colleges of supervisors for global banks. It told its new task forces to engage civil society experts. It outlined the roles and relationships of these institutions in a reformed global financial architecture.

Causes of the Washington Summit Performance

The Washington Summit's strong success on trade, fiscal stimulus, and IFI reform and its lesser performance on financial regulation was driven by six basic forces, with the first five also contained in the concert equality model of G8 governance and the sixth a distinct feature of the systemic hub model developed to explain G20 governance (Kirton 2012).

The first such force, seen above all in the initiation and institutionalization of a G20 summit to govern financial stability and the world economy, was the severe financial and ensuing economic shock that exposed the equal economic vulnerability of all systemically significant countries, and the social and even political vulnerability of some. In an era of financial hegemonic decline, financial crises had started on the periphery, with the debt crisis among developing countries in 1982, the 1994 peso crisis in Mexico, and the 1997–99 Asian-turned-financial crisis (Arrighi and Silver 1999). Now the shock was felt first and most forcefully in the core of America, Britain, and Europe, rather than in the G20's major emerging members of China, India, and Brazil.

The second force, seen in the G20 summit's creation and continuation and in its initial financial and economic performance, was the failure of American unilateralism, IMF hard-law multilateralism or EU regionalism, and G8, G7, or even G20 finance governance to cope with a crisis that began in America, Britain, and continental Europe, but spread quickly throughout a globalized world. G8 summits had failed to deal seriously with finance, economic, or trade, or even specific issues such as hedge funds for several years.

The third force, seen most clearly in the strong success on fiscal stimulus, IFI reform, and G20 institutionalization and in the lesser performance on financial regulation, was the equalization of globally predominant capability within the G20. The group contained a strong majority of the world's money, economy, and population, as a rising but financially closed China, with its $2 trillion in foreign exchange reserves, rivalled a financially open America rapidly adding $2 trillion to its substantial government debt. The world's financial centres and expertise, however, remained overwhelmingly within G7 members.

The fourth force, evident in the strong success on stimulus and trade and in the poor performance on financial regulation, was the common purpose among these otherwise diverse 20 members on the values of economic openness, social stability, and international cooperation rather than autarkic sovereignty to govern globalized finance. Here the EU, representing 27 democratic polities, several recently liberated from Soviet control and influence and also representing the Netherlands and Spain as newcomers to the G20, were important in strengthening the predominant democratic character of the G20. With regard to the anti-protectionist pledge, the first defection came from Russia, the G8's newest democracy, and a G20 member not yet bound by the World Trade Organization's international rule of law.

The fifth force, seen again in the strong success on fiscal stimulus, trade liberalization promises, and IFI reform and in the poorer performance on financial regulation, was the strong political capital, control, continuity, competence, and commitment, reinforced by the crisis, of the popularly elected leaders at Washington. Their voters supported the need for government spending and open trade.

The sixth force was the still constricted participation in a group of only 20 permanent members of the world's systemically significant states. They had a decade of proven process and performance at the finance level on the G20's core subjects of financial stability, reform for the Bretton Woods bodies, and macroeconomics. The 20 served as the hub of several other global networks governing global finance and economics at the summit and ministerials levels. Spain and the Netherlands, present only as part of the EU or French delegation, played no role at the Washington Summit. In contrast, the compact G8 club, both at the finance ministers' level and through an earlier statement issued by the leaders, provided the necessary leadership around which much larger and more actors could converge (Price 2009).

The April 2009 G20 London Summit

The G20's second summit took place in London on 1–2 April 2009, chaired and hosted by Gordon Brown (2010). The lead-up featured several high-profile differences among the members. Obama sought strong, swift fiscal stimulus. Sarkozy and Merkel instead emphasized strong, supranational financial regulation starting with tax havens and hedge funds. G7 members offered stimulus and financial regulation, while the emerging members called for trade openness, trade finance, development, and greater voice and vote for themselves at the IFIs. Britain and other members, largely from the G7, wanted action on climate change, while most emerging members did not.

In the end the London Summit was a very strong success. It brought an unpopular Brown widespread broad media acclaim and a small boost in the polls. The summit opened with a reception with Queen Elizabeth II. The leaders deliberated over dinner on 1 April and working sessions from breakfast to mid afternoon on 2 April. Their three concluding documents addressed economic growth, financial regulation, IFI reform, trade, social inclusion, and climate change. They endorsed economic and political openness.

The leaders made 88 commitments, close to the 95 they had made at Washington before. In their finance and economics work, they promised the fiscal and monetary stimulus required to restore growth, asked the IMF assess need, rejected competitive currency devaluation, and endorsed IMF surveillance of their economies and financial sectors. They called for stronger, high-standard, internationally consistent and cooperative regimes, embracing all systemically important institutions, instruments, and territories. The regimes would be developed by the Financial Stability Board (FSB), the IMF, and the Financial Action Task Force (FATF) for the November meeting of G20 finance ministers. They created $1.1 trillion in new stimulus, including $250 million in SDRs. They advanced the deadlines for quota and voice reform at the Bretton Woods bodies to spring 2010 for the World Bank and January 2011 for the IMF. They extended their anti-protectionist pledge through 2010, promised to redress past violations and to avoid fiscal and financial protectionism, endorsed notification to and monitoring by the WTO and other international institutions of their actions, and mobilized $250 million for trade finance.

By the time of the next G20 summit, in Pittsburgh in September 2009, the 13 assessed commitments had been complied with at a level of +0.35, led by the eight assessed trade commitments at +0.50, followed by one each on macroeconomic policy at +0.35, development at +0.30 and +0.05, financial regulation at 0, and green recovery at –0.1. The EU complied fully with the assessed commitments on trade, development, and a green recovery, but only partially with those on macroeconomic policy and financial regulation. The London leaders also developed global economic governance both inside and outside the G20, above all by turning the FSF into the FSB with all G20 members as full members.

These results flowed from a relatively balanced adjustment by all members. Different established and emerging countries led on different issues. The emerging powers and developing countries benefited a great deal from the agreements reached.

Obama, who had come to London to listen and learn, secured stimulus, relatively light financial regulation, and much on trade. Japan's offering of a $100 billion loan for the IFIs in November was matched the US and the EU; Europe's contribution came as an EU aggregate, equal to that of Japan and the United States. The EU total was later divided up among its member states.

China started to show leadership. The increase of SDRs was a response to a Chinese proposal. It expanded the existing stock of SDRs by eight times (Fratianni and Alessandrini 2009). China also had the G20's preferred a tax haven regime effectively exempt Hong Kong and Macau.

Causes of the London Summit Performance

The London Summit was driven to very strong success in the way outlined by the model of systemic hub governance. The first force was again shock-activated vulnerability. In particular, the 2008 shock had exposed the new vulnerability of all to processes arising from non-state or even non-human sources. It could speedily spread anywhere without intention, guidance or targeting, yet still inflict great damage on the national and human interests of the countries they touched. By the end of 2008 the crisis had plunged almost all of the G20 members into a severe growth contraction. By the first quarter of 2009, financial system seizure had spread to Russia, France, and Italy, leaving only the financial systems of Japan and Canada intact. Within the G8 by the first quarter of 2009, the scope, scale, and severity of the downturn had become the worst since the Great Depression in the 1930s. Especially with transmission mechanisms so complex and uncertain, and with the remedies such as quantitative easing in monetary policy so novel, no country could be confident that it could escape. All were equally vulnerable to a crisis so new, unpredictable, and large. Unlike 1997–99, where a largely untouched G7 could ride to the rescue of consequential affected countries outside the club, this time few suppliers of financial and economic security existed on the systemic scale required now.

The second force was the failure of the established multilateral organizations in response. The IMF had only $250 billion of its own resources to deploy when the crisis hit. Its governance structure had given only a slightly greater share of voice and vote to the emerging powers due to a deal done within the G20 finance ministers' forum. Its International Monetary and Finance Committee (IMFC), also created in 1999, was unable to respond to this fast-paced, complex crisis, with the domestic American housing and financial system at the core. Also constrained was the G20 finance ministers' forum, which was more of a consensus-oriented club than a decision-making and crisis-response one, and the FSF, which had left out the leading emerging powers of China, India, Brazil, Mexico, and South Africa. The G7 finance ministers and central bank governors, however, had sprung into inter-sessional action, moving boldly in October 2008 and again in early 2009.

The third force was the strengthening equalization of capability between the established and emerging economies and among those within the G7. First-ranked America saw its economy contract at seasonally adjusted annualized rates of 6.3 percent in the fourth quarter of 2008 and a further 6.1 percent in the first quarter of 2009. The contractions for second-ranked Japan were estimated in late April 2009 at 3.1 percent for the year ending in March and, by the IMF, at 6.2 percent for 2009. For third-ranked Germany the late April estimate was for a contraction of 5.4

percent in 2009. For the 27-member EU as a whole it was a 4 percent drop for 2009. Canada's economy was expected to contract by more than 7 percent annualized in the first quarter of 2009, the biggest fall on record, but would recover quickly after that. In sharp contrast, the strongest emerging economy member, China, where growth had fallen to almost zero in the fourth quarter of 2008, saw growth of 6.1 percent in the first quarter of 2009, with signs that it would accelerate even more. India, too, seemed likely to maintain growth above 5 percent. The only partial temporary offset to these changes in the real economy were those in exchange rates, as a flight to safety, or survival, gave the US dollar a temporary boost for a short while. But China's still controlled currency was appreciating as well. By spring 2009, the US dollar was dropping once again.

The fourth force was the common commitment to economic openness and political stability and, thus, for all but China and Saudi Arabia, the democracy that many had won or strengthened in the post-Cold War years. The EU and its G7 partners were concerned about the recent democracies in its many new and prospective members in Eastern and Central Europe. The newer democracies of Indonesia, Korea, and Mexico shared similar concerns. At their concluding news conferences, several leaders spoke of the unifying fear that economic distress would breed social unrest, political extremism, and authoritarianism, as it had in Europe and Japan in the 1930s. China had strong reasons to fear an intensification of its already widespread social instability.

The fifth force was the adequate political control, capital, competence and commitment of the G20 leaders at London. Within the G8, the leaders of America and Britain led the parties in control of their legislatures and no elections looming in the immediate future; the leaders of coalition governments in Japan and Germany would face general elections in the fall of 2009. Beyond the G8 the consequential leaders were secure, save for India's Singh, who faced a general election within weeks (which he won with a much stronger than expected majority). In light of the crisis, legislatures and central banks were willing to give their leaders the benefit of the doubt, except on populist issues such as executive pay. The major constraint from domestic politics came from the US Congress, which was unwilling to authorize another package of spending and bank bail-outs beyond the Troubled Asset Relief Program (TARP) signed into law by George Bush in October 2008 and the $787 billion recently committed by Obama. The G20 leaders were also reluctant to unleash a coordinated conventional fiscal stimulus. Importantly, two key leaders from established and emerging economies had extensive experience in the G20 finance club. Among the established members, Gordon Brown had served at the hub of several global financial networks, as British finance minister since 1997, a co-founder and participant in the ministerial G20 and IMFC since 1999, a participant in the quarterly G7 finance ministerials since 1997, and a participant in the annual G8 summit in 2008. India's Singh held a similar position in the emerging members' club. Moreover, in sharp contrast to G8 summits, at the London Summit G20 leaders had their finance ministers by their side.

The sixth force was the strengthened position of the G20 summit as a network hub. Brown added the Association of South East Asian Nations (ASEAN) and several other multilateral organizations, for a total of 29 summit participants. All the G20 participants except Obama and most of the guests were veterans of the Washington Summit only 14 weeks earlier. Jan Peter Balkenende of the Netherlands participated this time, and Spain's José Luis Rodríguez Zapatero returned.

More broadly, these G20 leaders collectively served as the hub of a global network that reached out to embrace all consequential plurilateral summit institutions that contained established and emerging countries and were of global relevance and trans-regional reach. Many of the key emerging economy leaders at London had longer experience in the G8 Plus Five than those of the G8 itself. There was no separate meeting among the emerging economy members to take up time and recreate the North-South divide. The G20's seminal structural principle of full equality among established and emerging members remained intact.

Conclusions

The 2008–09 financial crisis loomed large at the following G20 summits in Pittsburgh in September 2009, Toronto in June 2010, Seoul in November 2010, and Cannes in November 2011. With the global crisis receding and global growth returning, the G20 moved increasingly to serve as a steering committee rather than a crisis committee (see Appendix 10.2). Yet the threat of a new global crisis – now starting in Europe – grew. Bailouts were required for Greece the month before the Toronto Summit, Ireland on the eve of the Seoul Summit, and then Greece again and potentially Portugal, Spain and Italy, as 2011 unfolded. The EU was central to the management of these installments of the eurocrisis, with support for the bailout packages and policy guidance from the IMF. The G20 summits did just enough in crisis response, macroeconomic management, and financial regulation and supervision to keep the eurocrisis from going global, and thus allow time for the American economy to recover and for the emerging economy members of the G20 to adjust. By the Cannes Summit on 2–3 November 2011, the EU and G20 leaders were operating in close tandem at the summit itself, to ensure that both Greece and Italy, which would both soon have new governments, would solve their own problems before the global financial system once again seized up. Yet as host of the 2012 G20 summit, Mexico kept the eurocrisis at the centre of the agenda, just in case the efforts of the G20 leaders were called for again. And the G7 continued to contribute, primarily by coordination among its central bankers to inject liquidity as critical times.

During the global financial crises that afflicted a post–Cold War, globalizing world, the relationship between the EU and the G8/G20 has changed a great deal. At the start, over the Mexican peso crisis of 1994, the Europeans – reinforced by EU solidarity – successfully opposed a response by the G7 or even by the IMF, which the G7 controlled. By the end of 2010, the EU and its leading members were cooperating intensely at the G20 summit to prevent the escalating eurocrisis from generating another global one.

This transformation was defined by the growing membership on both sides. The EU was now a less cohesive club, containing many more members, with those beyond the 'original six' causing the regional financial crisis to erupt and cascade. At the level of finance ministers and central bankers the G7 continued to serve as a successful first responder, even as the G20 summit emerged to lead in the necessary fiscal stimulus and consolidation, macroeconomic adjustment, and financial regulation and supervision. On both sides this cooperative convergence was caused above all by the growing reality and recognition of the members' new vulnerability, first in Asia in 1997, then in America and Britain in 2008–09, and, finally, in Europe in 2010–11. Whether this common recognition of the vulnerability to financial crisis, economic recession, and the social and political instability that crisis and recession can bring, will continue to generate enough cooperative convergence to prevent a new global crisis will be the central challenge for the EU, the G7/G8 and the G20 in the years ahead.

References

Alexandroff, Alan S., and John J. Kirton (2010). 'The "Great Recession" and the Emergence of the G20 Leaders' Summit.' In *Rising States, Rising Institutions: Challenges for Global Governance*, edited by Alan S. Alexandroff and Andrew F. Cooper, pp. 178–95. Washington DC: Brookings Institution Press.

Arrighi, Giovanni, and Beverly Silver (1999). *Chaos and Governance in the Modern World System*. Minneapolis: University of Minnesota Press.

Bayne, Nicholas (1999). 'Continuity and Leadership in an Age of Globalisation.' In *The G8's Role in the New Millennium*, edited by Michael R. Hodges, John J. Kirton and Joseph P. Daniels, pp. 21–44. Aldershot: Ashgate.

Bayne, Nicholas (2000). *Hanging In There: The G7 and G8 Summit in Maturity and Renewal*. Aldershot: Ashgate.

Bayne, Nicholas (2011). 'Challenge and Response in the New Economic Diplomacy.' In *The New Economic Diplomacy*, edited by Nicholas Bayne and Stephen Woolcock, pp. 59–79. Farnham: Ashgate.

Bergsten, C. Fred, and C. Randall Henning (1996). *Global Economic Leadership and the Group of Seven*. Washington DC: Institute for International Economics.

Brookings Institution, ed. (2008). *The G20 Financial Summit: Seven Issues at Stake*. Washington DC: Brookings Institution. <www.brookings.edu/reports/2008/1112_g20_summit.aspx> (July 2011).

Brown, Gordon (2010). *Overcomng the First Crisis of Globalization: Beyond the Crash*. New York: Free Press.

Daniels, Joseph P. (1999). 'Supervising the International Financial System.' In *The G8's Role in the New Millennium*, edited by Michael R. Hodges, John J. Kirton and Joseph P. Daniels, pp. 107–18. Aldershot: Ashgate.

Eichengreen, Barry, and Richard Baldwin, eds (2008). *Rescuing Our Jobs and Savings: What G7/8 Leaders Can Do to Solve the Global Credit Crisis*. London: VoxEU. <www.voxeu.org/index.php?q=node/2327> (July 2011).

Engelen, Klaus C. (2008). 'Barely Contained Outrage.' *International Economy*, September, pp. 21-27, 80–83.

English, John, Ramesh Thakur, and Andrew F. Cooper, eds (2005). *Reforming from the Top: A Leaders' 20 Summit*. Tokyo: United Nations University.

Fratianni, Michele, and Pietro Alessandrini (2009). 'The Common Purse.' In *The G8 2009: From La Maddalena to L'Aquila*, edited by John J. Kirton and Madeline Koch, pp. 52–53. London: Newsdesk. <www.g8.utoronto.ca/newsdesk/g8-2009.html> (July 2011).

Freytag, Andreas, John J. Kirton, Razeen Sally, et al., eds (2011). *Securing the Global Economy: G8 Global Governance for a Post-Crisis World*. Farnham: Ashgate.

G7 (1998). 'G7 Leaders Statement on the World Economy.' 30 October. <www.g8.utoronto.ca/finance/g7_103098.html> (July 2011).

G7 Finance Ministers and Central Bank Governors (1998). 'Declaration by the G7 Finance Ministers and Central Bank Governors.' 30 October. <www.g8.utoronto.ca/finance/fm103098.htm> (July 2011).

G8 (2008). 'World Economy.' Hokkaido, 8 July. <www.g8.utoronto.ca/summit/2008hokkaido/2008-economy.html> (July 2011).

G20 (2008). 'Declaration of the Summit on Financial Markets and the World Economy.' Washington DC, 15 October. <www.g20.utoronto.ca/2008/2008declaration1115.html> (July 2011).

Hodges, Michael R., John J. Kirton, and Joseph P. Daniels, eds (1999). *The G8's Role in the New Millennium*. Aldershot: Ashgate.

Kirton, John J. (1995). 'The G7, the Halifax Summit, and International Financial System Reform.' *North American Outlook* 5 (June): 43–66.

Kirton, John J. (2002). 'Consensus and Coherence in G7 Financial Governance.' In *Governing Global Finance: New Challenges, G7 and IMF Contributions*, edited by Michele Fratianni, Paolo Savona and John J. Kirton, pp. 45–73. Aldershot: Ashgate.

Kirton, John J. (2006). 'Explaining Compliance with G8 Finance Commitments: Agency, Institutionalization, and Structure.' *Open Economies Review* 17(4): 459–75.

Kirton, John, J. (2008). '2008 Summit Grades.' Hokkaido, 9 July. <www.g8.utoronto.ca/evaluations/2008hokkaido/2008-kirton-grades.html> (July 2011).

Kirton, John J. (2009). 'G8 Financial Crisis Governance.' Paper prepared for workshop on 'Partnership for Building Global Public Goods', State University – Higher School of Economics, Moscow, 26 June.

Kirton, John J. (2011). 'The G8: Legacy, Limitations, and Lessons.' In *Global Leadership in Transition: Making the G20 More Effective and Responsive*, edited by Colin I. Bradford and Wonhyuk Lim, pp. 16–35. Washington DC: Brookings Institution.

Kirton, John J. (2012). *G20 Governance for a Globalized World*. Farnham: Ashgate.

Kirton, John J., and Madeline Koch, eds (2008). *Growth, Innovation, Inclusion: The G20 at Ten*. London: Newsdesk. <www.g8.utoronto.ca/newsdesk/G20at10.pdf> (July 2011).

Kirton, John J., and Madeline Koch, eds (2009). *The G20 London Summit: Growth, Stability, Jobs*. London: Newsdesk. <www.g8.utoronto.ca/newsdesk/g20london2009.pdf> (July 2011).

Kirton, John J., and Ella Kokotsis (1997/98). 'Revitalizing the G7: Prospects for the 1998 Birmingham Summit of the Eight.' *International Journal* 53(1): 38–56.

Kirton, John J., Nikolai Roudev, and Laura Sunderland (2007). 'Making G8 Leaders Deliver: An Analysis of Compliance and Health Commitments, 1996–2006.' *Bulletin of the World Health Organization* 85(3): 192–99.

Martin, Paul (2008). 'Time for the G20 to Take the Mantle from the G8.' In *Growth, Innovation, Inclusion: The G20 at Ten*, edited by John J. Kirton and Madeline Koch, pp. 22–27. London: Newsdesk. <www.g8.utoronto.ca/newsdesk/G20at10.pdf> (July 2011).

Price, Daniel M. (2009). 'Recovery and Reform.' In *The G8 2009: From La Maddalena to L'Aquila*, edited by John J. Kirton and Madeline Koch, pp. 24–26. London: Newsdesk. <www.g8.utoronto.ca/newsdesk/g8-2009.html> (July 2011).

Putnam, Robert, and Nicholas Bayne (1987). *Hanging Together: Co-operation and Conflict in the Seven-Power Summit*. 2nd ed. London: Sage Publications.

Rotman School of Management, ed. (2008). *The Finance Crisis and Rescue: What Went Wrong? Why? What Lessons Can Be Learned*. Toronto: University of Toronto Press.

Savona, Paolo, John J. Kirton, and Chiara Oldani, eds (2011). *Global Financial Crisis: Global Impact and Solutions*. Farnham: Ashgate.

Summers, Lawrence (2008). 'The Birth of the G20.' In *Growth, Innovation, Inclusion: The G20 at Ten*, edited by John J. Kirton and Madeline Koch, pp. 29–31. London: Newsdesk. <www.g8.utoronto.ca/newsdesk/G20at10.pdf> (July 2011).

Wood, Duncan (2005). *Governing Global Banking: The Basel Committee and the Politics of Financial Globalisation*. Aldershot: Ashgate.

Woolcock, Stephen (2011). 'European Union Economic Diplomacy.' In *The New Economic Diplomacy*, edited by Nicholas Bayne and Stephen Woolcock, pp. 169–86. Farnham: Ashgate.

Appendix 10.1   G8 Conclusions on Financial Crises, 1975–2011

Year	# of Words	% of Total Words	# of Paragraphs	% of Total Paragraphs	# of Documents	% of Total Documents	# of Dedicated Documents
1975	116	10.2	1	6.6	1	100	0
1976	602	37	9	36	1	100	0
1977	436	16.3	6	15.3	1	50	0
1978	296	9.8	4	8.1	1	50	0
1979	234	11.1	3	8.8	1	50	0
1980	318	7.9	3	6.2	1	20	0
1981	177	5.5	2	3.8	1	33.3	0
1982	600	33.4	10	50	1	50	0
1983	337	15.6	9	24.3	2	100	0
1984	240	7.3	2	4	1	20	0
1985	282	9	2	4.7	1	50	0
1986	469	13	5	15.6	1	25	0
1987	827	16.3	10	13.6	1	14.2	0
1988	1301	26.7	13	20	1	33.3	0
1989	378	5.3	8	6.6	1	9	0
1990	261	3.4	2	1.6	1	25	0
1991	266	3.2	4	7.1	1	14.2	0
1992	154	2.0	2	1.1	1	25	0
1993	170	5	1	2.3	1	33.3	0
1994	206	4.9	2	2.9	1	50	0
1995	812	11.2	12	8.9	1	33.3	0
1996	797	5.2	6	2.6	1	25	0
1997	181	1.4	1	.71	1	20	0
1998	508	8.3	6	9.3	1	25	0
1999	331	3.3	3	3.4	1	33.3	0
2000	463	3.4	6	4.1	2	40	0
2001	67	1	1	1.3	1	14.2	0
2002	198	1.6	4	2.7	1	12.5	0
2003	192	1.1	4	2.4	1	7.6	0
2004	0	0	0	0	0	0	0
2005	58	.26	1	.26	1	5	0
2006	0	0	0	0	0	0	0
2007	125	.48	2	.72	1	8.3	0
2008	81	0.4	1	0.7	1	14.2	0
2009	5,336	32	52	15.8	3	23	1
2010	268	2.5	2	2	1	33.3	0
2011	321	2.1	3	1.6	2	66.6	0
Average	470.49	8.57	5.46	7.98	1.08	32.8	0.03

Note: Data are drawn from all official English-language documents released by the G8 leaders as a group. Charts are excluded.

'# of Words' is the number of subjects to financial crises for the year specified, excluding document titles and references. Words are calculated by paragraph because the paragraph is the unit of analysis.

'% of Total Words' refers to the total number of words in all documents for the year specified.

'# of Paragraphs' is the number of paragraphs containing references to financial crises for the year specified. Each point is recorded as a separate paragraph.

'% of Total Paragraphs' refers to the total number of paragraphs in all documents for the year specified.

'# of Documents' is the number of documents that contain subjects related to financial crises and excludes dedicated documents.

'% of Total Documents' refers to the total number of documents for the year specified.

'# of Dedicated Documents' is the number of documents for the year that contain a subject related to financial crises in the title.

Appendix 10.2   G20 Leaders Conclusions on Financial Crises, 2008–09

Year	# of Words	% of Total Words	# of Paragraphs	% of Total Paragraphs	# of Documents	% of Total Documents	Total Dedicated Documents
2008	1,865	50.9	25	35.2	1	100	1
2009 London	2,135	34.1	30	32.6	3	100	3
2009 Pittsburgh	3,118	33.4	33	30.2	1	100	1
2010 Toronto	3,082	27.3	46	31.9	2	100	0
2010 Seoul	3,536	22.3	42	19.2	5	100	0
2011 Cannes	1,947	13.7	33	17.0	3	100	0
Average	2,614	30.2	34.8	27.7	2.5	100	0.83

Note: Data are drawn from all official English-language documents released by the G8 leaders as a group. Charts are excluded.

'# of Words' is the number of financial crises-related subjects for the year specified, excluding document titles and references. Words are calculated by paragraph because the paragraph is the unit of analysis.

'% of Total Words' refers to the total number of words in all documents for the year specified.

'# of Paragraphs' is the number of paragraphs containing references to financial crises for the year specified. Each point is recorded as a separate paragraph.

'% of Total Paragraphs' refers to the total number of paragraphs in all documents for the year specified.

'# of Documents' is the number of documents that contain financial crises subjects and excludes dedicated documents.

'% of Total Documents' refers to the total number of documents for the year specified.

'# of Dedicated Documents' is the number of documents for the year that contain a financial crises-related subject in the title.

Chapter 11

The European Union's Development Policy in the Context of the G8

Vitaliy Kartamyshev

The European Consensus on Development states that the primary goal of the European Union's development policy is to eradicate poverty in the context of sustainable development and universal achievement of Millennium Development Goals (MDGs) by 2015 (European Commission 2005). The EU implements this objective using a multidimensional approach that combines increasing aid volumes, aid effectiveness, and policy coherence for development.

The EU is among the world's largest providers of official development assistance (ODA). In 2010, it provided nearly €54 billion for financing development, which is 60 percent of global ODA and represents 0.43 percent of the EU's gross national income (GNI) (European Commission 2011a). Although the EU has reconfirmed its leading role, the prospects for reaching its collective commitment of devoting 0.7 percent of GNI to ODA by 2015 remain unlikely.

The EU's Aid Priorities

The international community's resolve to achieve the MDGs has been reconfirmed in several international venues, including the Doha trade liberalization negotiations of the World Trade Organization (WTO), the Accra High-Level Forum on Aid Effectiveness organized in 2008 by the Organisation for Economic Co-operation and Development (OECD), and the 2008 High-Level Meeting on Africa's Development Needs and the 2010 MDG Summit at the United Nations. At each, the EU's leadership and determined position were crucial for significant success in delivering positive and concrete outcomes for poor and developing countries. EU members share a consensus, underscored by the financial and economic crisis that began in 2008, that ODA is a long-term investment in more stable, prosperous, fair, and secure world.

However, there is growing concern that traditional approaches might not be sufficient. Concerted efforts are needed to ensure policy coherence in responding to crises, tackling corruption and tax reforms (including tax evasion), improving governance and the global financial architecture, untying aid from conditionality, establishing trade regimes conducive to poverty alleviation, and supporting the equitable development of rich and poor countries. Major donors increasingly recognize that progress on the MDGs depends on the developing countries taking ownership of the process themselves. Therefore, it is essential to provide more and better aid through general and sector-specific budget support. Because aid delivered as budget support goes directly into the development country's treasury, it is used according to that country's budgetary process. General budget support might be used to support a national development or poverty reduction strategy; sector-specific budget support can strengthen specific sectors such as health or education.

While disbursing aid directly to developing countries' treasuries runs the risk of mismanagement by corrupt governments, so do most types of program aid. However, the alternative – not providing aid at all – is unacceptable, given the highly volatile and insecure social conditions in many of the poorest and developing countries. The logic behind aid is that irrespective of the associated risks, there is a high return on the investment in terms of poverty alleviation. The kind of aid and the conditions under which it is disbursed are nonetheless significant. Recipient countries should have demonstrable track records and sound plans for poverty reduction, with healthy financial systems so they can use the resources effectively and account for them both to their parliaments and to civil society.

There is already ample evidence that countries that have received long-term, predictable budget support have made significant headway in reducing poverty. Indeed, the EU has provided high-quality budget support for public sector programmes in areas that have a direct effect on poverty reduction, specifically education and health. Oxfam's research has shown that this practice by the EU has produced positive outcomes in both those social sectors (Bökkerink 2008). More than half of the performance indicators linked to general budget support from the European Commission call for direct improvements in access to education and health. Eight of the countries that received large amounts of general budget support had increased government spending on education by 31 percent by 2005 (Bökkerink 2008, table 2).

While such an increase in social sector spending could have been possible without such aid, predictable, extended budget support encourages developing countries to pursue policies that have a high impact on poverty reduction. The counter-cyclical feature is also beneficial by making the budgets of poor countries less dependent on sudden external shocks such as a dramatic drop in revenue due to decreased demand for commodity exports, as has been seen as a result of the 2008 global financial crisis.

Global versus EU Aid Levels

Global ODA figures increased between 2000 and 2005, but decreased slightly in 2006 and 2007, due to the end of the debt relief programmes for Nigeria and Iraq, before resuming their upward trend in 2008 (OECD 2011b). Nonetheless, the EU fell short of its 2010 target by almost €15 billion (European Commission 2011a). That 2010 target was set at the Gleneagles Summit in 2005, when the G8 promised to deliver $50 billion in aid annually by 2010, with half of that aid to be directed at sub-Saharan Africa.

Although CONCORD, Eurodad, Oxfam and other development nongovernmental organizations (NGOs) criticize European governments for being behind schedule on aid quantity and quality, there are some signs for cautious optimism. According to the OECD (2010), total net ODA in 2010 rose to $128.7 billion, representing 0.32 percent of the GNI of the members of the OECD's Development Assistance Committee (DAC). The contribution of the 15 EU members of the DAC totalled $70.2 billion in 2010, which represented 54 percent of global DAC ODA. Of all the DAC members, only the EU set a clear timetable for reaching its goal of 0.7 percent of GNI for ODA by 2015. Figure 11.1 compares EU aid volumes with those of other non-European G7 donors, showing the EU remains a strong leader.

However, it remains to be seen in what form that aid will be given and what priority areas will benefit from this increasing trend. It is a challenge to untie aid from harmful economic conditions (especially those imposed by the IMF, which frequently offset the positive impact of aid on poverty). It is also challenging to provide more and better quality aid in the form of general and sector-specific budget support, especially in health and education, and to enhance efforts to provide aid over a extended, predictable period. There is already an encouraging policy shift to enter into MDG contracts with some African countries, to provide budget support for six years (as opposed to usual three years), and to reduce reporting requirements and improve delays in the EU's own bureaucratic processes for disbursing aid (see Appendix 11.1 for an explanation of an MDG contract).

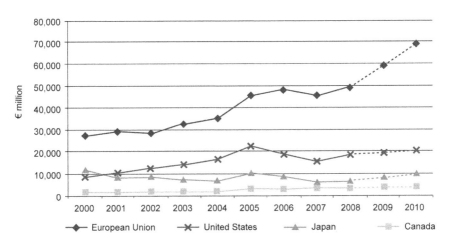

Figure 11.1   EU and Non-European G7 Aid Flows, 2000–10
(constant 2006 euros)
Source: European Commission (2009b).

Moreover, in light of the economic downturn that began as a result of the 2008 financial crisis, the EU's role and continued leadership in progressively fulfilling and increasing the ODA levels has gained special significance. More than ever, more and better aid is needed. The EU must demonstrate that its members have the collective responsibility, determination, political rigour, and resources continue to lead by example in fulfilling the promises.

At the G20 London Summit in April 2009, the leaders reaffirmed their willingness to reach their ODA targets, including on aid for trade, debt relief, and the Gleneagles commitments to sub-Saharan Africa. However, despite the renewed efforts of the international community, there are worrying signs that some countries are cutting their aid budgets in the face of adverse domestic economic conditions and growing political pressures to address unemployment and shrinking output at home, leading them further off-track from delivering what they had promised. Most notably, Italy, despite being the chair of the G8 in 2009, cut its ODA budget that same year. Its aid volume for 2010 was projected to be $4.03 billion, or 0.19 percent of GNI, making it unable to meet its EU promise to provide 0.51 percent of GNI as ODA by 2010 (OECD 2011a). Italy's ODA peaked in 2005 at 0.29 percent of its GNI.

The EU thus needs strong political determination, both collectively and individually, to set budgetary expenditures that would allow its members to meet their ODA commitments, despite growing constraints amid efforts to support financial sector and stimulate domestic industries, tackle unemployment, and implement tax reform. The EU should reassert its role as a world leader and avoid curtailing ODA at a time when developing countries need the support most, suffering from economic turmoil that has bee imported to them through increased food and fuel prices, tightened credit conditions, and reduced prospects for export-led growth.

The Impact of the Recession on the Gleneagles Promise

At the G8 Gleneagles Summit in 2005, eight rich countries and the EU committed to ensure aid increased by $50 billion by 2010. This promise was made in 2004 dollars, and it anticipated aid rising from $79 billion in 2004 to $129 billion in 2010. This amount represents the $50 billion promise to the poorest countries, of which $25 billion was to be disbursed to the poorest countries in sub-Saharan Africa.

Of the $50 billion promised, 85 percent ($42 billion) was to be delivered by the EU (see Figure 11.2). This was largely to be achieved by its commitment to reach 0.56 percent of GNI by 2010, made in May 2005. Key major countries also committed to go further, notably France, which aimed for 0.7 percent of GNI by 2012, and the UK, which aimed for 0.7 percent by 2013. While the UK remained on track to meet its pledge, France later pushed its deadline to 2015.

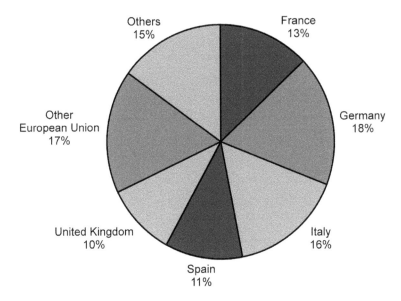

Figure 11.2   EU Member Shares of the Gleneagles Commitments

The 15 EU DAC members below 0.7 percent of GNI had promised to reach or exceed 0.51 percent by 2010. However, with GNI falling due to the global financial crisis, that amount would likely be less in cash terms than predicted at Gleneagles. The UK decided to commit at 2010 levels despite falling GNI, meaning that its ODA would reach as much as 0.6 percent in 2010 instead of 0.56 percent as originally promised.

As shown in Table 11.1, which includes the OECD's 2008 revised projections and France's changed deadline, the recession would decrease aid increases by as much as $9 billion, or $8 billion in 2004 terms. In other words, the $50 billion promise would become $42 billion. To keep the same level of aid to poor countries and avoid a cut, by 2010 the amount of the EU's GNI committed to aid should have been 0.63 percent of GNI, not 0.56 percent.

Aid for Trade: Enhancing the Coherence of the EU's Policy on Development

The EU policy on aid for trade (AfT) supports the developing and least developed countries in using trade as an instrument of poverty eradication and economic development. AfT complements trade negotiations and constitutes an important part of the Doha negotiations. Indeed, using the internationally agreed framework of trade agreements, it aims to help developing countries benefit from trade opportunities. In more concrete terms, the AfT strategy falls into the six categories,

Table 11.1   Impact of the Recession on Gleneagles Pledges (in millions)

	In 2008 dollars (euros)[a]			In 2004 dollars		
	Original pledge	Pledge predicted by OECD[b]	Difference	Original pledge	Projected pledge	Difference
Austria	2,165 (1,632)	1,945 (1,467)	220 (166)	1,805	1,614	191
Belgium	3,617 (2,727)	3,361 (2,534)	256 (193)	3,016	2,790	227
Denmark	2,939 (2,216)	2,623 (1,978)	316 (238)	2,451	2,177	274
Finland	1,423 (1,073)	1,300 (980)	123 (93)	1,187	1,079	108
France	17,863 (134,696)	13,909 (10,487)	3,954 (2,971)	14,895	11,544	3,350
Germany	19,440 (14,658)	17,687 (13,336)	1,753 (1,322)	16,210	14,680	1,530
Greece	1,716 (1,294)	1,145 (863)	571 (433)	1,431	950	481
Ireland	1,505 (1,135)	1,307 (985)	198 (150)	1,255	1,085	171
Italy	12,459 (9,394)	10,866 (8,193)	1,593 (1,201)	10,389	9,019	1,370
Luxembourg	452 (341)	395 (298)	57 (43)	377	328	49
Netherlands	7,068 (5,329)	6,647 (5,012	421 (317)	5,893	5,517	376
Portugal	1,248 (941)	1,119 (844)	129 (97)	1,040	929	112
Spain	9,711 (7,322)	8,271 (6,236)	1,440 (1,086)	8,098	6,865	1,233
Sweden	5,112 (3,854)	4,625 (3,487)	487 (367)	4,262	3,839	424
United Kingdom	15,570 (11,740)	15,570 (117,407)	0	12,983	12,923	60
Australia	3,497	3,266	231	2,916	2,711	205
Canada	4,701	4,875	−174	3,920	4,046	−126
Japan	11,177	13,310	−2,133	9,320	11,047	−1,728
New Zealand	394	415	−21	329	344	−16
Norway	4,443	4,295	148	3,705	3,565	140
Switzerland	2,162	1,862	300	1,803	1,545	257
United States	25,921	27,647	−1,726	21,614	22,947	−1,333
Total EU	102,277 (77,126)	90,770 (68,441)	11,518 (8,685)			
Total	154,081	145,110	8,971 (6,764)	128,481	120,441	8,040

Note: [a] Based on an exchange rate of \$0.754 to €1; [b] Figures drawn from Organisation for Economic Co-operation and Development (2009, table 4).

the first two being trade-related assistance and the rest referred to as the wider AfT agenda (see Appendix 11.2). The six categories are as follows:

1. trade policy and regulations;
2. trade development;
3. trade-related infrastructure;
4. productive capacity;
5. trade-related adjustment;
6. other trade-related needs.

In 2005, the EU pledged to spend collectively €2 billion per year on trade-related assistance as of 2010 (€1 billion from the European Commission and €1 billion in bilateral assistance from the European members). The principles that guide the EU's strategy call for AfT to be provided to all developing countries, particularly the poorest. It is to be linked to the MDGs and the broader development agenda. It should be part of other trade negotiations, including Doha, but must not substitute for them. Finally, it should operationalize the Paris Declaration on Aid Effectiveness and the EU's Code of Conduct on Complementary and the Division of Labour in Development Policy.

The Implementation of the EU's Aid for Trade Policy

The EU fulfilled its commitment to provide €2 billion annually in trade-related assistance by 2010 (European Commission 2010). By 2008, trade-related assistance from the EU and its member states had reached €2,150 billion, of which €1,143 came from the members and €1,007 billion from the EU (see Figure 11.3).

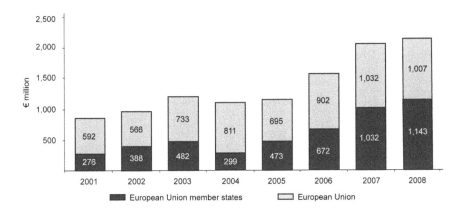

Figure 11.3   EU Commitments for Trade-Related Assistance, 2001–08
Source: European Commission (2010, chart 1).

The volume of trade-related assistance increased steadily from 2004 and then remained constant in 2007 and 2008.

On the wider AfT agenda, in 2008 the EU contributed €10.4 billion, of which €7.2 billion came from the member states and the balance from the EU (European Commission 2010). This was a substantial increase of €3.4 billion since 2007, and €3.9 billion since 2005 (see Figure 11.4).

AfT commitments are a priority for EU development cooperation (see Table 11.2). A comparison of aid volumes channelled through AfT instruments with the overall ODA shows that AfT has been a steady, significant part of EU assistance to developing countries. However, policy coherence of development agenda needs further strengthening. Donor governments need to mainstream the AfT agenda

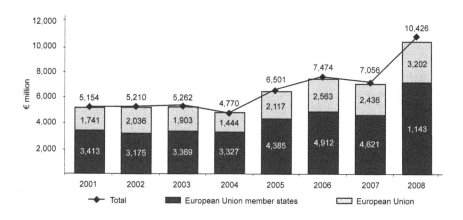

Figure 11.4   EU Commitments for Wider Aid for Trade Agenda, 2001–08
Source: European Commission (2010, chart 2).

Table 11.2   EU Aid for Trade versus Official Development Assistance (in € million)

EU commitments	2001	2002	2003	2004	2005	2006	2007
Aid for Trade	5,157	5,210	5,273	4,771	6,559	7,121	7,168
ODA: Bilateral sector	10,388	12,371	14,746	18,991	20,111	24,096	27,256
% Aid for Trade/ ODA bilateral sector	49.65	42.11	36.76	25.12	32.61	29.55	26.30
Total ODA	29,205	34,371	41,758	47,724	62,094	75,083	68,622
% Aid for Trade/total ODA	17.66	15.14	12.63	10	10.56	9.48	10.45

Source: European Commission (2009a, table 3).

in their policy dialogue with recipient countries, while the latter must ensure that AfT's instruments are made part of their national poverty reduction strategies.

Improving the Quality of Aid: The EU as a Leader

The EU has a unique opportunity once again to demonstrate to the world its capacity to lead on delivery and implementation of ODA commitments. Developing country governments desperately need more long-term and predictable ODA delivered directly to their budgets so it is not tied to various economic conditions that may undermine or offset poverty reduction strategies.

The EU, in its development policy, faces a number of issues:

- It must increase the quality and quantity of ODA to meet the Gleneagles targets, including increasing its allocation for budget support, as well as sector-specific budget support on education and health. Evidence shows that when ODA is tied to specific social sector outcomes, it produces the most effective poverty reduction strategies.
- It must continue to tie its general budget support contracts to increased allocations of recipients' budgets for health and education. Developing countries should be supported to spend 15 percent of their national budget on health (in line with 2001 Abuja Declaration of the African Union) and 20 percent on education (in line with the Global Campaign for Education target).
- In the aftermath of financial turmoil and economic downturn, it must pressure developing countries to improve accountability and transparency as part of the development package and as a condition for securing further budget support.
- It must extend general budget support over a predictable, long term for developing countries that meet the requirements for accountability and for tackling corruption, reducing tax evasion, and improving governance.
- It must give full support (including financial support) for the European Commission's plans to enter into MDG contracts with developing countries allowing for the extended length and predictability of aid.
- It must use its collective voice to implement reform at the IMF and the World Bank, including updating their governance structure, improving the quality of their policy advice, and ensuring the presence of the IMF's programmes in developing countries with sound macroeconomic policy. In particular, the IMF must relax its requirements on inflation targets and budget deficits provided that countries pursue poverty reduction policies linked to positive social outcomes in specific sectors, especially in health and education.

Conclusions and Recommendations

The EU's development policy over the past decade has undergone an important evolution. The EU rightfully enjoys a leadership role in providing ODA and financing development among its G8 partners and at the OECD. However, there remains room for improvement. EU members should take unambiguous steps to deliver their aid commitments by 0.7 percent of GNI by 2015. The EU should come up with a clear plan and a timetable to increase ODA volumes progressively to reach that milestone. It must resolve to provide genuine development assistance that is not inflated by expenditures that do not strictly correspond to true ODA.[1]

However, providing more aid is not enough. Providing the right kind is the EU's next big challenge. Such aid is not fragmented. It is predictable over a long term. It can become a powerful catalyst for developing strong public systems and setting in place the right development policies in developing countries. It can help send to school the 72 million children who currently have no access to education. It can help train nurses and pay doctors' salaries. And it can prevent the unnecessary deaths of mothers, babies, and children: at present, a woman during pregnancy or childbirth dies each minute, and every three minutes a child dies from a curable disease.

The EU should strengthen its policy coherence in all nine intervention areas that are crucial to eradicating poverty and achieving the MDGs.[2]

EU aid would be even more effective if it continues to be contingent on developing countries' successful implementation of their poverty reduction strategies, aligning ODA closer to countries' budgetary processes, making budget support (both general and sector-specific) more predictable and long term. Furthermore, provided that developing countries create a stable macroeconomic environment, achieve progress in the transparency and accountability of their financial systems, tackle corruption, and maintain budget expenditures that avoid inflation, the EU along with other donors should call for the termination of IMF programmes or, at least, for the fiscal flexibility that would enable developing countries to pursue strategies to reduce poverty in the context of sustainable development.

---

1 The EU has traditionally used technical assistance conditionality that required recipients to purchase goods and services – such as using consultants – from donor countries. Such conditionality does not contribute to local capacity building. More recently, EU members have included refugee costs and education costs for foreign students in their aid budgets (CONCORD 2008).

2 According to the 2005 European Consensus on Development, those nine areas are trade and regional integration; the environment and the management of natural resources; infrastructure, communications, and transport; water and energy; rural development; governance, democracy, and human rights; peace and security; human development; and social cohesion and employment (European Commission 2011b).

References

Bökkerink, Sasja (2008). 'Fast Forward: How the European Commission Can Take the Lead in Providing High-Quality Budget Support for Education and Health.' Oxfam International. <policy-practice.oxfam.org.uk/publications/fast-forward-how-the-european-commission-can-take-the-lead-in-providing-high-qu-114490> (July 2011).

CONCORD (2008). 'No Time to Waste: European Governments Behind Schedule on Aid Quantity and Quality.' CONCORD, Brussels. <www.eurodad.org/uploadedFiles/Whats_New/Reports/no_time_to_waste.pdf> (July 2011).

European Commission (2005). 'The European Consensus on Development.' Brussels. <ec.europa.eu/development/icenter/repository/european_consensus_2005_en.pdf> (July 2011).

European Commission (2009a). 'Aid for Trade Monitoring Report 2009.' Commission Staff Working Paper Accompanying the Communication from the Commission to the European Parliament, the Council, the European Economic and Social Committee and the Committee of the Regions: Supporting Developing Countries in Coping with the Crisis, Commission of the European Communities, Brussels. <eur-lex.europa.eu/LexUriserv/LexUriserv.do?uri=SEC:2009:0442:FIN:EN:PDF> (July 2011).

European Commission (2009b). 'Annual Progress Report 2009 on Financing for Development: Where Does the EU Go from Doha? What Prospects for Meeting the EU Targets of 2010 and 2015?' Communication from the Commission to the European Parliament, the Council, the European Economic and Social Committee and the Committee of the Regions: Supporting Developing Countries in Coping with the Crisis, Commission of the European Communities, Brussels. <eur-lex.europa.eu/LexUriserv/LexUriserv.do?uri=SEC:2009:0444:FIN:EN:PDF> (July 2011).

European Commission (2010). 'Aid for Trade Monitoring Report 2010: A Twelve-Point EU Action Plan in Support of the Millennium Development Goals' Commission staff working document accompanying the Communication from the Commission to the European Parliament, the Council, the European Economic and Social Committee and the Committee of the Regions, Commission of the European Communities, Brussels. <eur-lex.europa.eu/LexUriserv/LexUriserv.do?uri=SEC:2010:0419:FIN:EN:PDF> (July 2011).

European Commission (2011a). 'EU Accountability Report 2011 on Financing for Development: Review of Progress to the EU and Its Member States.' Communication from the Commission to the European Parliament, the Council, the European Economic and Social Committee and the Committee of the Regions, Commission of the European Communities, Brussels. <ec.europa.eu/europeaid/how/accountability/eu-annual-accountability-reports/documents/working-document-vol1_en.pdf> (July 2011).

European Commission (2011b). 'Intervention Areas.' Development and Cooperation DG – EuropeAid, Brussels. <ec.europa.eu/europeaid/what/development-policies/intervention-areas/index_en.htm> (July 2011).

European Commission (2011c). 'MDG Contract.' <ec.europa.eu/europeaid/what/millenium-development-goals/contract_mdg_en.htm> (July 2011).

Organisation for Economic Co-operation and Development (2009). 'Development Aid at Its Highest Level Ever in 2008.' Paris. <www.oecd.org/document/35/0,3343,en_2649_34447_42458595_1_1_1_1,00.html> (July 2011).

Organisation for Economic Co-operation and Development (2010). 'Development Aid Reaches an Historic High in 2010.' Paris. <www.oecd.org/document/35/0,3746,en_2649_34447_47515235_1_1_1_1,00.html> (July 2011).

Organisation for Economic Co-operation and Development (2011a). 'Development Assistance Committee Peer Review: Italy.' Paris. <www.oecd.org/dataoecd/54/59/44403908.pdf> (October 2011).

Organisation for Economic Co-operation and Development (2011b). 'Trends in Development Co-operation, 1960–2010.' In *Development Co-operation Report 2011: 50th Anniversary Edition*. Paris: Organisation for Economic Co-operation and Development. doi: 10.1787/dcr-2011-45-en (October 2011).

Appendix 11.1   Key Features of the EU's MDG Contracts

The MDG contract is a long-term, predictable form of general budget support launched by the European Commission as part of its response to international commitments to provide more predictable assistance to developing countries. It has the following key features:

- A six-year commitment of funds.
- A base component of at least 70 percent of the total commitment.
- A variable performance component of up to 30 percent, which would comprise two elements:
  - MDG-based tranche: at least 15 percent of the total commitment would be used specifically to reward performance against MDG-related outcome indicators and reforms following a mid-contract review of progress against those indicators, with adjustments deferred to the second half of the programme.
  - Annual performance tranche: Up to 15 percent of the annual allocation could be withheld in the case of concerns about performance with respect to implementation, performance monitoring, progress with improvements, and macroeconomic stabilization.

Eligible countries have a successful track record in implementing budget support. They show a commitment to monitoring and achieving the MDGs and to improving domestic accountability for budgetary resources. They also have active donor coordination mechanisms to support performance review and dialogue.

Source: European Commission (2011c).

Appendix 11.2   Categories of Aid for Trade Activities

The European Union uses six categories for Aid for Trade (AfT) activities, which are useful for coherent reporting and monitoring. Each category is linked to specific codes in the general Creditor Reporting System through which overall ODA is reported.

- Trade-related assistance:
  - Trade policy and regulations: trade policy and planning, trade facilitation, regional trade agreements, multilateral trade negotiations, multi-sector wholesale/retail trade, and trade promotion. Includes training of trade officials, analysis of proposals and positions and their impact, support for national stakeholders to articulate commercial interest and identify trade-offs, dispute issues, and institutional and technical support to facilitate implementation of trade agreements and to adapt to and comply with rules and standards.
  - Trade development: investment promotion, analysis and institutional support for trade in services, business support services and institutions, public-private sector networking, e-commerce, trade finance, trade promotion, and market analysis and development. This is largely a subset of building productive capacity, covering specifically its most trade-related part.
- Wider AfT agenda: trade-related assistance plus the following:
  - Trade-related infrastructure: physical infrastructure including transport and storage, communications, and energy generation and supply.
  - Productive capacity: business development and activities aimed at improving the business climate, privatization, assistance to banking and financial services, agriculture, forestry, fishing, industry, mineral resources and mining, tourism. Includes trade-related and non-trade–related capacity building.
  - Trade-related adjustment: contributions to the government budget to assist with the implementation of recipients' trade reforms and adjustments to trade policy measures by other countries, assistance to manage shortfalls in the balance of payments due to changes in the world trading environment.
  - Other trade-related needs: trade-related support not captured under the above-mentioned categories.

Source: European Commission (2010).

Chapter 12

Security as a Global Public Good: Common Issues for the European Union and the G8

Sergey Medvedev and Igor Tomashov

Security is one of the most contested issues on the political agenda. However, interpretations of security often differ, and the subjects of the discourse (the individual, the group, the country, the state, the international community) sometimes have conflicting interests. For example, in the name of security, it is possible both to increase the defensive capabilities of the state and to attack the human rights of its population. In order to promote security as a global public good, it is important to analyse different political and military conflicts from the perspectives of the collective good and the international community. Global and regional international institutions, such as the European Union and the G8, possess enough authority to speak on behalf of the common good. Based on this assumption and in pursuit of the rationale of the security policies of the key actors, this chapter takes stock of EU and G8 attempts to resolve conflicts in different parts of the world.

Security and International Peace as Global Public Goods

The provision of international peace and security is perhaps the most important global public good. In fact, conflicts and wars are usually accompanied by the violation of human rights, destruction of the environment, erosion of institutions, and other public bads. Moreover, they cause negative effects that may be destabilizing at both the regional and global levels.

Civil wars and ethnic conflicts trigger refugee flows and increased crime and may directly or indirectly influence the situation in neighbouring countries. For example, the genocide in Rwanda in 1994 led to the destabilization of Burundi and Zaire (Collier 2006). As pointed out by the International Task Force on Global Public Goods: 'In the absence of an effective collective security system, not only will the levels of war, terrorism and other forms of strife increase, but international prosperity will be at risk or even reversed. War, conflict and terrorism will erode international confidence, weakening financial markets. And isolationism and distrust between peoples will infect trade regimes, bringing protectionism and economic reversal. International public health and efforts to combat climate change will suffer in an atmosphere of eroding security' (International Task Force on Global Public Goods 2006, 55).

Security and international peace are essential global pubic goods, non-excludable in provision and non-rival in consumption. The only argument against this thesis is the geographical remoteness of a region in conflict. However, although geography to some extent influences the perception of the situation, it does not change the basic characteristics of this type of global public good. Moreover, the geographical factor is decreasing, considering the 'globalization' of the notion of security and peace, and the elimination of the problem of 'free rider' in international politics: in today's world, there are no free riders in the context of international security.

However, the study of concrete examples reveals, first, different interpretations of security and peace as global public goods and, second, an absence of mutual dependence between security and peace. When only a few countries possess nuclear weapons, it may be seen as a global public good because the nuclear weapons play a stabilizing role in the international system. But the borderline between good and bad in this situation is thin: in theory, the aspiration of North Korea and Iran to possess nuclear weapons strengthens their national defence capacity (which may be not the case in reality) at the price of international security. Another fundamental question is to what extent the existence of armies guarantees security and peace and to what extent it precludes security and peace. The 'military lobby' has a vested interest in the accumulation of arms and the perpetuation of conflicts; millions of people all over the world earn their living by working in the military industry or dealing in the 'markets of violence'. For them, wars are a kind of 'corporate good'.

The example of the USSR is an extreme case of the overproduction of the defence capability of the state and security of the whole Soviet bloc. The situation in the second half of the 20th century was hardly peaceful. The United States and the USSR faced each other during the Cold War, intensifying the arms race and engaging in numerous peripheral conflicts. At times, the world was on the brink of a nuclear catastrophe, as happened in the 1962 Cuban missile crisis. The military might of each forced the two parties into peace but did not establish it. This situation is broader than it looks at first glance: the search for balance between guaranteeing security and the development of peace requires a reassessment of the role of the military; meanwhile conflict management and institution building require different types of political management.

In the era of globalization, the concepts of security and international peace are evolving as well. On the one hand, the notion of security acquires a 'civil' dimension and becomes more elusive: in addition to the prevention of wars, terrorism, organized crime, and the proliferation of the weapons of mass destruction, it includes financial and energy security and the struggle against infectious diseases and against environment degradation. On the other hand, the prospects for international peace are slim where global growth is unequal and the world order erodes, discrediting of western 'liberal imperialism'.

During the Cold War, security was a one-dimensional and homogeneous issue. It existed in a single political and geographical space, determined by the ideological rivalry between capitalism and socialism. These days, the provision of global security is a multidimensional and multilateral process. This is perfectly illustrated by the case of Europe, where security is provided by such different organizations as the North Atlantic Treaty Organization (NATO), the Organization for Security and Cooperation in Europe, the European Union, and the Collective Security Treaty Organisation. The United Nations is gradually losing its legitimacy at the global level, being unable to assume the role of the universal mechanism for resolving all security problems. States tend to resort to unilateral actions, or build 'coalitions of willing', when engaging in military actions or in conflict management. In these circumstances, the role of new actors such as the EU in security is coming to the fore.

The EU's Common Foreign and Security Policy: Providing for Global Security?

The EU has always moved gradually and consistently in pursuit of its goals. The move from being an economic community to a political union was not easy and took several decades. This process still continues. In adapting to the consequences of enlargement and overcoming the crisis of integration, the EU now faces the challenge of political institutionalization and the implementation of the Common Foreign and Security Policy (CFSP). Although citizens of the European countries are not ready to see any further weakening of their national sovereignties – as indicated by the hardships of the ratification of the European constitution and the Lisbon Treaty – at the level of values, the conditions for further integration are all in place. The aspiration for peace, the peaceful resolution of conflicts, the rule of law, human rights, and democracy are essential elements of the European identity. Opinion polls show that Europeans would favour the adoption by the EU of a more effective foreign and defence policy in order to pursue these goals (Emerson 2008).

The establishment of the Western European Union (WEU) in 1948 and of NATO in 1949 are notable landmarks in the history of cooperation among European countries in the field of security. These two organizations have guaranteed security of Europe during the second half of the 20th century, until the WEU and the EU merged in 2000 and NATO became oriented towards global rather than regional problems. The EU now plays a more active role on the international stage, pursuing its foreign policy goals within the framework of the CFSP and the European Security and Defence Policy (ESDP) (Barabanov 2000). In 2010, in accordance with the Treaty of Lisbon, the European External Action Service was created, headed by the High Representative for Foreign Affairs and Security Policy Catherine Ashton (Council of the EU 2009).

The members of the European Council first discussed the prospects of implementing a common European foreign policy through more active intergovernmental consultation and exchange of information at the end of 1960s, when the idea of European political cooperation was discussed at the European Council summit in the Hague (Barabanov 2000). The *Single European Act* adopted in 1986 formalized this intergovernmental cooperation in foreign policy and confirmed the aspirations of the member states to 'endeavour jointly to formulate and implement a European foreign policy'.[1] Massive changes at the end of 1980s and beginning of the 1990s further enhanced this desire.

After the signing of the Maastricht Treaty, a common foreign and defence policy became one of the pillars of integration. Shortly thereafter, the WEU defined new objectives of foreign and defence policy: humanitarian and rescue tasks, peacekeeping tasks, and the tasks of combat forces in crisis management, including peacemaking (Barabanov 2000). The EU began to position itself as a 'supplier' of security as a global public good: building the success of Western Europe. it aspired to 'export' security to the global markets. The EU has since become a significant international actor and has participated in conflict management in the Balkans, Africa, and the Middle East. Another important step was the Amsterdam Treaty, which established the post of a High Representative for Common Foreign and Security Policy. Javier Solana, former secretary general of NATO, held this position from 1999 to 2009.

The priorities of the EU's foreign policy are defined in the European security strategy adopted in 2003 (EU 2003). The document specifies the main contemporary security threats: terrorism, the proliferation of the weapons of mass destruction, regional conflicts, and organized crime. It calls for a more active, efficient, coherent foreign policy in which its partners cooperate. It states that the EU 'should be ready to share in the responsibility for global security and in building a better world'. In this sense, European foreign policy aims at providing security as a global public good rather than at building an isolationist 'fortress Europe'.

Since the beginning of the 21st century, the EU has led more than 20 anti-crisis missions. Among them are military operations in Libya, Bosnia and Herzegovina, Chad, the Democratic Republic of Congo, Somalia, as well as civil operations in Kosovo, Georgia, Palestine, Iraq, and Afghanistan (EU 2011c). Moreover, the activity of the high representative in foreign affairs and security policy is supported by eight special representatives of the EU, working in Afghanistan, the African Union, Bosnia and Herzegovina, Central Asia, Kosovo, the South Caucasus, Georgia, the Southern Mediterranean region, and Sudan (Council of the EU 2011).

The scale and tasks of the CFSP are gradually widening. Mission EULEX in Kosovo was organized in 2008 and remains the largest civil operation in the

---

1   'Single European Act, Title III: Treaty Provisions on European Co-operation in the Sphere of Foreign Policy, Article 30.' (1986). Official Journal L 169, 29 June 1987. <eur-lex.europa.eu/LexUriServ/LexUriServ.do?uri=CELEX:11986U030:EN:HTML> (July 2011).

EU history: 1950 international police officers, judges, prosecutors, and customs officials are contributing to the institution building on the territory of the newly declared state (EU2011a). The important role of the EU in the settlement of the conflict in Abkhazia and South Ossetia is also worth mentioning: it was Nicolas Sarkozy, president of France when France held the rotating presidency of the EU, who mediated in the conflict management between Russia and Georgia in August-September 2008. Stability is the region is backed by the EU Monitoring Mission in Georgia. In 2008 the EU announced its first naval operation and sent around 20 ships and aircraft to fight piracy in Somalia (EU 2011b).

The Role of the EU and the G8 in the Provision of Global Public Goods

The domain of public policy is no longer limited by the borders of nation-states. Public policy has gone global, which opens up new opportunities for collective action but also causes new problems. Guaranteeing international peace and security is a top issue on the global agenda. However, although all significant international actors recognize security as a priority, the level of violence in the world does not decrease, new conflict areas continue to emerge, and the number of terrorist acts grows every year. Although western countries make a considerable effort to fight these types of global public bads, the demand for security and peace by far exceeds the supply.

Many actions by the West, and their long-term consequences, also provoke ambiguous interpretations. The lack of aid to the poorest countries is seen as evidence of the predatory nature of capitalism, but the increase of assistance that comes with conditions for political and economic reforms is often considered another manifestation of neocolonialism. Moreover, research indicates that humanitarian aid and official development assistance may not have their intended impact because irresponsible leaders in the recipient countries co-opt the resources to increase their military spending (Collier 2006, 10). The G8 members are also criticized for undermining their declared intentions to ensure global security and reduce poverty by maintaining their material interests in selling arms to the same countries that receive their humanitarian aid, such as Congo, Sudan, and Myanmar (Lenta.ru 2005). But even should the day come that they refuse to sell weapons, developed countries will likely be accused anew of seeking to preserve their hegemony by preventing the developing countries from guaranteeing their security.

One of the most disturbing trends of the 2000s is a slowdown in the pace of world's democratization. The number of democracies today is roughly the same as it was ten years ago. The US attempt to establish democratic regime in Iraq did not only taint its global image but also seriously destabilized global security. The question is paradoxical: is it possible to wage wars for the sake of the ideal that democracies do not fight each other?[2]

However, difficulties in finding the consensus are no reason to give up. The EU provides an example of best practice here. The amount of European aid, which comes from the EU budget and the budgets of its member-states, amounts to €54 billion, making it among the largest donors of global official development assistance (European Commission 2011). Moreover, the EU is the largest trading partner for the world's poorest countries. The EU also supports non-governmental organizations and fulfils the commitments it undertakes at G8 summits. For instance, the EU (2007) committed more than €840 million to the G8's Global Partnership against the Spread of Nuclear Weapons and Materials of Mass Destruction for more effective control over chemical, biological, radiological, and nuclear weapons and materials.

Through humanitarian and military missions, the EU uses its authority and resources to provide global security. It is nonetheless often criticized for its inability and even fear of more active engagement in international affairs. Yet can the dispatch of a few dozen police officers and diplomats change anything in reality? The exception is the Balkans, but the states in this region could possibly join the EU, so operations there cannot be seen as the accomplishment of a purely global public good mission. And even in the Balkans the EU follows the principle of the 'visibility' of the uniformed military and police forces, whose symbolic presence should prevent new violent conflicts (Emerson and Gross 2007). Such a 'post-heroic' approach of the EU can be either praised as a new post-modern type of foreign policy or criticized for its passivity. The reality is that it is in many ways predetermined by US military might, which makes it possible for Europe not to think about the military aspects of its security.

In general, today the EU is one of the largest suppliers of global public goods. Establishing peace in Europe and creating a stable zone of freedom and security on the continent belong to greatest achievements of humanity in the second half of the 20th century. The tasks for the 21st century include a further accumulation of these goods and the spread of European values and high political and economic standards at least to the territory of 'wider Europe', which includes the Mediterranean region, the Middle East, Russia, and Central Asia. The development of the CFSP is undoubtedly the main instrument of international peace and security as global public goods.

---

2 A striking answer to this question was given in 2002 by Robert Cooper (2002), who argued for the positive role of the idea of 'double standards' in international relations: 'Among ourselves, we operate on the basis of laws and open cooperative security. But when dealing with more old-fashioned kinds of states outside the postmodern continent of Europe, we need to revert to the rougher methods of an earlier era – force, pre-emptive attack, deception, whatever is necessary to deal with those who still live in the nineteenth-century world of every state for itself. Among ourselves, we keep the law but when we are operating in the jungle, we must also use the laws of the jungle.'

References

Barabanov, Oleg (2000). 'Tendencii razvitiya OVPB ES i ZES: nezhdannyi vyzov dlya Rossii? [Main Trends in EU Common Foreign and Security Policy Development and the WEU: An Unexpected Challenge for Russia?].' In *Russia and European Security Institutions: Entering the Twenty-First Century*, edited by Dmitri Trenin. Moscow: Carnegie Moscow Center.

Collier, Paul (2006). *Peace and Security*. Stockholm: Secretariat of the International Task Force on Global Public Goods.

Cooper, Richard (2002). 'The New Liberal Imperialism.' *Guardian*, 7 April. <www.guardian.co.uk/world/2002/apr/07/1> (July 2011).

Council of the European Union (2009). 'Background: The High Representative for Foreign Affairs and Security Policy/The European External Action Service.' Brussels. <www.consilium.europa.eu/uedocs/cms_data/docs/pressdata/en/ec/111301.pdf> (July 2011).

Council of the European Union (2011). 'EU Special Representatives.' Brussels. <ue.eu.int/policies/foreign-policy/eu-special-representatives?lang=en> (July 2011).

Emerson, Michael (2008). 'The Struggle for a Civilised Wider European Order: Elements for European Security Strategy.' CEPS Working Dcoument No. 307, Centre for European Policy Studies, Brussels. <www.ceps.be/ceps/download/1576> (July 2011).

Emerson, Michael, and Eva Gross, eds (2007). *Evaluating the EU's Crisis Missions in the Balkans*. Brussels: Center for European Policy Studies. <www.ceps.be/ceps/download/1576> (July 2011).

European Commission (2011). 'EU Accountability Report 2011 on Financing for Development: Review of Progress to the EU and Its Member States.' Communication from the Commission to the European Parliament, the Council, the European Economic and Social Committee and the Committee of the Regions, Commission of the European Communities, Brussels. <ec.europa.eu/europeaid/how/accountability/eu-annual-accountability-reports/documents/working-document-vol1_en.pdf> (July 2011).

European Union (2003). 'A Secure Europe in a Better World.' European Energy Strategy, Brussels. <www.consilium.europa.eu/uedocs/cmsUpload/78367.pdf> (July 2011).

European Union (2007). 'G8 Global Partnership.' Brussels. <ue.eu.int/eeas/foreign-policy/non-proliferation,-disarmament-and-export-control-/g8-global-partnership?lang=en> (July 2011).

European Union (2011a). 'EULEX Kosovo: EU Rule of Law Mission in Kosovo.' EU Common Security and Defence Policy, 18 November, Brussels. <www.consilium.europa.eu/eeas/security-defence/eu-operations/eulex-kosovo/factsheets?lang=en> (July 2011).

European Union (2011b). 'EUNAVFOR Somalia.' EU Common Security and Defence Policy, Brussels. <www.consilium.europa.eu/eeas/security-defence/eu-operations/eunavfor-somalia?lang=en> (July 2011).

European Union (2011c). 'Overview of the Missions and Operations of the European Union.' EU Operations, Brussels, November. <www.consilium.europa.eu/eeas/security-defence/eu-operations?lang=en> (July 2011).

International Task Force on Global Public Goods (2006). 'Meeting Global Challenges: International Cooperation in the National Interest.' Final Report, Stockholm.

Lenta.ru (2005). '"Большая восьмерка" разоряет беднейшие страны при помощи поставок оружия.' ['G8 Ruins the Poorest Countries by Selling Them Arms.'], 22 June. <www.lenta.ru/news/2005/06/22/g8> (July 2011).

Chapter 13

Knowledge and Education as Global Public Goods

Sergey Medvedev and Igor Tomashov

Knowledge and education are increasingly important elements in development. They go hand in hand, and while new technologies allow free access to information, education provides people with tools to analyse that information and create new knowledge. However, key international actors need to do a lot of work in this field. In fact, a consistent effort over the next few decades is required for knowledge and education to become de facto global public goods. This chapter assesses some initiatives of the European Union and the G8 to promote knowledge and education as global public goods.

Knowledge and Education as Global Public Goods

The growth of the knowledge economy is a significant characteristic of the changes that have occurred globally in recent decades. Education, invention, and the accumulation of knowledge have always been important to progress. But the main sources of power have traditionally been violence and wealth. However, this balance is changing: as Alvin Toffler (1990) has written, because the nature of power has changed, wealth and violence have become dependent on knowledge.

As a result, knowledge and education have become globalized public goods. In the past the development of an education system was primarily the task of the nation-state, but today universal primary education and gender equality in access to education are set out in the Millennium Development Goals (MDGs). It is an ambiguous situation: knowledge in the broad sense is a driving force for the development of civilization, but it is also a source of growing global inequality. While the developed countries have all the opportunities for the advancement of science, the rest must depend on imported technologies as well as humanitarian and financial assistance.

Knowledge is a non-excludable and non-rival global public good. Everyone can learn a mathematical theorem and this does not prevent others from learning it. The more well-educated people there are in society, the higher the potential of its development. So the source of the problem of global inequality lies not in knowledge as such but in access to it and in the transaction costs associated with gaining access. Primary education is still not universally available: in 2009,

32 million children in sub-Saharan Africa were not in school; 53 percent of the children around the world who are excluded from the school system are girls (United Nations 2011).

MDG 2 is to achieve universal primary education by 2015. Obviously, this is impossible without the participation and assistance of states and international organizations that exercise global governance – first of all, the members of the G8 and the EU, which have the financial and technological capacity for initiatives to reach that goal. Indeed, success depends on the realization of projects such as the One Laptop Per Child Mission to provide children in developing countries with inexpensive computers to improve the quality and efficiency of their education and to overcome the digital divide.[1]

Access to primary education is one of the most difficult challenges among those related to education and science, but it is far from the only one. The issue of copyright protection and patenting is still pertinent. The work of researchers should be well paid, although doing so might contradicts the principles of non-excludability and non-rivalry that guarantee the existence of knowledge as a global public good. In search of a solution to this problem, a system of state and private support for research and system patenting has emerged. Patenting supports the material incentive of scientists, limiting the non-excludability of knowledge for a certain period.

In this sense, the interaction among key actors in the fields of knowledge and education has a somewhat contradictory character. On the one hand, in recent years such interaction has been determined by growing international cooperation and by the understanding of the necessity of narrowing the global social and economic gap. On the other hand, countries, organizations, and individuals cooperate but also compete with each other. The accumulation of knowledge as a global public good is difficult because of the huge costs of access to high-quality education and the lack of universal educational standards and proper infrastructure.

Education in the G8 Agenda

The problems of education have drawn steadily more attention in recent years. International actors have realized the critical importance of education for the development of modern society. It has become obvious that it is impossible to achieve ambitious political, economic, and social goals without adapting education to today's realities. The G8, which has evolved from being an informal economic club to an important mechanism for global governance, and the intensification of its cooperation and dialogue among international institutions such as the EU, the United Nations, and the World Bank are key to this adaptation.

The number of references to education in the communiqués and documents produced at G8 summits has been rising from year to year (G8 Research Group

---

1   See One Laptop Per Child at <laptop.org/en>.

2009). It has frequently been closely associated with other issues such as developing information technologies, fighting unemployment, and providing assistance to the developing countries. Having been included in the G8 agenda since the second half of the 1990s, it received the most attention when Russia made it a theme of the 2006 St Petersburg Summit, but was also a key topic at the 1999 Cologne Summit and the 2002 Kananaskis Summit. The G8 ministers of education met in 2000 and 2006, and the G8 economy ministers also discuss the issue.

The EU has been participating in the G7 and G8 since 1977. It engages in the multilateral forum, promoting its interests and supporting the initiatives of the European countries. Having had a positive experience of cooperation in the field of education, the EU and the European members of the G8 play an important role in defining the G8's approach. At the initiative of European leaders, the topic of 'lifelong learning' became a topic of discussions at the Cologne Summit, where the leaders adopted the 'Cologne Charter: Aims and Ambitions for Lifelong Learning', which emphasized the role of education in achieving economic success, civic responsibility, and social cohesion (G8 1999).

The following year, when Japan assumed the presidency of the G8, it suggested continuing the dialogue on education as one of the issues on the agenda of the 2000 Okinawa Summit. At the first ever G8 education ministerial meeting, in April 2000 in Tokyo, the ministers discussed the challenges facing educational systems in the era of globalization, the use of information and communication technologies in education, and the promotion of lifelong-learning programmes, and international exchanges among students, teachers, researchers, and administrators (G8 Education Ministers 2000).

Also in 2000, UNESCO held the World Education Forum in Dakar, which confirmed the MDGs and adopted new commitments: 'achieving a 50 per cent improvement in levels of adult literacy by 2015, especially for women, and equitable access to basic and continuing education for all adults' and 'eliminating gender disparities in primary and secondary education by 2005, and achieving gender equality in education by 2015, with a focus on ensuring girls' full and equal access to and achievement in basic education of good quality' (World Education Forum 2000). The strategy was called Education For All and became the main global initiative for education.

G8 members including the EU participate actively in the programme implementation. They addressed it at the 2002 Kananaskis Summit, when they agreed on a document called 'A New Focus on Education for All', in which they supported the joint plan of the World Bank and International Monetary Fund (IMF) to accelerate progress on Education for All and announced their commitment to raise the amount of aid for developing countries (G8 2002). The launch of the Education For All Fast Track Initiative was a result of joint efforts. This programme is implemented by the World Bank but financed from different sources, including the EU budget. In addition, as one of the world's largest donors of official development assistance, the EU implements its own assistance programmes (European Commission 2011a).

Discussions became especially active in 2006, when Russia chaired the G8. The EU was one of the main initiators of ideas and proposals. Jan Figel, the commissioner responsible for education, training, culture, and multilingualism, participated in the G8 education ministers' meeting in Moscow in June 2006. The European perspective was reflected in the declaration that was issued at the meeting, which emphasizes the importance of the internationalization of education, increased international educational mobility, and improved transparency and compatibility among educational systems – all the priorities of the EU, as pointed out by Figel (G8 Education Ministers 2006; European Union 2006). Special attention was paid to the role of education in the adaptation and integration of immigrants, a highly sensitive topic for the EU.

At St Petersburg, the G8 (2006) issued the 'Education for Innovative Societies in the 21st Century', which stresses the important role played by knowledge in the modern societies and defines the key goals of the development of education. These goals are generating new knowledge and innovations, building skills for life and work, overcoming global inequality in access to education, and advancing social cohesion and immigrant integration. The declaration stresses the fact that education is a public good on a global scale, and should be created and provided by states in close cooperation with the private sector through international projects and the harmonization of the educational systems.

A Common European Educational Space as a Global Public Good

The G8's 'Education for Innovative Societies in the 21st Century' mentions the Bologna Process as one of the most successful international educational projects. The Bologna Process is an ambitious initiative to create a common European higher education area. While it is not formally an EU project, its initiation and implementation cannot be analysed outside the context of European integration, which has created the institutional prerequisites for cooperation in education and changed the mind-set of people who have realized the benefits from the regionalization of national public goods.

More than 40 countries participate in the Bologna Process, which aims to harmonize educational systems across a vast region from Reykjavik to Vladivostok. One direct result of reforms should be the 'adoption of a system of easily readable and comparable degrees, also through the implementation of the Diploma Supplement, in order to promote European citizens employability' (European Ministers of Education 1999). The internationalization of education, fostered by the Bologna Process, contributes to cooperation among universities and research centres within Europe and among other countries. A global educational space and infrastructure have gradually emerged, equalizing access to high-quality education. These factors foster the achievement of goals formulated by the G8 education ministers in Tokyo in 2000: doubling the mobility of students and teachers in the 2000s and easing the transfer of qualifications and credits for students participating in international exchanges (Gorbunova and Larionova 2006).

The EU plays a key role in promoting the European higher education area. Projects such as Erasmus Mundus, the Jean Monnet Programme, and 7th Framework Programme for Research encourage the emergence of a European identity and brings the EU closer to its mid-term aims to build a knowledge-based economy. In the international arena, these education and training initiatives provide Europe with an intellectual and technological superiority and highlight the role of the EU in setting best practices in the creation of global public goods.

The EU pays special attention to the concept of lifelong learning. Understanding its strategic advantages, as stated in the 1999 Cologne Charter and reaffirmed in many other documents by the world leaders, in 2007 the EU implemented a five-year Lifelong Learning Programme (European Commission 2011c). This programme will support the development of the European economy and the knowledge-based society and strengthen social cohesion. It brings together four existing EU projects: Comenius, stimulating mobility and cooperation among secondary schools; Erasmus, promoting international student mobility in higher education; Leonardo da Vinci, supporting the development of professional skills and vocational training; and Grundtvig, focusing on international initiatives in adult education.

The EU also contributes to developing the educational systems of other countries. Since 1990, it has implements Tempus, a programme that supports institutional reforms in education in neighbouring countries in the Balkans, Northern Africa, Eastern Europe, and the Middle East. The EU promotes cooperation not only with developed countries, but also with the developing ones, thus contributing to the achievement of the MDGs and the Dakar Framework for Action on Education for All. For example, the Edulink programme supports joint projects among European higher educational institutions and the states and regions of African, Caribbean, and Pacific countries.

The Erasmus Mundus programme, one of the largest global projects to promote international cooperation in the education and make high-quality European education accessible to international youth, is a significant global public good. While it is far from being non-excludable, its very existence testifies to the globalization of higher education as a public good. The scale of this programme is growing: it now has an annual budget in excess of €450 million and more than 2.2 million students have participated (European Commission 2010). The target group of the program includes doctoral candidates, and the number of supported post-graduate programmes and the size of scholarships for students, teachers, and researchers are also growing (European Commission 2011b).

The EU has become a global leader in higher education and science as global public goods. And although Europe still lags behind the US in the total number of foreign students and researchers, it has accumulated unique experience in institutionalizing cooperation in all segments of the triangle of knowledge – education, research, and innovation – necessary for the development of modern societies. The EU thus plays a key role in the internationalization of knowledge as a global public good.

References

European Commission (2010). 'The ERASMUS Programme: Studying in Europe and More.' Education and Culture Directorate General, Brussels. <ec.europa. eu/education/lifelong-learning-programme/doc80_en.htm> (July 2011).

European Commission (2011a). 'Development Policies.' Brussels. <ec.europa.eu/ europeaid/what/development-policies/index_en.htm> (July 2011).

European Commission (2011b). 'ERASMUS for Students: Get a New Perspective.' Education and Culture Directorate General, Brussels. <ec.europa.eu/education/ erasmus/doc1051_en.htm> (July 2011).

European Commission (2011c). 'The Lifelong Learning Programme: Education and Training Opportunities for All.' Education and Culture Directorate General, Brussels. <ec.europa.eu/education/lifelong-learning-programme/ doc78_en.htm> (July 2011).

European Ministers of Education (1999). 'Bologna Declaration.' Bologna, 19 June. <www.bologna-bergen2005.no/Docs/00-Main_doc/990719BOLOGNA_ DECLARATION.PDF> (July 2011).

European Union (2006). 'G8 on Education: Commissioner Figel to Present the EU's Experiences in Moscow.' Press release IP/06/702, Brussels, 31 May. <europa.eu/rapid/pressReleasesAction.do?reference=IP/06/702&format=HT ML&aged=0&langu> (July 2011).

G8 (1999). 'Köln Charter: Aims and Ambitions for Lifelong Learning.' Cologne, 18 June. <www.g8.utoronto.ca/summit/1999koln/charter.htm> (July 2011).

G8 (2002). 'A New Focus on Education for All.' Kananaskis, 26 June. <www. g8.utoronto.ca/summit/2002kananaskis/education.html> (July 2011).

G8 (2006). 'Education for Innovative Societies in the 21st Century.' St. Petersburg, 16 July. <www.g8.utoronto.ca/summit/2006stpetersburg/education.html> (July 2011).

G8 Education Ministers (2000). 'G8 Education Ministers' Meeting and Forum: Chair's Summary.' Tokyo, 4 April. <www.g8.utoronto.ca/education/ education0400.html> (July 2011).

G8 Education Ministers (2006). 'G8 Ministerial Meeting on Education.' Moscow, 1–2 June. <www.g8.utoronto.ca/education/education2006.html> (July 2011).

G8 Research Group (2009). 'G8 Education Conclusions, 1975–2009.' Toronto, November. <www.g8.utoronto.ca/conclusions/education.pdf> (July 2011).

Gorbunova, Ekaterina, and Marina Larionova (2006). 'Эволюция проблематики образования в контексте приоритетов и обязательств «Группы восьми».' ['Evolution of Educational Topic in the Context of G8 Priorities and Commitments.'] *International Organisations Research Journal* (3): 8–38. <iorj.hse.ru/data/2011/05/12/1208596979/evolprobl.PDF> (July 2011).

Toffler, Alvin (1990). *Powershift:Knowledge, Wealth, and Violence at the Edge of the Twenty-First Century*. New York: Bantam Books.

United Nations (2011). 'The Millennium Development Goals Report 2011.' New York. <www.un.org/millenniumgoals/11_MDG%20Report_EN.pdf> (July 2011).

World Education Forum (2000). 'Education For All: Meeting Our Collective Commitments.' Dakar Framework for Action, 26–28 April, Dakar. <unesdoc. unesco.org/images/0012/001202/120240e.pdf> (July 2011).

PART V
Trends in Leadership
and Models of Engagement

Chapter 14

The European Union as a Model for Global Governance

Vladimir Zuev

The 2008 global financial crisis has made it imperative to rethink the existing model of global economic governance. The crisis revealed one striking inadequacy among others: insufficient global financial regulation.

Yet experts do not share a common view on the functioning of the system of global governance. Some say that it was not ready to respond to the crisis and withstand the pressure of critical events. Others defend the system, admitting that it required only slight changes to cope. The truth, as so often, lies probably somewhere in between.

However, it is clear that the functioning of the global financial institutions must be modified. The institutions themselves should be made more efficient and their capacity to manage different aspects of the global economy should be substantially enhanced.

The EU as a Role Model for Global Governance

Critics of the European Union have examples of unsuccessful European projects in mind, and there are many to choose from. But it is also true that the EU's accomplishments are unique. Never before has there been such an advanced level of economic integration. The EU has several features that no other group of countries in the world possesses.

According to the World Trade Organization (WTO) (2011), by 2010 the number of preferential trade agreements in force was close to 300. In reality there are even more of them, as some states do not notify the WTO of their agreements. Nonetheless, not one compares with the EU in terms of scale of economic cooperation and depth of integration.

The EU has a history of more than 50 years of success. Membership has increased from the initial six to 27 members. More countries are waiting to be accepted as members. Would an unsuccessful venture enjoy such popularity? The mere fact that ever more countries want to join the European integration process is a testimony of the value of this unique union.

The EU model can be useful to various types of regional and international organizations in addition to countries. One spectacular case of a hard-won consensus is the European Monetary Union, created by countries with different interests and traditions, including national currencies. This compromise changed the members' role in the world's monetary and financial system, as well as the geometry of the global financial system itself. The European Monetary Union put an end to the domination of the US dollar in the international monetary system, making way for a new era of a bi-monetary system.

On the eve of the G20 summit in London in April 2009, Russia, China, and Kazakhstan proposed a new supranational currency for international settlements. The role of currencies has remained a topic of discussion among the leaders at subsequent G20 summits. Here, the EU experience could be particularly helpful in improving the international currency system in one way or another.

However, a supranational currency is unlikely to top the current list of the common global challenges to be addressed. The key actors in the international community still have far to go along a long road before that issue will dominate the global agenda.

It is nonetheless helpful to concentrate on aspects of the EU experience that could apply more realistically and rationally to the different economic and political interactions among global governance institutions.

The Structure of the Institutional System of Global Governance

Several innovative features of the EU institutional system can be singled out as relevant for the international system of global governance, beginning with the establishment of the European Council.

While the institutions of the European Union were navigating the troubled seas of setting the terms and conditions of integration and cooperation, regular informal meetings of members' heads of state and government helped to address the most controversial issues and map out the way forward. Although those meetings were not formally part of the institutional system, they contributed much to the evolution of a legal order within the European community. Only since the 1986 *Single European Act* and then the 1991 Maastricht Treaty came into effect has the European Council been the highest official institution within the EU. Until then, those informal meetings had been functioning in parallel with official institutions and steering the European Union. The emergence of the European Council within the EU structure is thus an example of the EU institutional system adapting effectively to the emerging needs of integration.

In a way, the system of global economic governance follows a similar pattern. The G8 was created in parallel to the United Nations system as an informal institution to respond to critical international problems and coordinate the policies of the world's leading countries. Existing UN institutions were not sufficiently effective, similar to the way that European institutions were far from efficient. An informal body in the form of the G8 filled the void.

Similarly, the G20 meetings of finance ministers and central bank governors of the most systemically significant economies from all continents filled in the gap in the functioning of the established global financial institutions since 1999. Moreover, the recent voice and vote reform of the International Monetary Fund (IMF) is the beginning of a long process of making this global institution more legitimate, with the ultimate goal of being able to resolve the most acute financial problems of the modern world economy.

Another useful EU experience lies in its unique combination of supranational institutions and intergovernmental structures. There is a delicate balance between the intergovernmental structures representing national interests of the member states (the European Council and the Council of Ministers) and the supranational institutions working for a common interest (the European Parliament, the European Commission, and the European Court of Justice). This balance, however, is not constant. But within a non-linear trend there is a clear tendency to increase the powers and competences of the supranational institutions within the EU. The roles of the European Parliament, the European Commission, and the European Court of Justice are gradually increasing, which in turn means that the potential for integration is increasing, as is the ability to find common solutions to the difficult problems of interdependent economies of the EU members.

Decision Making as Accommodation

Effective decision making is at the heart of any structure. An organization cannot function without a system for working out and agreeing on decisions, nor can it progress. Many international structures, facing challenges, search for the new ways to make their work more efficient. They must also consider the other aspect of success, namely implementing those decisions.

The EU engages in decision making in a unique way. No other international institution can boast of a similar system, which is one of the greatest achievements of European integration. While there are arguments for and against its application to the global governance system, until now there is no better mechanism to manage the priorities of different countries collectively within international institutions in an increasingly interdependent global environment. The EU's decision-making process has much potential for compromise, with clauses and safeguards that allow for countries to operate at different speeds.

One factor of its success is the mechanism for accommodating the interests of both big and small countries, which differ in national priorities, traditions, and cultures. The EU's decision-making system serves big and small business, suits different social groups, and allows for varying political and economic factors (both domestic and external). Agrarian and industrial countries alike find their interests reflected in developing common structures, and economies of scale and degrees of development are organically unified within the system. Countries that within recent history were in a state of war – or even more recently in a state of Cold

War – now work out common decisions in a common structure of vital importance common to all of them. Moreover, the proportion of those who are dissatisfied with the EU is smaller than the proportion of those who favour it.

But can these achievements be reproduced at a global scale? To learn the secret is, as usual, both simple and difficult.

In simple terms, the EU's decision-making process can be summarized as a system of four times three, where:

- 1×3 = there are three major institutions for making decisions: the European Parliament, the Council of Ministers, and the European Commission;
- 2×3 = there are three major procedures to reach a decision: consultation, consent, and co-decision;
- 3×3 = there are three stages in the process: proposal, discussion, and acceptance;
- 4×3 = there are three major voting outcomes: unanimity, simple majority, or qualified majority.

Critics argue that this process is too complex. Yet it could not be more simple and logical, given the objectives of integration and the complexity of the problems, and the ambition required of the solutions.

The process differs depending on the area and subject of cooperation. Interaction among the EU decision-making bodies varies and the mode of interaction is not always the same. The more intensive cooperation in a particular area, the more operational the system should be. Thus with more supranational mechanisms, it is harder for the members to hamper the compromise for the prescribed procedure.

Decisions can be more or less binding according to the circumstance. There are five categories of decisions – from complex regulations and directives to simple recommendations – that assure necessary flexibility for member states while securing the required legal order within the EU.

Effective decision-making processes in many intergovernmental organizations is often associated with the right to veto. In the EU, however, a system of 'majority and qualified majority' voting is used more extensively. Otherwise, decisions would be very difficult to make and take a very long time agree upon.

The distribution of votes among the countries must also be arranged properly. On the one hand, small countries possess a smaller share of votes, although not as small as their size might suggest. In this way they are 'overrepresented' in the formulation of common policies, and their influence is much stronger than it would have been, had they not joined the EU. On the other hand, large countries have larger proportion of votes and thus a 'bigger say'. In most intergovernmental organizations, the common practice is to find ways to accommodate small countries and avoid the dominance of big ones. But true success is possible if and when the interests of the big participants are also fairly represented. Would it be just if a small state could decide on common industrial policies on equal terms with a big industrial economy? Or, if recipients of IMF assistance could determine the lending policy for the countries that fund the IMF? Influential countries are not likely to be satisfied with such an equation, and smaller European states have been wise enough to accept the realities.

Another positive feature of EU governance lies in the competences of its common institutions. While EU members determine both the degree and range of competences for those institutions, the institutions themselves accrue some power. However, they can exercise their authority relatively independently without asking for permission from the members. This autonomy is an important prerequisite for the success of the EU's common policies.

To ensure that EU members feel secure, according to legislation a member can opt out of a common policy if its major national interests are at risk. This encourages a state that might hesitate about the future consequences of cooperation in a particular field to proceed in a more decisive manner.

The principle of subsidiarity, integrated into the EU legal's system, means that decisions should be taken at an appropriate level. Common institutions come into play only if national or regional structures are incapable or less efficient in dealing with the issue. This is a useful lesson for many international structures, which tend to grab as much power as possible without consideration for efficiency.

Even with the EU's variable speeds and cautious approach to decision making and legislative implementation, members sometimes remain reluctant to engage in new areas of cooperation for fear of unpredictable economic and social consequences for their respective economies and societies. While such hesitation is understandable, especially given the unprecedented level of regional integration, the EU has a safeguard system of 'variable geometry' to accommodate those fears.

One such example is the European monetary system with a single currency of the euro at its heart, as Britain and other EU members have not chosen to join the monetary union. Another example is the Schengen agreement for visa-free travel within the EU borders, which only some member have signed. The list of such examples drawn from the EU experience is long. However, with time, cooperation among all the members will gather momentum and lure in new members that will realize the advantages of cooperation while, at the same time, assuming the responsibilities that come with it.

Some analysts tend to speak about the core and periphery of the European integration, sometimes in a negative sense. It would be more appropriate to view variable geometry of cooperation positively. As many areas of integration are sensitive, the EU's ability to allow for a degree of liberty in choosing to enter into binding common policies is a valuable feature of this modern model of global economic governance. Even a partial application of such features could improve the efficiency of global governance.

The Challenge of Economic Governance

The world needs global governance institutions. The task of global economic governance is already high on the global agenda. It is becoming all the more urgent with increased pressure to find quick solutions to the most acute global problems. One major obstacle to upgrading their effectiveness is a lack of efficiency in decision making and in implementing the resulting decisions.

There are several ways to enhance the efficiency of global economic governance. To upgrade the level of governance, institutions with variable geometry should operate in parallel to existing ones. This process already occurs at the regional level, where new intergovernmental organizations are created in addition to existing ones with a different range of competences. Thus alongside the Commonwealth of Independent States, the Eurasian Economic Community and the customs union have been created with a different composition to give a new impetus to regional cooperation within the post-Soviet space. Time will tell which of these organizations will be more resistant to global changes and to what extent they can cope with those changes.

In the history of European integration there was a similar process. The European Free Trade Association (EFTA) was created as an alternative to the quickly developing cooperation within the European community. Soft and binding options were offered to European countries at that time, with the more binding commitments eventually demonstrating greater efficiency and success. As a result, most of the countries on the continent chose in favour of the European communities – European Union – over the EFTA.

Another example related to the development of global governance institutions is the establishment of the G20 forum of finance ministers and central bank governors in parallel to the existing and influential IMF. There was some duplication in their missions. But the G20 format was different, with a less formal and less structured dialogue that made up for the inefficiency of IMF activities. The IMF's 187 members cannot react to rapid changes on international financial markets as quickly as needed, while the G20, being more compact in composition and less formal in procedure, has more flexibility.

The G20 is a product of the G7/G8 system, itself a parallel structure to the UN bodies. G8 priorities sometimes duplicate those of the UN Security Council or General Assembly. Again the G8 provides another tool for dealing with the same challenges, as it too is more compact and less formal and has proven to be effective at forging solutions to the hardest issues on the global agenda.

In general, an expansion of the role of different informal structures is another way of enhancing the efficiency of the global governance system. Different kinds of forums become important channels of information about existing challenges. As a result, the discussions that take place in those forums lead to decisions that increase of the level of global governance. Another example is the World Economic Forum, which has become an opportunity not only to debate the issues on the global economic agenda, but also to seek solutions and initiate decisions relating to sustainable economic development.

A 'multi-speed integration' method could be especially appropriate in the work of global institutions when unanimity is extremely difficult to achieve among member states with divergent interests. In the case of the UN Framework Convention on Climate Change, which aimed to protect the environment by limiting greenhouse gas emissions, some of the major polluters such as the Canada, Russia, and the US, were slow to ratify the Kyoto Protocol. The Kyoto Protocol was adopted in Japan on 11 December 1997. The detailed rules for implementation were adopted in Marrakesh in 2001. According to the UN (2011), the protocol is subject to ratification, acceptance, approval, or accession by Parties to the United Nations Framework Convention on Climate Change. Parties to the UNFCCC that have not signed the Protocol may accede to it at any time. When the protocol entered into force on 16 February 2005, after it had been ratified by Russia, the necessary threshold of a minimum 55 percent of the total carbon dioxide emissions for 1990 was reached. There are now 193 parties (192 states and one regional economic integration organization) to the Kyoto Protocol, which account for 63.7 percent of total emissions.

An important requirement in the multi-speed approach is the accumulation of a critical mass for a policy to be implemented. The countries that should assume responsibility could initiate an arrangement that is then followed by the others.

There is reason to assume that in the years to come, under pressure to reach their global goals countries will have to delegate some national competences to international organizations in order to make global economic governance more operational. A state on its own cannot manage global issues that extend beyond its jurisdiction.

Such an evolution would be similar to the EU process. In particular, a limited number of national competences could be partially transferred to international economic organizations in clearly defined cases, with limitations on the scope of the application of these competences. That would be the only reasonable approach to manage the 21st century's interdependent global economy. Otherwise, more economic disasters are inevitable. As in the case of European integration, this trend will likely start to develop within the system of global economic structures, but not political or military structures.

The application of the EU model presents some practical challenges. One such issue is how to distribute votes in a qualified majority decision-making procedure within a given structure. For example, at the UN, if population is the criterion, then all decisions will be made by India and China; if economic potential is considered, then it will be the United States and Europe that make the decisions; if raw materials are taken into account, it will be some other configuration. A complex formula is required to combine them all.

It thus seems necessary to depart from the unanimity rule in certain cases. Not all countries, however, may be ready to do so, at least not to the extent that has been done within the EU. But some aspects of the EU experience could be incorporated gradually into the global economic governance system. Many regional groupings already actively apply the EU experience, sometimes using the same procedures for cooperation.

One significant concern of most nation-states is the possible loss of control over their national economies. International institutions are perceived as a threat to national sovereignty. Many politicians and analysts support this fear. As Vacláv Klaus (2007), former president of the Czech Republic, has said, one of the biggest challenges is the trend towards an increase in the supranational aspects of EU policies: 'I have many times pointed out that the move toward an ever-closer Europe, the so-called deepening of the EU, as well as rapid political integration and Europe's supranational tendencies … are damaging to democracy and freedom'.

It remains unclear how a supranational trend could endanger civil freedoms and democracy. The degree of democratic freedoms within the system would need to be analysed. The supranational mechanism itself does not increase or diminish democracy. It could be either more or less democratic compared to individual national systems. For instance, the Lisbon Treaty has introduced democratic elements to reduce the democratic deficit that exists in the EU.

The fear of lost sovereignty over the economy as a result of a supranational institutional system seems not well founded. A nation-state already loses some control over part of its economy as it becomes transnational. Global institutions partially restore some of that control, as a result of the process of globalization.

Global institutions could compensate for the loss of control over some offshore activities. For this reason, cooperation with offshore jurisdictions was on the G20 agenda at the 2009 London Summit, and followed up by international institutions. Individual states cannot manage the problem efficiently.

In this case, as in many others, it becomes clear that the state is, to a certain extent, compelled to pass some of its national competences up to a regional or international level. It is an objective necessity. Global issues cannot be treated efficiently by individual nation-states. Indeed, as Nicholas Bayne and Stephen Woolcock (2003) have written, governance systems require national governments to share part of their sovereignty. But the penetration of international capital into national economies questions those nation-states' sovereignty nonetheless.

The more the nation-states are prepared to share their competences with international institutions, the more efficient the global governance system will be. The more interdependent and fragile the sectors of economic activity are (such as environment protection, climate change, biodiversity, fishing quotas, or atomic energy security), the more the need for a transfer of competences. The EU countries have realized – earlier, perhaps, than the rest of the world – that more competences need to be transferred to common institutions in order to achieve progress in common policies. In this sense, the EU shows the way ahead for today's global governance institutions.

References

Bayne, Nicholas, and Stephen Woolcock, eds (2003). *The New Economic Diplomacy: Decision Making and Negotiation in International Economic Relations*. Aldershot: Ashgate.

Klaus, Václav (2007). 'Environmentalism and Other Challenges of the Current Era.' Economic Development Bulletin No. 10, Cato Institute, Washington DC. <www.cato.org/pubs/edb/edb10.pdf> (July 2011).

United Nations (2011). 'Status of Ratification of the Kyoto Protocol.' <unfccc.int/kyoto_protocol/status_of_ratification/items/2613.php> (July 2011).

World Trade Organization (2011). 'World Trade Report 2011.' Geneva. <www.wto.org/english/res_e/booksp_e/anrep_e/world_trade_report11_e.pdf> (July 2011).

Chapter 15

The European Union and the G8: Priorities, Functions, Values

Marina Larionova and Mark Rakhmangulov

The European Union has been committed to effective multilateralism and global governance since early 1970s. It sought and secured membership in the G7 in 1977. Since then, the EU's role in economic summitry has grown substantially. Given its singular importance, the unique nature of its participation in the G8, and its increasing prominence there, the EU provides 'an excellent case study for the examination of the [European Union's] increasingly defined presence in the international arena' (Hainsworth 1990).[1]

Nonetheless, the role of the EU in the G8 has not been well explored. Although several seminal studies have addressed the EU's involvement and influence in summit negotiations and outcomes, they have reflected on the first two decades of G8 summitry (see Hainsworth 1990; Bonvicini and Wessels 1984; Ullrich and Donnelly 1998). Yet since the beginning of the 21st century, there have been global structural shifts and internal changes in the EU. Now, with 27 member states, the EU has more power, a much enhanced image, and increased legitimacy.

Objectives and Methodology

This chapter examines the EU's contribution to global governance, in large part by focusing on its evolving role in the G8. Covering the period from 1998 to 2008, it picks up where the earlier studies left off. It thus reflects the EU's changing identity as a global player following the 1997 signing of the Treaty of Amsterdam, the birth and development of the European Security and Defence Policy and the European Security Strategy, the enlargement that increased its representative weight in international institutions, and the further extension of its competencies, as well as the changing world order. It presents the findings from a functional analysis of EU and G8 contributions in four areas of comparison: the performance of global governance functions, the definition of global agenda priorities, the promotion

---

1   For the purposes of this chapter, in general terms G8 refers to both the G7 and the G8 unless referring directly to the period before Russia began participating at the summit level.

of shared values, and the intensity of the EU's engagement with international institutions.

Using an approach first developed by John Kirton (2007) to assess the G8's performance and role in global governance, this chapter explores and measures the EU's contribution to achieving its objectives of community political management, deliberation, direction setting, decision making, delivery, and the development of global governance.

Community political management is an extension of Kirton's dimension of domestic political governance, which does not apply to the EU. This analysis of the EU thus considers cases where the G8 has been instrumental in contributing to the EU's implementation of its policy objectives.

With regard to deliberation, the analysis examines the EU contribution to the debate on priority setting for global governance and forging a shared understanding of the issues and their value and place on the agenda. Similarly, on direction setting, it considers if, how, and to what extent the EU as a member of the G8 possesses the capacity to project its core priorities in shaping G8 priorities, normative statements, and values-based targets. On decision making, it focuses on the EU's contribution to crafting commitments made in G8 summits. On delivery, it assesses EU compliance with G8 commitments and compares the EU's compliance performance with that of the other G8 members.

To conduct this analysis, this chapter draws on an evidence base developed to document the changing role of the EU in the G8 system of institutions over the last decade, with the EU sharing with its G8 partners the responsibility for global security and well-being. The quantitative and qualitative analysis of the evidence focused on the issues and statements common to the G8 and EU priorities, values, decisions, commitments, and actions. The G8 performance assessment methodology designed by John Kirton, Ella Kokotsis, Jenilee Guebert, and Caroline Bracht (2011) was used in collecting and assessing the evidence in order to ensure consistency and coherency.

Consistency demanded that the same indicators be used where possible, although the objectives of this analysis required those indicators to be fine-tuned to reflect the nature of the data and respond to the specific needs of the research. Not all indicators of the G8 performance assessment methodology applied to the EU, so a different set of indicators was adopted.

With regard to community political management, the study used two indicators:

- Communiqué recognition – the number of references to the EU and its institutions in G8 communiqués (in a positive context that implicitly recognizes and verbally rewards the contribution). The unit of analysis was a reference; if the EU was mentioned twice in one sentence, it was scored as one.
- References to the G8 in the EU documents, including direct references to G8-specific summits and indirect references to G8 summits where the summit was implied in the policy documents, statements, or address (or equivalent).

With regard to deliberation, direction setting, and delivery, the analysis used absolute and relative data based on the number of characters relating to the function in documents. (The character account includes spaces and punctuation marks.) Relative parameters were defined as the share of the function in the total of all functions and expressed in percentages. The comparison focused on the share of functions in G8 and EU documents and the correlation between them.

On delivery, an additional indicator was the EU score published in the G8 final compliance reports produced by the G8 Research Group. These reports assess compliance over the period between each annual summit, starting with the summit at which the commitments were made and ending on the eve of the next summit.[2]

On global governance development, EU and G8 contributions were assessed on the basis of comparative analysis of the share of discourse devoted to the function.

On shared values, the analysis focused on EU and G8 values in the discourse on direction setting. Data were not restricted to the G8's 'democratic values' and included open markets, investment, free trade, climate and environmental protection, development, peace, and anti-corruption. The study examined similar normative statements that recurred in EU and G8 documents and the correlation between the two sets of references.

On priorities, the analysis assessed 13 broad priorities present on the agendas of both institutions. In the content analysis, a text unit could be earmarked as implementing only one of those priorities. The comparison was based on absolute cumulative data on the number of characters and the relative data on the issues shared in the EU and G8 discourse over the period under study.

To assess the EU and G8 engagement with other international institutions, references to a list of 186 such institutions were identified in the documents in the data base. The data contained the number of references made in that period and the correlation of the number of references to the number of characters in the documents:

$$I_i = \frac{R_i}{C}$$

where I_i is the intensity of references to international institutions in a certain year (period), R_i is number of references made to the institution $(_i)$ in that period, C is the total number of characters in the documents in that period, multiplied by 10,000 for ease of interpretation.

A cross-institutional comparison was made using the data on intensity and dynamics. A combination of the parameters on intensity and dynamics allowed an assessment of the EU and G8 contributions to developing multilateralism on key issues of global governance.

The content analysis suggested that the documents would not necessarily render explicit evidence of the EU's influence and its contribution to G8 performance.

---

2   See 'Analytical and Compliance Studies' on the website of the G8 Information Centre at <www.g8.utoronto.ca/compliance>.

Simultaneously the data provided evidence of G8-EU interdependence and mutual reinforcement, as well as G8 being instrumental in making the EU an international actor. There remains a question of which leads which. The response depends on the policy sphere as well as on other factors. Thus not only was careful analysis of the wording required to build the evidence base, but in-depth knowledge of EU/G8 processes and history was also necessary to interpret the data.

The Data Base

The data base contains documents produced by EU institutions and the G8 between 1998 and 2008. Sources included the official websites of G8 chairs, the G8 Information Centre website at the University of Toronto, and websites of think tanks. EU documents were drawn from the online archive of press releases published by the Council of the European Union and the European Commission website.

The evidence base contains 1,927 documents, most of which (1,676) belong to the EU. The remaining 251 belong to the G8. The number of EU documents differs significantly over the years and reflects both a pattern in EU processes and the intensity of deliberation on priorities shared with the G8. The number of G8 documents reflects the formally adopted summit documents.

The materials analysed include:

- documents issued at G8 summits and ministerial meetings, reports from working groups and task forces, and joint statements with the Outreach members of Brazil, China, India, Mexico, and South Africa, whose leaders participated in summits from 2005 to 2008.
- documentation and data pertaining to the involvement of EU institutions (the European Council, the council presidency, the high representative for the Common Foreign and Security Policy [CFSP], and the European Commission) in G8 processes and legal texts on role of the EU in the world.

In selecting EU priorities, the study focused on issues with an international and global character, as well as internal issues with foreign policy implications. It also included, but was not be limited to, the following configurations within the European Commission:

- the General Affairs and External Relations Council;
- the Directorate-General for Economic and Financial Affairs at the European Commission and the European Central Bank;
- the directorates-general for transport, telecommunications, and energy where relevant; and
- the Directorate-General for the Environment.

The data base also included documents referred to in presidency conclusions and annexed to them. Documents on the CFSP received special attention although the essential authority for the policy remains with EU member states, unlike in the cases of economy, finance, external trade, and development. With regard to CFSP issues, the documents included but were not limited to those of the European Council, the EU foreign ministers and the meetings of the European Commissioner for External Relations, the presidency of the European Council, and the high representative for the CFSP.

There are relatively few European Commission documents because they are used to prepare the subsequent decisions of the Council, which were the major source of data.

Key Findings

Functions

Deliberation dominates in both the EU and the G8 according to the absolute data and within the total discourse (see Figure 15.1). The EU outperforms the G8 on average over the period under study, except, notably, in 1999 and 2007 when Germany held both the presidency of the European Commission and the chair of the G8 (see Appendix 15.1). The share of references related to the deliberation function is similar for both institutions for these two periods, which can be attributed to the capacity of the German chancellors' teams to find synergies among the national, regional, and global priorities on the summit agendas. The G8 and EU summits in those years focused on economic issues, but regional security constituted a substantial part of the deliberation. In 1999 under Gerhard Schröder, it was in the form of an EU initiative on the Stability Pact for South Eastern Europe;

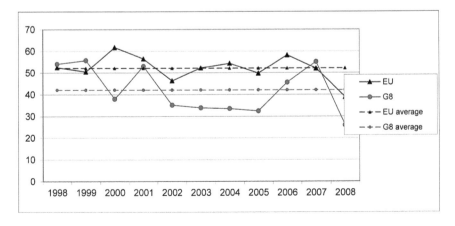

Figure 15.1   Deliberation Characters (%)

in 2007 under Angela Merkel, the G8 leaders debated the future status of Kosovo and United Nations Special Envoy Martti Ahtisaari's proposal for a settlement, as well as other security challenges high on the EU agenda, namely the Middle East peace process, Iran, Iraq, Afghanistan, Sudan and Darfur, non-proliferation, nuclear safety, and security.

The dynamics of direction setting in the EU and G8 converge in a way that is especially characteristic of dual EU/G8 presidencies (see Figure 15.2). The exception is in 2005, when the United Kingdom was unable to use the dual presidency to promote a European response to issues high on the public agenda. The UK had an internal agenda fraught with divisions over the financing of the EU budget for the 2007–13 period. The EU also was midway through its multi-annual strategic programme for the period 2004–06, with economic reform and social justice, security and stability, and Europe's role in the world as its main objectives. There was little real linkage between these two presidencies, not 'because of the very different nature of the decision-making processes in the two organizations' but because 'the G-8 Presidency … provided an opportunity to focus on the big themes of Third World poverty and climate change, and to work for progress in these key areas with some of the most internationally significant states. The EU Presidency is much less glamorous; it requires working in a much more circumscribed manner in a more complicated set of institutional arrangements and with more limited objectives. The UK … tended to treat the G-8 Presidency as something to be celebrated; and the EU Presidency as something to be endured' (Whitman and Thomas 2005).

There is also some convergence on both decision making and global governance development (see Figures 15.3 and 15.4). The G8 decision-making average is higher than that of the EU. However, during the UK and the German dual presidencies in 1998 and 2007 respectively there was almost the same level of consensus in both institutions.

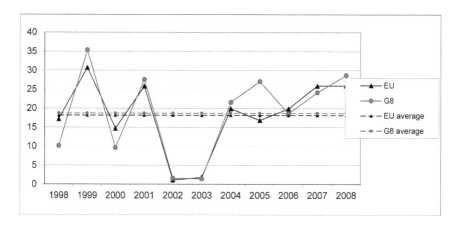

Figure 15.2   Direction-Setting Characters (%)

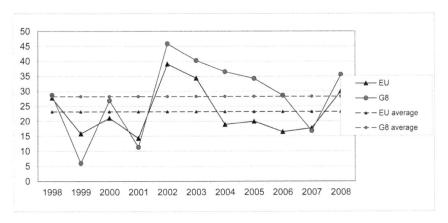

Figure 15.3 Decision-Making Characters (%)

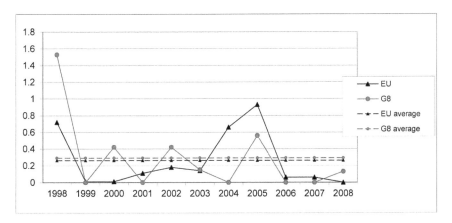

Figure 15.4 Global Governance Development Characters (%)

On global governance development, the average performance for the G8 and EU is also close, with the G8 leading and scoring a record high during the 1998 UK presidency. Issues on the leaders' agenda related to the historic decision to establish the EU's monetary union, efforts to re-establish stability and growth in Asia, the role of the international financial institutions in managing the financial crisis that had begun in 1997, and commitments to the 21st Century Strategy of the Organisation for Economic Co-operation and Development (OECD) to support reforms in developing countries and to reach goals for economic and social development.

The EU, however, demonstrates a higher level of delivery (see Figure 15.5). This conclusion is confirmed by the EU performance on compliance with its commitments: the EU scores higher than the G8 in the assessments conducted

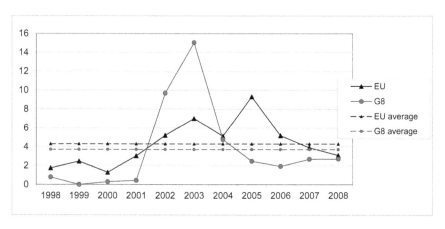

Figure 15.5 Delivery Characters (%)

by the G8 Research Group since 2004.[3] Because the performance of the two institutions differs depending on the area of collaboration, the data indicate a downward trend in the EU's performance on its commitments on development (see Figure 15.6).

On the political agenda, the G8 and the EU contribute equally in terms of direction setting. Once again, the G8 leads on decision making, but here it also leads on the development of global governance. On compliance, there is a downward trend for both forums, although the G8 outperforms by almost 20 percent (see Figure 15.7).

On the security agenda, again there is parity with regard to direction setting, with a higher degree of discourse intensity in the G8 (see Figure 15.8). The G8 leads on decision making and global governance development, and the EU average on delivery slightly exceeds the G8's.

In the issue area of the environment, the picture varies from year to year (see Figure 15.9). On average, G8 and EU contributions are about equal on deliberation, direction setting, decision making, and global governance development. In part, this parity can be attributed to the fact that the EU member chairing the G8 included the environment and climate change on the G8 agenda. Indeed, this is confirmed by similarity in global governance functions for both institutions in the years with dual presidencies. On delivery, again the EU demonstrates a higher level of performance.

On the function of delivery, the EU's contribution is consistently higher than the G8's (see Figure 15.10). This performance confirms the commitment of the EU to multilateralism through action and to extending a culture of compliance with collective decisions beyond the EU.

---

3   See 'Analytical and Compliance Studies' on the website of the G8 Information Centre at <www.g8.utoronto.ca/compliance>.

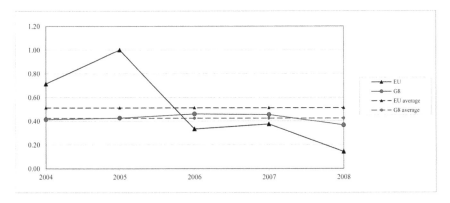

Figure 15.6   EU and G8 Compliance with Commitments on Development

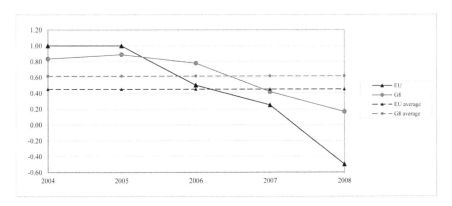

Figure 15.7   EU and G8 Compliance with Commitments on Political Issues

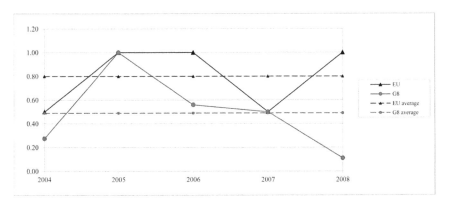

Figure 15.8   EU and G8 Compliance with Commitments on Security

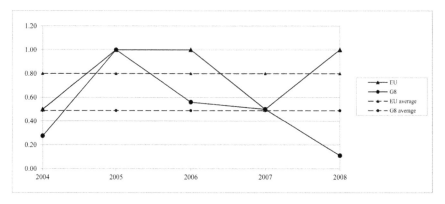

Figure 15.9   EU and G8 Compliance with Commitments on the Environment

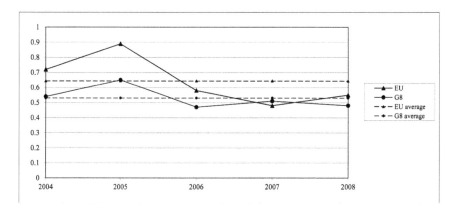

Figure 15.10 EU and G8 Overall Compliance

Because the EU does not preside over G8 summits, it does not possess the essential instrument for community political management. It thus comes fourth in the number of references to it in the G8 documents, after Russia, Japan, and the United States. The G8 addresses the EU most often during the dual presidencies under the UK and Germany (see Table 15.1). However, the peak was in 2006, the year of the Russian G8 presidency, which indicates the importance placed by Russia on its partnership with the EU, especially in implementing the St. Petersburg Plan of Action Global Energy Security. Nonetheless, content analysis reveals that most references to the EU are in the documents on political issues and health, confirming the role of the EU in the G8 on these issues and its overall importance for Russia as a partner.

Table 15.1   References to G8 Members and the EU in G8 Documents

	1998	1999	2000	2001	2002	2003	2004	2005	2006	2007	2008	Total	Share (%)
Russia	7	11	4	31	21	26	3	15	92	33	14	257	22.04
Japan	13	3	25	11	2	28	4	11	12	27	63	199	17.07
United States	11	11	10	18	11	28	2	13	29	28	15	176	15.09
European Union	21	13	6	11	0	0	4	14	29	18	9	125	10.72
Canada	4	0	2	11	9	20	1	4	27	22	2	102	8.75
United Kingdom	8	1	1	7	1	13	2	10	28	16	6	93	7.98
France	4	0	0	0	5	26	3	9	28	8	5	88	7.55
Germany	5	0	0	0	3	11	1	9	24	9	8	70	6.00
Italy	6	0	2	3	5	11	4	2	12	7	4	56	4.80
Total	79	39	50	92	57	163	24	87	281	168	126	1,166	100.00

The G8 frequently refers to the EU on political issues, finance, economy, and the environment – issue areas where it deems the EU intervention to be vital (see Table 15.2). The number of EU references to the G8 is significantly lower than that of G8 references to the EU, and much lower than the number of the EU references to other key international institutions (see Figure 15.11). However, a positive trend is clearly traceable, likely the result of the EU considering the G8 to be increasingly useful for influencing the global agenda and thus for community political management. Furthermore, this analysis does not confirm the assertion that multilateral institutions are effective for domestic or community political management. The share of this function is low for both the G8 and the EU compared to the other functions (see Figure 15.12).

Table 15.2   References to the EU in G8 Documents by Priority

	1998	1999	2000	2001	2002	2003	2004	2005	2006	2007	2008	Total	Share (%)
Political Issues	0	10	4	1	0	0	2	7	12	10	1	47	37.6
Finance	8	0	0	5	0	0	0	0	0	2	0	15	12.0
Health	0	0	0	0	0	0	1	0	14	0	0	15	12.0
Economy	5	2	2	3	0	0	0	0	1	0	0	13	10.4
Environment/ Climate change	2	0	0	1	0	0	0	0	0	3	5	11	8.8
Security	4	1	0	1	0	0	1	0	0	0	0	7	5.6
Energy	0	0	0	0	0	0	0	3	0	3	0	6	4.8
Development	0	0	0	0	0	0	0	4	2	0	0	6	4.8
Uncategorized	2	0	0	0	0	0	0	0	0	0	3	5	4.0
Total	21	13	6	11	0	0	4	14	29	18	9	125	100

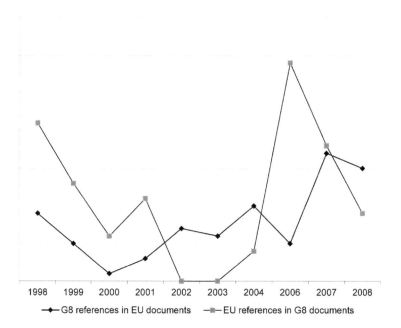

Figure 15.11 G8 and EU References

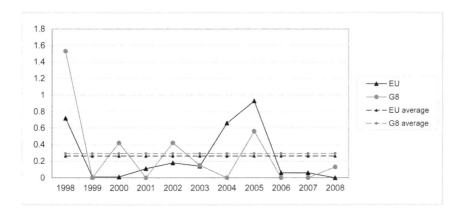

Figure 15.12 Community Political Management Characters (%)

Clearly the EU contribution to the global governance function differs according to issue area (see Table 15.3). On the economy, the intensity of deliberation for both the EU and the G8 is higher than average on all priorities. The share of decision-making function on economic issues is much higher for the EU, and higher than the EU average.

Table 15.3   Priorities by Function (% characters)

	Economy		Finance	
	EU	G8	EU	G8
Deliberation	53.95	58.42	55.44	54.76
Direction setting	15.45	17.96	15.02	15.30
Decision making	28.37	17.78	26.61	12.41
Delivery	1.79	0.50	2.32	3.44
Development of global governance	0.29	5.33	0.61	13.54
Community political management	0.15	0	0.00	0.54
	Trade		Development	
	EU	G8	EU	G8
Deliberation	54.37	27.61	49.70	43.91
Direction setting	11.52	27.88	17.36	16.24
Decision making	32.06	41.19	28.45	31.44
Delivery	1.60	0.00	2.96	3.36
Development of global governance	0.38	3.32	1.53	4.82
Community political management	0.07	0	0.00	0.22

On finance, the intensity of deliberation and the share of direction setting for both institutions are about even, but the EU share of decision-making function is significantly higher. On trade policy, the share of deliberation in the EU is significantly higher than that in the G8. Given the EU competencies on trade policy it is surprising that G8 exceeds the EU substantially on direction setting and decision making.

On development assistance, the levels on deliberation are higher for the EU and about equal on decision making. On the global governance development the G8 performance is higher. And although on delivery they are close, EU compliance is consistently higher than that of the G8.[4]

To sum up, the EU contribution to all global governance functions has been increasing. It leads on the intensity of the discourse and level of delivery, and thus influences consensus building and compliance. The analysis revealed the EU had an increasing impact on direction setting and global governance development. The dynamics of the direction-setting function support the argument for the extra clout of dual G8-EU presidencies: 1998 with the UK, 1999 with Germany, 2005 with the UK, and 2007 with Germany.

The EU has a limited capacity for using the G8 as a mechanism for community political management. Consequently, it is difficult to assess its contribution to developing global governance. Nevertheless, the high number of references made by the G8 to the EU supports the assumption that the G8 is an effective opportunity for the EU's community political management. It is also evidence of the EU's substantial contribution to the G8 agenda.

Values

Two processes were observed over the period under study: the consolidation of the shared values system and its transformation. Peace, democracy, open markets, and trade liberalization remain pillars for both the G8 and the EU. The environment, human well-being, and development gain new prominence for both. In the EU, deliberation on free trade and open markets acquired higher significance over time, with peaks in growth from 1998 to 2000, during a period of systemic and institutional changes, followed by a stabilization in growth.

According to a comparative analysis of the intensity of dynamics of values, the EU leads on the values of peace and democracy (see Figures 15.13 and 15.14). On freedom, its contribution exceeds that of the G8 by far (see Figure 15.15).

On the values of human well-being and development, however, the G8 discourse defines the trend, although on the former there is the exception of a surge in the year of the 2002 Kananaskis Summit (see Figure 15.16). The G8 leads on development, despite convergence during the dual presidencies of 2005 and 2007 (see Figure 15.17).

A special picture develops with regard to values relating to the environment. Although the average parameters are close, the dynamics of the two curves indicate the driving force of the EU (see Figure 15.18).

---

4   See 'Analytical and Compliance Studies' on the website of the G8 Information Centre at <www.g8.utoronto.ca/compliance>.

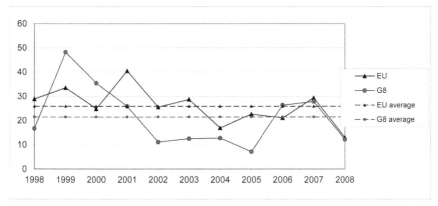

Figure 15.13 References to Peace (%)

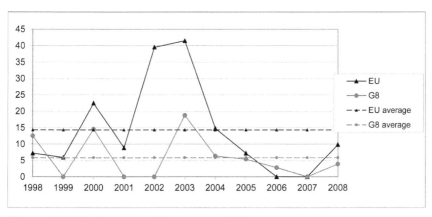

Figure 15.14 References to Democracy (%)

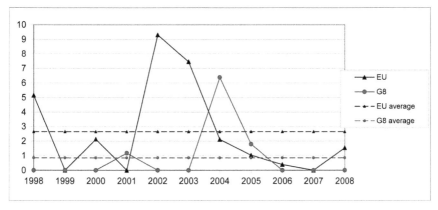

Figure 15.15 References to Freedom (%)

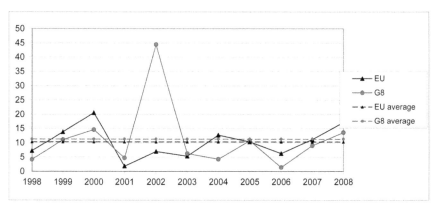

Figure 15.16 References to Well-Being (%)

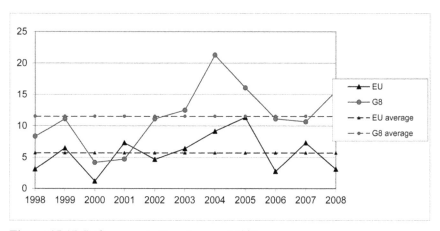

Figure 15.17 References to Development (%)

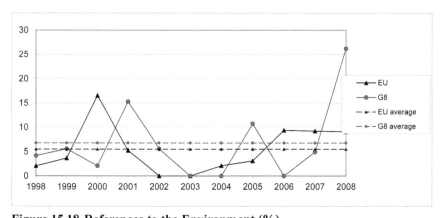

Figure 15.18 References to the Environment (%)

The G8 maintains its leadership in the values of free trade, investment, and anti-corruption (see Figure 15.19). However, on free trade there is a marked increase in the G8 parameters in 1998 and 2003, and a convergence of G8 and EU parameters in 2005 and 2007 (see Figure 15.20). Given that 1998, 2005, and 2007 were years with dual G8-EU presidencies, it is not possible to disentangle the two contributions.

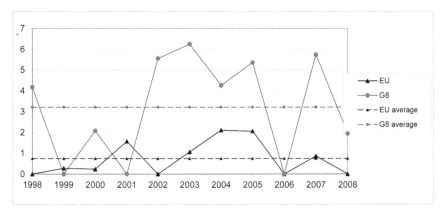

Figure 15.19 References to Investment (%)

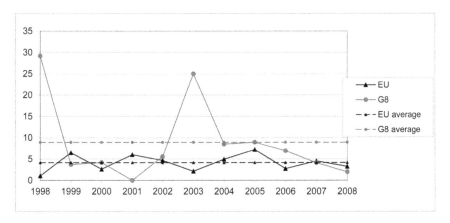

Figure 15.20 References to Free Trade and Open Markets (%)

On anti-corruption, although the G8 average is higher, given that the peaks fall in 2001, when Italy chaired the G8, and in 2005, when the UK chaired the G8 and the EU, some of the anti-corruption discourse in the EU was carried over to the G8 setting (see Figure 15.21).

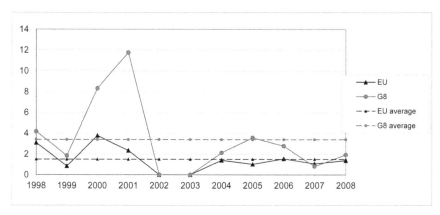

Figure 15.21 References to Anti-corruption (%)

To sum up, the EU's contribution to consolidating the shared values system is greater on peace, democracy, and freedom, and it tends to lead on the environment. The G8, however, continues to define the global dialogue on development, and its traditional values of free trade and open markets, investment, and anti-corruption.

Priorities

It is little surprise that the absolute discourse intensity and cumulative parameters for the EU exceed those for the G8 by far, thanks to the specific nature of G8 and EU processes. An analysis of those parameters reveals increasing convergence on most priorities, including political issues and security, economy, trade, energy, education, and science and innovation. However, it is unclear whether the intensity of the discourse on priority issues in the EU influences the agenda of other international institutions – namely the G8.

The absolute cumulative data confirm the assumption that intra-EU political and institutional transformations influence the EU's contributions to the development of global governance on major policy issues. This tendency is especially pronounced in the increasing intensity on finance and monetary policy, security and political issues, energy policy, and cooperation in the sphere of education and science. The trends are related accordingly to implementing the third phase of economic and monetary union, strengthening the institutional foundation of the security and defence policy (with the entry into force of the Amsterdam Treaty in 1999), enhancing cooperation on energy (with regard to trans-European networks in the energy sector, investment in projects in the petroleum, natural gas, and electricity sectors, and the creation in 2001 of the European Energy and Transport Forum), and strengthening the institutional foundations for education (with the launch of the Education and Training 2010 work programme).

The data also reveal differences between the EU and G8 in terms of setting priorities. Whereas political issues and security, finance, and environment occupy nearly equal shares of both institutions' agendas, the issue of development assistance – regardless of the unit of measurement – is inevitably among the top three issues on the G8 agenda (see Appendices 15.2 and 15.3). The relative parameters confirm the G8's leading role on development, although after the 2002 Kananaskis Summit the intensity of G8 deliberation decreased in the total number of documents, references, and characters (see Figure 15.22). The EU and G8 parameters are close in 2005 and 2007. However, given the dual presidencies of the UK and Germany in those years, it is hard to attribute the rising tendency solely to EU leadership. Nevertheless, the dual presidency allowed for the mutual reinforcement of making Africa a priority on both agendas.

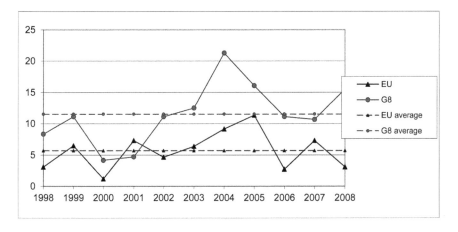

Figure 15.22 Development Characters (%)

Although the G8 leads in shaping the global agenda on economy and finance, after the EU established its monetary union and launched the Lisbon strategy the trend fluctuates towards a convergence of parameters on economy (see Figure 15.23). Moreover, the EU contribution to global dialogue on finance remains surprisingly modest (see Figure 15.24). Nonetheless, given that three of the four peaks in the G8's score fall during dual G8-EU presidencies – in 1998, 2001, and 2007 – it appears that EU priorities were reflected in the G8 agenda.

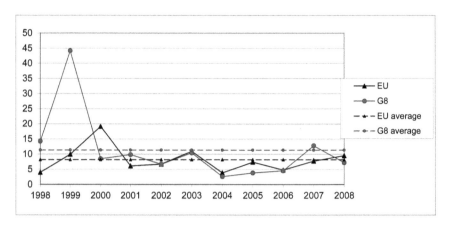

Figure 15.23 Economy Characters (%)

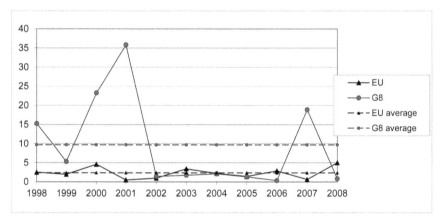

Figure 15.24 Finance Characters (%)

The EU dominates in the discourse on trade policy, reflecting the facts that this issue figures only ninth on the G8's list of priorities, the EU accounts for 19 percent of global imports and exports, and through the European Commission the EU acts as a single entity on the international scene (see Figure 15.25).

On energy, there is a consistent trend of the EU agenda strengthening since 2005, more prominently since 2006 after the adoption of the St Petersburg action plan (see Figure 15.26). The G8 dominates on average in terms of the total number of documents, references, and characters. However, the EU leads in terms of the intensity of dynamics, which can be attributed to the UK's dual presidencies in 1998 and 2005, and partially to Germany's in 2007, when energy efficiency and environment were on the G8 agenda, as well as the general prominence these issues gain in both intra-EU cooperation and EU external dialogue.

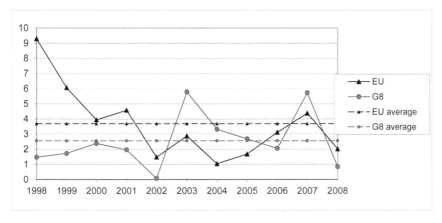

Figure 15.25 Trade Characters (%)

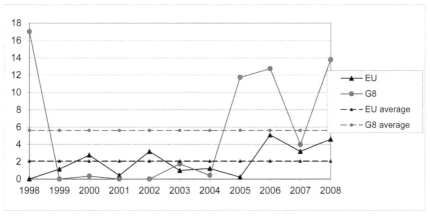

Figure 15.26 Energy Characters (%)

While the EU agenda on environmental protection is consistently strengthened, the G8 has a greater priority share in the documents, references, and characters in 2008, the last year included in this analysis (see Figure 15.27). As with energy, the EU led by intensity on environmental issues, which is directly related to their prominence in intra-EU cooperation and EU external dialogue.

Although the political agenda features high in the EU documents included in this analysis, the average intensity of deliberation on security on the G8 agenda is much higher (see Figures 15.28 and 15.29). However, there is convergence on the degree of the discourse intensity, which is most apparent on political issues.

There is also a convergence on discourse intensity on the issue of health, with the G8 leading (see Figure 15.30). The peak of G8 leadership occurred in 2006, when

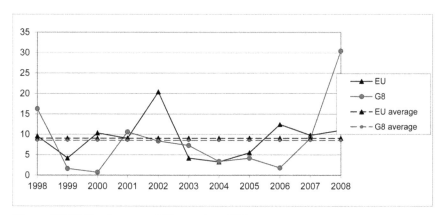

Figure 15.27 Environment Characters (%)

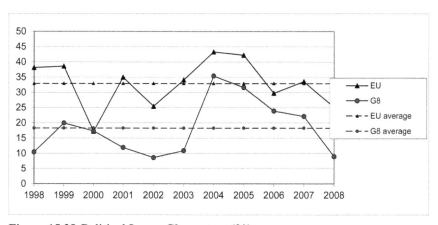

Figure 15.28 Political Issues Characters (%)

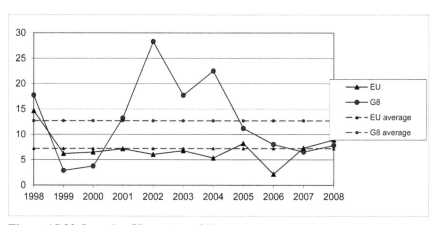

Figure 15.29 Security Characters (%)

the Russian chair placed both education and health on the St. Petersburg Summit agenda. This trend confirms the growing role of 'new issues' on the agendas of both the G8 and the EU in response to new global governance challenges. The tendency confirms an increasing role of the 'new issues' of science, information technology, education, and innovation in both institutions' agendas in response to new global governance challenges (see Figure 15.31).

Thus, according to the relative balance in discourse intensity on global public goods, there is generally a positive dynamic with regard to development, environment, trade, and anti-corruption, as well as education and science.

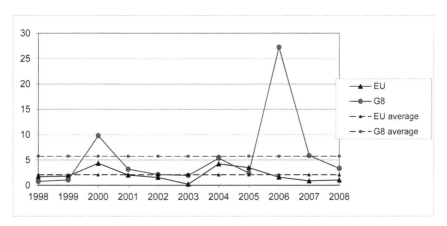

Figure 15.30 Health Characters (%)

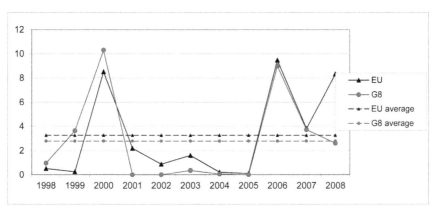

Figure 15.31 Characters for Science, Information Technology, Education, and Innovation (%)

Engagement with International Institutions

Because there are more EU documents included in this study, the number of EU references to international institutions significantly surpasses the comparative number for the G8 (see Figure 15.32).

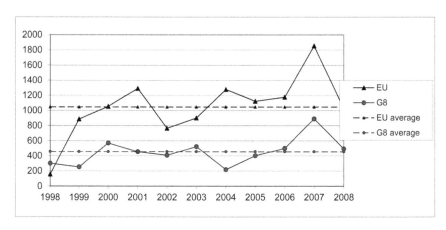

Figure 15.32 References to International Institutions (%)

However, the intensity of references to international institutions in G8 documents exceeds the intensity of the EU by far (see Figure 15.33).[5] This reflects the G8's reliance on international mechanisms to implement summit decisions. The level of intensity of EU references to international institutions remains stable over time. For the G8, the 1998 peak is related to several factors, including G8 reform, decisions made on the international financial architecture following the beginning of the Asian financial crisis, and decisions on development, climate change, and the fight against infectious disease. It is also related to the inclusive approach to 'global alliance for global values' taken by British prime minister and G8 host Tony Blair (2006). The lowest intensity is observed in the 2004 US presidency of the G8, which can probably be attributed to the preference of the Bush administration for unilateralism and reliance on its own resources and mechanisms, as well as tensions among the G8 members over the Iraq war, which made forging a consensus on international mechanisms for implementing commitments more difficult.

For both the EU and the G8, the UN remains the key partner, with 12 percent of references in the EU documents and almost 46 percent in G8 documents (see

5   Intensity of references to international institutions is measured as the relation between the number of references to international institutions in one year and the number of characters of the documents issued in that year, multiplied by 10,000.

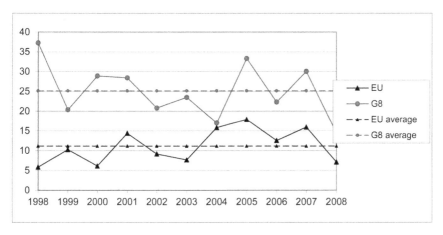

Figure 15.33 Intensity of References to International Institutions (%)

Tables 15.4 and 15.5). Of all other institutions included in this analysis, only the World Trade Organization features among the top five, at 8 percent for the EU and 3.5 percent for the G8. The International Monetary Fund and the World Bank, which are the main partners for the G8 agenda not only on finance but also on development, climate change, and economics, rank 17th for the G8 and 11th for the EU between 1998 and 2008 – before the issues of preventing financial crises or post-crises measures arose on the agenda, and before reform of the global governance architecture including the G20 and Financial Stability Board gained such prominence. Another frequent G8 partner is the OECD, which ranked tenth

Table 15.4   EU References to International Organizations

Organization	1998	1999	2000	2001	2002	2003	2004	2005	2006	2007	2008	Total	Share, %
United Nations	55	356	526	670	356	379	563	557	555	767	475	5,259	45.75
World Trade Organization	13	122	61	116	66	91	71	69	100	156	74	939	8.17
African Union	0	0	0	2	4	35	119	92	154	294	101	801	6.97
Organization for Security and Co-operation in Europe	13	89	57	62	42	69	69	24	24	28	42	519	4.52
International Criminal Tribunal for the former Yugoslavia	3	13	4	31	20	43	36	70	29	37	29	315	2.74

Table 15.5   G8 References to International Organizations

	1998	1999	2000	2001	2002	2003	2004	2005	2006	2007	2008	2009	Total	Share, %
United Nations	67	44	76	68	85	82	21	90	111	134	245	149	1,172	12.02
International Monetary Fund	37	52	112	88	47	29	13	45	11	56	13	35	538	9.66
World Bank	18	33	36	50	42	33	21	66	41	90	69	39	538	7.91
Organization for Economic Co-operation and Development	29	11	36	34	9	37	4	22	18	44	64	92	400	5.39
World Trade Organization	16	8	13	22	8	40	19	32	21	28	20	18	245	3.53

in EU documents, likely because the EU is defined within the organization as a member without a vote. Whereas at 5 percent the OECD comes fourth in the G8 list, the Organization for Security and Co-operation in Europe ranks fourth in the EU list, with an almost equal 4.5 percent. This variation in institutional engagement results from the differences in priority setting, as well as the nature of EU membership in these institutions and their links with the G8.

Conclusions

Several overall conclusions can be drawn from the analysis contained in this chapter. First, on all functions measured, the EU's contribution to global governance is growing. Its average dynamics is highest on global governance development, direction setting, deliberation, and delivery. On average, the EU scores higher than the G8 on deliberation and delivery, influencing the processes of forging consensus and the level of compliance with commitments made at G8 summits, whereas the dynamics of the EU and the G8 converge on direction setting. There is overlap, or near overlap, on the functions of decision making and global governance development.

Second, the EU significantly contributes to the consolidation and transformation of a shared system of values. With regard to the discourse intensity, the EU leads in promoting the values of peace, freedom, and democracy. Its defining influence is also evident on the environment, whereas the G8 continues to lead the global dialogue on development and its traditional values of free trade and open markets, investment, and anti-corruption.

Third, the data indicate increasing convergence in the discourse dynamics of both institutions on the main priorities, foremost, of political and security issues, economy and trade, energy, and, more recently, education, science, and innovation. The intensity of the EU discourse contributes to the developing the global governance agenda and may influence the inclusion of priorities in the G8 agenda. However, there are clear differences in priority setting between the two institutions. Thus, development, political issues, and security are top priorities for the G8, whereas for the EU the top three are political issues, the economy, and the environment.

Fourth, the discourse dynamics confirm the impact of intra-EU political and institutional transformations on the EU's contribution to shaping global governance processes on key policy issues. Thus, although the G8 leads on economy and finance, after the establishment of the European monetary union and the launch of the Lisbon strategy, there is a slow convergence on these issues. The EU dominates in intensity of deliberation on trade. There is a clear trend of its growing impact on energy policy and the environment, and indeed the EU defines dynamics of the value system on the latter.

On security, financial crisis management, and the fight against corruption, the levels of discourse intensity converge. In spite of the EU's steadily and significantly growing contribution to development assistance, the G8 leads on agenda setting for development and its consolidation as a core value.

Because the G8 relies on international institutions to implement its commitments, there is a much greater intensity of references to international institutions in G8 documents than in EU documents. However, the steady, growing number of references to international institutions in EU documents confirms the EU's commitment to effective multilateralism.

Fifth, the dynamics of data on all areas of analysis (priorities, functions, and values) affirms that the dual presidency of the EU and the G8 constitutes an indisputable resource for the EU to influence the global discourse and implement global governance functions.

References

Blair, Tony (2006). 'A Global Alliance for Global Values.' Foreign Policy Cenre, London. <fpc.org.uk/fsblob/798.pdf> (July 2011).

Bonvicini, Gianni, and Wolfgang Wessels (1984). 'The European Community and the Seven.' In *Economic Summits and Western Decision-Making*, edited by Cesare Merlini, pp. 167–93. London: Croom Helm.

Hainsworth, Susan (1990). 'Coming of Age: The European Community and the Economic Summit.' Country Study No. 7, G7 Research Group. <www.g8.utoronto.ca/scholar/hainsworth1990/index.html> (July 2011).

Kirton, John J. (2007). 'The Bottom Line: Has the G8 Achieved Its Goals?' Paper prepared for a workshop on "The Future of the G8: Global Economic

Governance and the Potential for a Revision of Institutional Arrangements," Stiftung Wissenschaft und Politik, Berlin, 6 June. <www.g8.utoronto.ca/scholar/kirton2007/kirton_goals.pdf> (July 2011).

Kirton, John J., Ella Kokotsis, Jenilee Guebert, et al. (2011). 'G8/G20 Reference Manual for Commitment and Compliance Coding.' Toronto, 22 September. <www.g8.utoronto.ca/evaluations/compliancemanual-110922.pdf> (September 2011).

Ullrich, Heidi K., and Alan Donnelly (1998). 'The Group of Eight and the European Union: The Evolving Partnership.' No. 5, November. <www.g8.utoronto.ca/governance/gov5> (July 2011).

Whitman, Richard, and Gareth Thomas (2005). 'Two Cheers for the UK's EU Presidency.' December, Chatham House, London. <www.chathamhouse.org/sites/default/files/public/Research/Europe/bpukeupresidency.pdf> (July 2011).

Appendix 15.1   EU and G8 Presidencies

Year	G8	Council of the European Union
1998	United Kingdom	United Kingdom
		Austria
1999	Germany	Germany
		Finland
2000	Japan	Portugal
		France
2001	Italy	Sweden
		Belgium
2002	Canada	Spain
		Denmark
2003	France	Greece
		Italy
2004	United States	Ireland
		Netherlands
2005	United Kingdom	Luxembourg
		United Kingdom
2006	Russia	Austria
		Finland
2007	Germany	Germany
		Portugal
2008	Japan	Slovenia
		France

Appendix 15.2 Priorities in EU Documents (thousands of characters)

	1998	1999	2000	2001	2002	2003	2004	2005	2006	2007	2008	Total	Share, %
Political issues	102.5	333.7	296.0	313.6	212.1	400.4	349.5	264.9	279.2	390.4	360.6	3303.1	30.78
Economy	10.7	85.8	328.4	54.7	55.8	128.0	31.0	46.2	44.8	89.6	136.1	1011.1	9.42
Environment/Climate change	25.7	36.1	177.2	80.7	170.4	48.9	26.4	34.4	116.4	113.5	157.6	987.4	9.20
EU-specific issues	24.7	75.7	100.7	99.1	108.6	112.5	67.5	54.9	59.7	66.7	70.9	840.9	7.84
Bilateral relations	16.2	45.0	30.9	56.9	84.9	136.5	135.1	45.3	66.2	73.0	93.7	783.8	7.30
Security	39.4	53.6	111.6	64.2	50.5	79.7	43.1	51.6	20.4	84.9	128.1	727.1	6.77
Development	4.7	95.7	27.9	79.1	55.8	51.8	33.0	44.3	53.2	117.7	61.4	624.6	5.82
Uncategorized	3.4	27.2	157.9	58.7	23.2	57.3	45.8	21.7	58.3	61.8	72.3	587.6	5.48
Science, information technology, education, innovation	1.4	2.2	146.4	19.6	7.4	18.8	1.8	0.6	88.8	44.3	119.5	450.8	4.20
Trade	25.0	52.4	67.7	41.1	12.4	33.7	8.4	10.5	29.2	51.0	28.9	360.4	3.36
Finance	6.6	16.9	78.4	4.3	8.2	39.9	17.7	8.8	26.9	7.3	71.5	286.4	2.67
Energy	0.0	9.9	47.4	3.7	26.5	11.5	9.9	1.4	47.5	37.0	65.8	260.7	2.43
Health	4.5	15.6	74.6	18.1	12.9	2.7	34.1	21.8	15.0	10.3	15.1	224.9	2.10
Crisis management	2.0	3.3	20.6	3.0	1.5	45.6	3.1	20.8	27.9	12.5	19.0	159.5	1.49
Corruption	1.9	12.0	54.7	0.4	4.6	7.1	0.7	0.0	4.8	3.2	35.0	124.3	1.16
Total	268.8	865.1	1,720.3	897.3	834.9	1,174.5	807.3	627.3	938.4	1,163.1	1,435.6	10,732.6	100.00

Appendix 15.3　Priorities in G8 Documents (thousands of characters)

	1998	1999	2000	2001	2002	2003	2004	2005	2006	2007	2008	Total	Share, %
Development	3.3	23.4	22.3	20.4	86.4	74.0	22.1	28.2	15.0	13.3	72.5	380.8	18.22
Political issues	8.4	24.7	34.3	19.0	16.9	24.3	45.2	38.1	53.6	65.5	30.6	360.6	17.25
Security	14.3	3.6	7.4	21.1	55.4	39.5	28.7	13.5	18.0	19.3	26.7	247.4	11.83
Economy	11.4	54.7	16.7	15.7	13.1	23.2	3.3	4.6	10.2	37.8	24.6	215.2	10.30
Environment/ Climate change	13.1	2.0	1.4	16.9	16.4	16.2	4.3	5.0	4.1	26.7	103.8	209.9	10.04
Finance	12.3	6.5	45.9	57.2	2.8	3.9	2.7	1.6	0.8	56.0	2.7	192.3	9.20
Health	0.6	1.3	19.4	5.1	4.1	4.4	6.8	2.9	61.2	17.4	11.4	134.5	6.44
Energy	13.7	0.0	0.7	0.0	0.0	3.9	0.5	14.1	28.6	11.8	47.1	120.3	5.76
Science, information technology, education, innovation	0.8	4.5	20.3	0.0	0.0	0.8	0.1	0.0	20.2	11.0	8.9	66.6	3.19
Trade	1.2	2.1	4.7	3.1	0.2	12.9	4.2	3.2	4.6	17.0	2.9	56.2	2.69
Corruption	0.0	0.5	18.4	1.2	0.0	7.5	9.5	0.0	6.6	4.1	2.4	50.1	2.40
Uncategorized	1.4	0.5	6.2	0.1	0.2	8.7	0.2	0.6	0.0	16.5	7.6	41.9	2.00
Crisis management	0.0	0.0	0.0	0.0	0.3	3.7	0.0	8.6	1.7	0.0	0.0	14.3	0.69
Total	80.5	123.8	197.7	159.8	195.6	222.7	127.6	120.4	224.4	296.4	341.0	2,090.1	100.00

Index

Global Finance Series

Full series list

Sustaining Global Growth and Development:
G7 and IMF Governance
Edited by Michele Fratianni,
Paolo Savona and John J. Kirton
ISBN 978-0-7546-3529-1

Governing Global Finance
New Challenges, G7 and IMF Contributions
Edited by Michele Fratianni,
Paolo Savona and John J. Kirton
ISBN 978-0-7546-0880-6